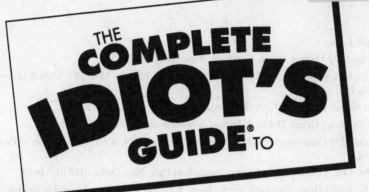

THE COMPLETE **IDIOT'S** GUIDE® TO

Country Living

by Kimberley Willis

ALPHA

A member of Penguin Group (USA) Inc.

ALPHA BOOKS

Published by the Penguin Group

Penguin Group (USA) Inc., 375 Hudson Street, New York, New York 10014, USA

Penguin Group (Canada), 90 Eglinton Avenue East, Suite 700, Toronto, Ontario M4P 2Y3, Canada (a division of Pearson Penguin Canada Inc.)

Penguin Books Ltd., 80 Strand, London WC2R 0RL, England

Penguin Ireland, 25 St. Stephen's Green, Dublin 2, Ireland (a division of Penguin Books Ltd.)

Penguin Group (Australia), 250 Camberwell Road, Camberwell, Victoria 3124, Australia (a division of Pearson Australia Group Pty. Ltd.)

Penguin Books India Pvt. Ltd., 11 Community Centre, Panchsheel Park, New Delhi—110 017, India

Penguin Group (NZ), 67 Apollo Drive, Rosedale, North Shore, Auckland 1311, New Zealand (a division of Pearson New Zealand Ltd.)

Penguin Books (South Africa) (Pty.) Ltd., 24 Sturdee Avenue, Rosebank, Johannesburg 2196, South Africa

Penguin Books Ltd., Registered Offices: 80 Strand, London WC2R 0RL, England

International Standard Book Number: 978-1-59257-801-6
Library of Congress Catalog Card Number: 2008927328

11   8   7   6   5   4   3

Interpretation of the printing code: The rightmost number of the first series of numbers is the year of the book's printing; the rightmost number of the second series of numbers is the number of the book's printing. For example, a printing code of 08-1 shows that the first printing occurred in 2008.

Printed in the United States of America

Publisher: *Marie Butler-Knight*
Editorial Director: *Mike Sanders*
Senior Managing Editor: *Billy Fields*
Senior Acquisitions Editor: *Paul Dinas*
Senior Development Editor: *Christy Wagner*
Production Editor: *Kayla Dugger*
Copy Editor: *Tricia Liebig*

Cartoonist: *Steve Barr*
Cover Designer: *Kurt Owens*
Book Designer: *Trina Wurst*
Indexer: *Heather McNeil*
Layout: *Chad Dressler*
Proofreader: *Mary Hunt*

Contents at a Glance

Contents

Introduction

If you picked up this book, you're probably thinking about or at least dreaming of moving to the country. This book was written to nudge all of you who want to move to the country "someday" to make it sooner rather than later. If questions about what to do and how things work are holding you back from your dream, this book helps you make the right decision.

There's a lot more to moving to the country than learning about raising chickens. The country community is different from the city and suburbs, and you're not only going to learn new "hands-on" skills, but also new "people" skills when you move. I cover both aspects in the following chapters.

The person who moves to the country today is different from the "back-to-the-lander" who moved in the 1970s. Today people are more likely to commute long distances to a job so they can raise their family in the country but continue a standard of living close to what they left behind—only in a better place. This book addresses the issues these new country dwellers face.

As America's baby boomers age, more and more of them long for a simpler, quieter lifestyle. They're nostalgic for a lifestyle some of them remember from Grandma's house. They want to feel safe again. This book welcomes you home.

And for those of you who are younger, who have a strong sense of wanting something better in life for yourself and your family, who want your kids to be able to play outside and breathe clean air, this book is for you, too.

When I moved to the country many years ago, I often wished someone had written a guide to country living that covered everything I needed to know in one easy-to-read book. I hope I have provided that reference for you.

If you really want to, you can do it. Don't let it be just a dream. Turn the page and find out that it isn't that hard or scary. Come on home to the country. We'll leave the lights off so you can see the stars.

How to Use This Book

This book is divided into six parts:

In **Part 1, "Your Country Dream,"** I discuss the dream of moving to the country. This book was written to nudge dreamers into reality and to get them to come home to the country. This part is where we begin the journey.

After you make the decision to move to the country, in **Part 2, "Your Home in the Country,"** I discuss all the things you need to consider—choosing a home or building one, landscaping, and perhaps building a pond.

In **Part 3, "Adjusting to the Country,"** I discuss what happens after you move into your new country community. There are some adjustments in thinking to be made. These chapters help you through it.

If you lived in the city all your life, home systems like wells and septic systems may baffle you. **Part 4, "How Things Work in the Country,"** gives you an overview of those systems and also covers a few other topics like fencing and building a pole barn.

In **Part 5, "Farm Fresh Food,"** I discuss the process of providing some of your own food, including vegetables and fruit, eggs, and maple syrup.

What's the country without animals? In **Part 6, "Country Pets and Other Critters,"** I discuss common pets and their adjustment to the country. Then we look at wildlife, both invited and uninvited.

In the back of the book, the appendixes give you additional information. Appendix A is a glossary. And in Appendix B, I list some websites, organizations, and books that give you more detailed information about living in the country.

I hope you enjoy the book.

More Help

Throughout this book you'll see boxed sidebars that call your attention to one of four things.

def•i•ni•tion

These boxes give you the meanings of country words that may be new to you.

Rural Rule

Look here for tips about country life.

Country Color

These sidebars give you tidbits about life in the country you might not know.

Sinkhole

Heed these warnings about possible dangers.

Acknowledgments

I'd like to thank my husband, Steve, for agreeing to move to the country with me many years ago and letting me live the life I'd always dreamed of and who encouraged me and prompted my memory as I wrote this book.

Trademarks

All terms mentioned in this book that are known to be or are suspected of being trademarks or service marks have been appropriately capitalized. Alpha Books and Penguin Group (USA) Inc. cannot attest to the accuracy of this information. Use of a term in this book should not be regarded as affecting the validity of any trademark or service mark.

Part 1

Your Country Dream

You have a dream. You want to move to the country. Fresh air. Peace and quiet. Space to roam. You're ready to stop dreaming and just do it. But maybe you're feeling a little overwhelmed. You have so many things to consider and so much to learn.

In Part 1, we take the first step to fulfilling your dream. In the next two chapters, I cover the many decisions you need to make before you pursue your country dream, including the wants and wishes of others in your family. Be sure you're using your head as well as your heart in your decision to move to the country. To help you with that, I've included some things about the country you might not have considered. It's not all perfect out here.

Why Do You Want to Live in the Country?

In This Chapter

♦ Exploring what country means to you

♦ Deciding what you want from the country

♦ Using your head to make decisions

Country means something different to each person. In this chapter, we explore what you think country is, why you want to be there, and your expectations of country living.

This is the chapter where your dreams are stroked and you realize you want to move to the country as soon as you can. The rest of the book is written to slow you down and guide your choices. That way, you aren't as likely to make a mistake and will truly enjoy your move to the country.

What's Your Definition of *Country*?

Close your eyes and picture yourself in the country. What do you see? A small cabin among towering pines? A white house and a big red barn silhouetted against golden wheat fields? A little house on the shores of a beautiful lake? An adobe home overlooking miles of desert? A stone house with a white picket fence and a tire swing in the yard? The country is all these and more. And country is not just the right house; it's a feeling you get when you're in the right place.

Many of you probably believe that a move to the country will improve your quality of life. You'll breathe cleaner air, experience quiet nights, and watch glorious sunrises. Your children will play outside safely, and your neighbors will wave to you. If you want those things, you *can* have them in the country.

Some people think country means 40 acres and a farm. Others think country is a $1/_2$-acre lot with beach access. Some people are in the country when they live in a small village or in a rural subdivision with large lots. We each have an idea of what a country lifestyle is. Some might not be very realistic, but if you're reading this book, you're at least thinking about coming home to the country.

> **Country Color**
>
> How does the government define country? The U.S. Office of Management and Budget defines a rural county as one that does not have a city of 50,000 people or more and is not next to a county that depends on it socially and economically.

Some of you are basing your idea of a country life-style on a memory, either your own from childhood or memories passed down to you from a parent or grandparent. Do you remember running through the fields playing games, catching frogs at the swamp, sitting on a porch swing watching the rain, or waving at neighbors driving by? Do you remember catching fireflies in a jar, finding crabs at the beach, watching Dad put up a fence, or helping Mom pick corn from the garden? How about going barefoot or swimming in a pond? Sledding down a snowy hill? Playing hockey on the frozen lake? Your kids could do these things. You can still do these things.

Maybe it's a desire to move out of a climate you find unpleasant. Is winter in the city just too much to bear anymore? Do you want to experience four seasons or have snow on the ground for Christmas? A life in the country might be for you.

Classic Country or New Country?

Forget about *Little House on the Prairie* or *The Waltons*. Today, most if not all country homes have flush toilets and electricity—at least if the owner wants them. (If your idea of country involves growing your own food, heating with wood, and putting up an outhouse, you just need to find the right spot.)

Shopping and medical care may require a long trip, depending on where you settle in the country, but better roads make the trip a little easier. Phone lines reach most country homes, and cell phones make communication available where the lines don't reach.

And thanks to computers, many people can move far from their physical office and still work. You can write to, hear, and even see co-workers and loved ones far away almost instantly. Although some areas don't have high-speed Internet connections, in almost every area of the country, a satellite dish or a land-line phone can keep you connected. That same technology can bring you distance learning or entertainment even far up in the mountains or out on the desert. The good thing about this technology is that when you want to be alone, you can just turn it off and disconnect from the world.

In rural areas today, fewer than 7 percent of inhabitants are employed in agriculture. Many are employed in some other area and commute from their country home to their job. Those who work in the community are in service-related jobs; artistic endeavors; tourism; or professional jobs such as teaching, medical care, etc. Still, many who have full-time jobs do a little farming on the side.

Although it's *possible*, it's very hard to move to the country and make a living from conventional farming. If you've never farmed and have no agricultural education, it's even harder. If your dream is to move to the country and actually farm for a living, you need to do a lot of learning, save your money, and do some intense planning before you actually move.

> **Sinkhole**
> Some people believe they can buy farmland and then get paid not to grow crops. Most of these programs are gone now, and the remaining ones have rigorous rules and restrictions. You will not make a living this way.

Jobs may be harder to find in country areas, and the pay might be less. In your dream, you may plan to move to the country and work there, too. It's not that you can't make a living in the country; you may just have to be a little innovative to have the best of both worlds, a good paying job and a place in the country.

Country Expectations

So back to closing your eyes and picturing that perfect country place. Think about what's important to you, and why you are unsatisfied with where you are living now. Country is not so much a piece of land and a certain type of house; it's about a lifestyle.

Some people are energized and happy with a bustling, crowded, urban lifestyle. For others, it's stressful and tiring. You don't have to be totally depressed and frightened to want to move to the country, but you must be seeking a change that feels better to you.

Music to Your Ears

Noise—the city is always filled with noise. Sirens screaming, stereos booming, neighbors fighting, TVs blaring, traffic—it's endless. Sometimes you can push it to the background and only realize it's there when there's an absence of it. But noise is a stress factor. We need to hear the sounds of nature that are drowned out when so many of us are jammed in a small area.

It's not always quiet in the country, but most areas of the country have considerably lower noise levels than the city. And much of the noise is nature's noise, which is much better for us. You can hear birds singing, frogs croaking, the rain coming across the fields, water lapping the shores, wind rustling through the leaves, or maybe the crackle of the northern lights. These noises make the stress pour out of you, help you relax, and keep you calm.

Privacy and Safety Matters

In the city, do you feel like you're always being watched? Even if no one is really trying to keep track of you, you're probably being watched. From cameras mounted on poles and buildings to the neighbor peering from behind the blinds, someone is watching you. When you work in your yard, you do so in front of many people, most of them strangers. When you walk to your car, when you collect your mail, and when you carry out your trash, someone is watching you.

But sometimes those who are watching you make you feel very uneasy. You put double locks on your doors and always walk with a friend. You carry mace in your purse or even a concealed weapon. Because so many people are around, you feel you need to be on guard all the time. It's hard to tell which stranger is harmless and which is not. You may not recognize the stress of this constantly vigilant behavior, but it does impact your life.

It's not always safe in the country, and crime does occur. But all of a sudden you realize that you can go outside and fewer, if any, people are around to see anything you do. There are fewer strangers to monitor, and you don't constantly have to be checking people coming near you for signs of danger. And when something is out of place or not right, your neighbor is likely to notice, and in the country, he or she is more likely to do something about it.

Country Color

When I first moved to the country, I was working nights and my husband was working days. We had adopted the practice of leaving our doors unlocked because one of us was always home. I, of course, slept during the day. Imagine my shock when I got up one day and found a package on the kitchen table. The mail lady had brought it in quietly because it was too big for the mailbox and she knew I was sleeping and didn't want to wake me. That's what living in the country is all about.

Do You See What I See?

Close your eyes and imagine what you want to see from your country home. Is it the desert hills painted in the tawny colors of a sunset? Rolling green hills dotted with fat cattle? Tall trees stretching toward a blue sky? Your children splashing in blue water on a milky white beach? The stars so close you can touch them?

Our eyes need to see something besides concrete walls and anemic street trees, freeways littered with fast-food trash, the neighbor's garage wall, and neon lights glaring through the night. Our eyes need to stretch toward distant horizons, across ripening fields, and deep into the night sky.

Stress comes from a constantly noisy environment. Stress comes from not seeing beautiful things daily. Stress comes from living where you have to be constantly vigilant and worried about your and your family's safety. The country can reduce that stress and restore peace in your life. Reducing stress by restoring peace, quiet, and safety can definitely improve your quality of life. So will breathing cleaner air.

But moving to the country may improve your quality of life in other ways. You may feel more connected to your community and more in charge of your community's fate.

Hobbies and Recreation

Many times a move to the country lets you afford a better home for your family. Families and couples often spend more time together in country settings, with recreational activities or just enjoying quiet times, if you choose to live where that type of activity is available.

Wouldn't it be nice just to walk outside with a fishing pole and down to a nice trout stream? Or saddle up your horse and take a quick ride down a sleepy country road after work? You could walk out the door after breakfast and take a hike, looking for arrowheads. Or get up early Sunday morning to ski down fresh snow on the nearby hills. Your children will be able to do things outdoors without you having to drive them somewhere. You can have a compost pile by your garden and an apple tree in the backyard. You can lay on your own beach with a good book and not have to listen to someone's stereo booming 2 feet from you. If you want these things, you can have them.

Sinkhole

Remember, some country areas may have restrictions on what kinds of activities can be done at your home, just as city and suburban areas do. Check out the regulations in the area you're thinking of moving to before you pack up and head out.

The country allows many people to pursue another dream—a hobby they couldn't do at their city home or that they have outgrown the space allotted to it. Maybe you want to breed and train hunting dogs or have a pottery kiln. Perhaps your dream is to have lots of land to explore your passion for gardening. Or maybe you need a pole barn to store your antique cars and quiet roads to drive them on.

All kinds of hobbies make too much noise, dust, or smells, or take too much room for a city home. If you look long enough, you can find a place that will allow you to pursue that hobby.

Farm Fresh Food

If you want to move to the country to grow at least some of your own food, you are doing a great thing. The food you produce will be more nutritious, cleaner, and safer than food you buy in stores. Growing your own food is often hard work, but it's the best feeling in the world to fill your cupboards with food you've grown yourself.

You may even be considering raising some of your own meat or hunting to provide meat for the family. For vegetables and maybe a few chickens for eggs, you will need very little land. For raising larger livestock, you'll need considerably more land. However, a family who has good land and a good system can probably raise most of their food on 5 acres.

If you're considering moving to the country to "live off the land," take time to learn all you can before stepping into the adventure. A slow and gradual approach to self-sufficiency works better than jumping in with both feet.

Even if you find that raising your own food is too hard when you move to the country, or that you don't have enough time at first, you'll still be closer to people who do raise

the food. You can purchase sides of beef
from the farmer down the road and bushels
of tomatoes to can from the corner farm
stand. These people are your neighbors,
so you can see how they raise the food and
know if they are the person you want to
support. If you buy in the community and
support local farmers, you're doing as much
good for yourself and the environment as
growing your own food.

Rural Rule

Later in this book, I talk a
little about growing your own
food and raising chickens, but
learning all about raising your
own food would take several
books. Check out Appendix B for
a list of several books that can
help you.

Starting a Country Business

Dreaming about a move to the country to start your own business is much like dreaming about the right spot to pursue a hobby. First, be sure you can set up the business
in the area you decide to move to by checking zoning regulations.

If you want to start a dairy, breed horses, raise Christmas trees, or build a campground, you'll need to be in the country, of course. But you can run other types of
businesses from a country home.

An artist or writer can work from his or her country home office, thanks to today's
technology. A lawyer or doctor may be dreaming of setting up a practice from a
country home or in a nearby small town. You could sell candy from a small shop in a
tourist town, or take visitors out to fish from your boat. You might start a mail-order
plant nursery or grow cut flowers for the florist trade. You could run a cider mill or a
bed and breakfast. All these things may be part of the reason you want to move to the
country.

Reality Check

That all sounds lovely, doesn't it? But before you pack up and move, let's break for a
bit of a reality check.

Get out a pen and some paper, and write down what your country dream is. It may
seem silly, but just do it. It'll help you clarify just what you want from a country move.
Write down the physical things you want, like a log cabin in the middle of a forest, a
big greenhouse, or a horse, and also the intangible things, like "I want to feel safe," "I
want to feel part of a community," or "I want to feel less stressed."

I don't mean to discourage you from moving to the country. But sometimes we have to put our dreams on hold until the time is right. We need to plan and learn so we can have what we dream of. On the other hand, if you're always dreaming and never doing, you'll never fulfill your dream. It's a delicate balance of wanting, needing, and really being able to do it. Sometimes your heart screams "Yes, just do it!" but your mind screams back, "Don't be a fool!" The trick is to get your heart and mind to use one calm and sure voice and make a decision. Let's talk to both.

Is Now the Right Time?

You may be very ready to flee to the country because you are stressed or frightened in the city. You may be getting anxious because time is going by and you aren't getting any younger. A major life event may have occurred—death of a parent or spouse, a divorce, a serious illness, or retirement—and you might want a change. But don't let events drive you to do things you aren't prepared for. Sometimes the time just isn't right.

If you have a parent who is relying on you for help, would it be wise to move far from them? If you have a child with special needs who is happy and contented where he or she is, should you uproot them? If you or a spouse is deeply immersed in a job that requires a quick on-the-job response in emergency situations, can you handle that after a move?

Stop and think. Will time eventually change things so the move isn't so disruptive? If a major life event has sparked an interest in a move, give it a few months to see if you're still as interested.

What About Money?

All moves cost money. There are short-term costs, such as hiring a truck to move and getting new phone lines or satellite dishes. Most of those are manageable. But it's the long-term costs that must be considered before you decide to move. Moving to the country may save you money in the long run—or cost you more, depending on your current circumstances.

Will your new country life come with a house payment larger than the one you have? If you want to buy or rent a home in the country, how is your credit? If your credit score isn't that great, you might want to work on repairing your credit before looking for a new home.

It's very romantic to read about people who sell everything to buy a piece of land. They then live on the land for 6 years in a tent while they build a mortgage-free home between commuting to jobs in the city and raising all their own food. Some people can do this, but most of us cannot. For every person who does this and writes that inspiring story, probably 100 others quickly fail at it. It's far better to try to reduce your current living expenses and save enough money to buy some land. In a few years, you'll be better prepared to make the move.

Sometimes you have to compromise a little with your dream. Maybe you can't afford a lakeside cottage, but maybe you can afford one with lake access. Maybe you could purchase some land with a smaller, older home and save money to someday build that larger stone house on your land. Maybe you could even rent a home in the area of your dreams while you search for the perfect place.

To know whether you have enough money to move, you need to go back to the list of what you want from the country and do some research.

If you've chosen an area of the country to move to, find out what property is selling for in that area. Will you need a bigger mortgage payment to have the home you want? If your move involves starting a business, do some research to see what a greenhouse costs to build and operate in your chosen area, what stores rent for, or what type of business the community needs and what it already has.

> ### Country Color
>
> Property is usually cheaper the farther away you go from urban areas or recreational destinations. Property on dirt or gravel roads is also cheaper than that on paved roads.

Make lists of expected costs, and compare them to your current living costs. Will you need another or better car to make a commute or navigate country roads? On the other hand, maybe you won't need to spend money on certain things, such as country club fees, homeowner association dues, or boarding your horse at a stable.

How's the Commute?

Unless you're able to retire, have a career you can work on from home, or are starting your own business, you'll probably need to commute to a job in a larger urban area. Many people commute long distances so they can make a good living and enjoy a country lifestyle.

You'll be happier with your country home if you don't spend hours every day driving to and from it, so if you can, try to locate your country home within an hour's drive of your job. Long commutes can be as stressful as living in the city, and the cost of gas

Rural Rule

When you've found a country area where you want to live, try driving from your workplace to the area at rush hour or the time you'd be coming home or going to work. How long does it take? Can you stand that drive every day?

and maintaining your car can be added expenses. And remember that an hour's commute in good weather can take 2 or more hours in bad weather.

If your country dream home means you need to move too far to keep your present job, how do you plan to support yourself? The wisest thing to do when planning a move to a distant area is to line up a job there first. You may need to take a job in a different field or learn some new skills. Really think about this. You don't want to lose your dream home almost as soon as you get it.

After you've carefully thought about a move to the country, using your head and doing your homework, you'll have a better picture of whether you should go ahead with the move now. Sometimes just waiting a year or two makes the move go more smoothly. And sometimes waiting only makes you older. But if your heart and mind are harmonizing a country tune, it's time to sing it.

The Least You Need to Know

- *Country* means something different to everyone. You need to determine what it means to you before you pack up and move.

- A country lifestyle is not just about owning land and a type of house. It's about embracing a new community and taking full advantage of the natural beauty around you.

- If commuting to your present job won't be practical, take some time to decide how you intend to make a living.

- The decision to move to the country must be made with your head and your heart.

2

What Else Should You Consider?

In This Chapter

- Involving the family in a country move
- Considerations for families, singles, retirees, and other lifestyles
- Country concerns for everyone

You've made the decision with your heart and mind that you want to move to the country. But what about the other significant people in your life? Unless you're single, other people will be affected by your desire to have a country lifestyle.

You know you want to move to the country, but maybe other members of your family aren't so sure. You've thought about what you want, but what about what they want? It's time to involve the other members of your family in the planning.

Is Everyone on the Same Page?

Maybe you've talked about moving to the country so much that everyone from your family to your boss knows exactly what you want to do. Or maybe you've just dreamed about it, occasionally mentioning little things, such as "I'd like to do that some day …."

You may know exactly what your significant other wants because you share the same dream—or think you do. But here's the rub: you might want to move to the country this year, as soon as you can get a moving truck lined up, but your significant other might be thinking about the move as something you'll do when the kids are out of school or when you retire. Your kids might think you're just talking to scare them into obeying their curfew.

Sinkhole

If you've decided you definitely want to move to the country but know that significant other people in your life are opposed to the move, don't think you can beg, plead, reason, and order everyone to move. It won't be as smooth and happy as you planned.

It's time to gather everyone who will be affected by the move and tell them what you want. Be sure they know your exact plans, whether it's to find a place and move this year, to begin saving and plan to move in the next 3 years, or to retire early and move. Tell them the kind of country lifestyle you want, where you want to move, how you plan to finance the move, where you intend to work, etc. And then listen to what they have to say.

Your wife may tell you firmly that she is not moving until this baby is born. Your husband may tell you he is not going to leave his dad alone and move 250 miles away. Some of your kids may say "Cool!" while others may start crying and slam some doors. Now you need to talk.

Sometimes compromise is in order. Can you be happy moving out of the city but close enough to your wife's family that she's happy? Can you wait until your son finishes his senior year at the city high school? Talking with the family may make you realize that there are considerable problems to be overcome before a move is possible. Your dream might need to be altered or put on hold.

In the rest of this chapter, I discuss some other things for the whole family to consider. A country move is in your future, and if you're prepared and knowledgeable, the move will be much smoother.

Considerations for Families

The age of your children makes a difference in what you need to consider about moving to the country. Very young children should adjust easily. Teens have the hardest time, especially if they're moving too far away to keep in touch with their friends.

If you want your kids to participate in more wholesome activities, say 4-H instead of hanging out at the mall, you'll need to gently nudge them into it. Sure, the mall may be too far away, but they could substitute hanging out at the local McDonald's instead.

Long Commutes to Schools

In some country areas, the distance a child has to go to school may be much farther than it was in the city. Country schools have consolidated in the last 50 years, so instead of many small schools in many places, you'll find one larger school in a central location. The idea is to provide more educational opportunities at less cost.

This can mean a long commute for even small children. They may be on buses for 2 or more hours a day. Driving your kids to school may save some time, if you can do it.

Country schools have fewer snow days than many city schools, maybe because bus-route roads seem to be cleared first. In really bad weather, though, country buses probably won't run.

Fewer Educational and Recreational Opportunities

Country schools usually prepare their students for college and careers as well as, if not better than, city schools. But some activities and classes might not be offered in smaller country schools.

Programs for gifted children or special needs children may be lacking in smaller school districts. Art, drama, and music may not be offered because of the cost. Sometimes it's possible to make up for these classes by allowing your child to attend a club—or even begin a club for these activities if none exists.

You can probably count on a football team at your country school, and probably wrestling, but other sports may not be played at the school. Some areas are big on baseball, others basketball, and a few have soccer teams. In general, there are fewer tennis, golf, and track opportunities at country schools.

Rural Rule

If your child is dreaming of a career in basketball, cheerleading, or another activity and the county school doesn't have a team, maybe you can help by volunteering to be a coach, or at least help a coach get a team started.

Extracurricular recreational activities may be different, too. Instead of playing pool at the YWCA, your kids might want to swing on a rope in the hayloft. They can go fishing instead of to the playground. There are more opportunities to enjoy outside sports in the country, and you should encourage your child to do so. Help them see that there aren't *fewer* things to do for fun, just *different* ones.

Dealing With Isolation

In the good old days, country children were generally part of large families and they played with each other. Today's country child is probably from a smaller family and has fewer things to do to keep busy. For some children, playing alone is just fine, but for some, being far from neighbors and friends is very hard.

When you think about it, country children are often no more isolated than city children. In the city, children aren't allowed to go out and play after school because someone may hurt them. They often aren't allowed to go places within easy walking distance because it's too dangerous.

As a parent, you often have to go the extra mile, city or country, to be sure your child can have fun with friends. That might mean you provide transportation to a friend's house or invite old and new friends to your house. (See Chapter 10 for more about helping children adjust to country life.)

Considerations for Singles and Couples

If you're single, probably the only person you have to worry about pleasing with your new country lifestyle is you. If you're a couple with no kids and both of you agree you want a country lifestyle, there should be nothing to worry about. Right?

Not so fast. What seemed so inviting—fewer neighbors—might soon worry you. What will happen if you have an accident or need help? Sure, there may be other single guys and gals in this area of the woods, but how do you meet them?

Unfriendly to Some Lifestyles

Country folk are, in general, on the conservative side. Much of mainstream America is more accepting to different lifestyles these days, but there may still be some resistance in country areas to people of different colors and religions, homosexuals, and trans-sexuals. Each area differs, and so do the people in it.

It's your right to choose anywhere you want to live in America. Be friendly and answer questions honestly if asked. Give your new neighbors time to know you as a person, before they think about how you are different from them. Don't move into an area and expect to change everyone overnight, and don't say or do things to shock or anger people deliberately. You're less likely to be harmed because you have a different life-style in the country, but you might not be welcomed with open arms either, at least at first.

Limited Shopping and Recreation Opportunities

If your lifestyle includes fine dining, theater, and time at the gym, you might feel a little lost in the country for a while. You can find these things by going to a larger urban area when you want to, but you might have to consider how often you like to shop at high-scale stores or dance until dawn as you're narrowing down locations for a country home.

If you have to drive an hour each way to find a good restaurant, how often will you want to go? You may learn to love the Dew Drop Inn for its Friday night fish fry but still crave a little sushi once in a while.

If you work in the city and have plenty of people around you all day, you might not mind being alone at night at your country home. But if you're a single who works from home, or a couple who have moved far from friends and relatives, you might go through times when isolation from the world feels a little depressing. When you get to know your country neighbors, those feelings will lessen.

Considerations for Retirees

Retirees may not have to worry about a long commute, but there are things they will want to consider when making a move to the country. The move may take even more consideration if it means moving a long distance to another climate.

You may be perfectly healthy now, but what happens if you develop a serious illness? It can happen to anyone, old or young. What kind of medical care is available in the community you want to move to? If you already have medical issues that need regular care, can you get it in the community you choose?

> **Sinkhole**
>
> A 2003 study published by the American Academy of Family Physicians stated that only 76 percent of doctors accept new Medicare patients, and in rural areas, the figure is higher. You might want to check out doctors when looking for a place to retire.

A 50-mile drive to the hospital can seem awfully long when you're ill, especially in bad weather. Ambulance and EMT services may take much longer in the country, also. There are, however, many country areas with good hospitals and medical care reasonably close.

Large, urban areas often have senior citizen programs that provide health screenings, recreational and social opportunities, and transportation. Some country areas also provide such services, but some may not. If those things are important to you, choose your country place with that in mind.

Family Ties

Although the kids may want to visit you in sunny Arizona for Christmas, their jobs or finances may not allow them to. And if you are on a tight budget or have difficulty traveling, you may not be able to visit them.

If you rely on children or other relatives to help you with certain things, you'll have to find other support if you move far away. If being close to family at holidays and other special times is important to you, plan your move to the country so you aren't too far away.

Sometimes when you move to the country you may get more visits from relatives and friends than you want or need. Free vacations in a beautiful spot interest a lot of people. You might want to downplay how beautiful your beach is or how wonderful the skiing is. You may have to actually set limits on who can visit and for how long.

> **Rural Rule**
>
> If you don't like sharing your home with visiting relatives and friends, you might want to buy a smaller home in an area farther from popular attractions or recreational areas.

Transportation Issues

In the city, drives may be short, walking and bicycling are good for quick trips to the store, and cabs and buses provide transportation for longer distances. In the country, a car is almost always needed to get to shopping, church, and medical appointments. If you move to areas where harsh winter weather isn't a factor, driving may be easier. But if you have difficulty driving, a move to the country may drastically change your lifestyle. Some country areas, usually those in warm areas where lots of seniors live, do provide reasonably good bus service.

More Physical Demands

Some retirees have worked hard all their lives and are in good physical shape. Others are used to a desk job and a lawn service. It can be a problem when someone who isn't used to physical work moves to the country and has to split wood to heat the house.

You know what level of physical activity you are used to and what you can handle. Be realistic in picking a country lifestyle that suits your abilities. Remember that as you get older, you want to enjoy life more and work less. Then again, one man's work is another man's pleasure ….

Considerations for Organic Living

For some people, a dream home in the country includes a lifestyle of pesticide-free food they grow themselves. They want to breathe clean air, chop their own wood for heating, and hang their laundry out to dry in the sun. These are admirable goals, but you may have to ease into this lifestyle gradually.

Don't Grow There

You could grow much of your family's food on an acre of land. But it needs to be reasonably fertile land, with adequate water and a long-enough growing season for basic crops.

Dry, desert conditions without a good well would make growing your own food very hard, as would rocky mountainous areas with thin soil and a chance for surprise frosts. Heavily wooded land would have to be cleared before much food can be grown, and there might even be laws saying whether or not you can remove the trees in the first place.

Country Color
Old cropland would seem to be ideal for gardeners but often isn't. It can be so depleted of nutrients that it will take years to restore organic matter and soil fertility.

The soil where conventional cash crops have been grown may be heavily contaminated with chemicals. The crops grown on that land will not be considered organic for up to 6 years. Old pasture and feedlot areas often have compacted soil full of weeds.

It's Harder Than You Think

If you've never raised animals for meat or counted on your garden to provide most of your winter food supply, you may be in for a surprise. The fun and novelty wears a little thin in the winter when the hose is frozen and you're lugging bucket after bucket of water from the house to the barn through knee-high snow drifts. Or when the sheep get out in the road in the pouring rain or a raccoon gets in the chickens and kills them all. When you're canning that 500th jar of tomatoes or looking at the $1/2$ bushel of potatoes that was supposed to last you through the winter, things just don't look so rosy. And forget vacations or sleeping in if there's an animal waiting to be milked.

People who intend to commute back and forth to city jobs should be especially careful of how much farming work they decide to take on. Start with a small garden and a few chickens, and get a routine and a feel for the process. Build up your soil, and learn the growing conditions before trying to replace the grocery store with your garden. Only then should you gradually expand to grow more of your food.

Many people get several types of animals and put in a huge garden almost as soon as they move in to their country home. Usually after a few years, they are down to a few things they know they can do well—and have time to do.

It's better to have the right equipment and housing, and the time to do a few things well, rather than trying to do everything and wearing yourself out while making a huge mess.

Considerations for Everyone

Some city people have unrealistic expectations of the country because they've not experienced it at all times of the year. Others have never spent any time in the area of the country where they're considering moving. Land just 1 or 2 miles apart can have vastly different qualities and problems.

I think one of the things country people dread the most is having someone from the city move next to them who then starts complaining about noise or smell or sights. Roosters crow, pigs smell, and farm machinery is noisy. Those are normal parts of country life, even if they don't seem so normal to you.

You don't move into an area and demand that accepted, normal farming practices be changed. There are some not-so-pleasant things about the country you and your family may experience. This isn't to scare you or change your mind about a country move. It's to prepare you so you think about and know what to expect. The more you know beforehand, the less likely you are to get upset later.

A Room with a View

You may have moved to your home to watch the deer feeding in the fields, but when the leaves fall off the trees, the junk cars and old bed frames in the neighbor's woods are revealed. Or maybe the crop farmer has left six fluorescent orange grain wagons in the field next to your house for a month. You may build a new home in the country with a gorgeous view of the mountains from your front window. Then a new neighbor builds a house right in your line of sight. A friend once had a nice view of a small pond and some woods. Now she looks at an old semi-truck with a soft drink logo that a neighbor moved in for storage.

Don't buy your country home just for the view. Country views may change with the seasons or the landowner's whim, and there's often nothing you can do about it.

Country Color
A friend of ours raises mules and sells them to the Amish population in our area. He keeps several mares in a pasture with a large stud donkey. New neighbors with young children built a home in view of one of his pastures. The man in this family showed up early one morning, banging on our friend's door. He was furious that the stud was breeding the mares in front of his children. He demanded that the animals be locked up, out of view of the children. This man had unrealistic attitudes and views about the country.

Country Noise

We often move to the country to escape all the noise that surrounds us in the city, but there can be noise in the country, too. Most country noise is seasonal or temporary, but there are times when country noise can be annoying.

Harvest and planting times can be very noisy in country areas. At our house this week, we've listened to the rumble of huge trucks and felt our house shake as they pass about every 15 minutes from sun up to well after dark. It's sugar beet harvest time here, and the trucks are going to the sugar factories from the fields. I've learned to be patient with this because I know it'll be over soon and it's part of our country life here.

Roosters crow—that's a fact of country life. What you may not know is they just don't crow in the morning; the crowing can go on all day. Even hens can make a lot of noise when they're announcing they just laid an egg or squabbling with each other. Geese honk and ducks quack—sometimes quite loudly. Animals often get noisy every day around feeding or milking time. When farmers separate young calves, lambs, or foals from their mothers, the animals may spend a few days calling frantically back and forth to each other.

Country homeowners who live near big wind mills, grain elevators, working gas or oil wells, or gravel pits are also subjected to noise. It's better not to move close to these things, and to choose areas where the zoning doesn't allow them, if quiet is important to you.

What's That Smell?

Many smells newcomers may find objectionable are seasonal or temporary in nature, but some country smells can persist. If your home is anywhere near large animals or poultry, you will, at some point, smell them. This is normal. Manure smells worst in wet weather, and fall and spring rains often intensify livestock smells.

> **Country Color**
>
> Some people find the smell of one type of animal manure more objectionable than another. The smell of cow and pig manure is stronger and more objectionable to most people than the smell of horse, goat, or sheep manure.

When a farmer spreads or sprays his field with manure, even those living far from the animals may notice the smell. Living near where manure is stored in piles or lagoons is not recommended. Factory farms and confined feedlots are also not good choices for neighbors.

Animals have other smells, too. Male goats, or bucks, have a very powerful smell. Sheep with wool also smell. Wet feathers and rotten eggs smell. In ocean side and lakeside property, dead fish and other things that wash up on shore can be a problem for your nose.

Other seasonal temporary smells can come from pesticides, fertilizers, and herbicides sprayed on crops. Sometimes seasonal processing plants, like the sugar beet factories, can put off a powerful smell. Natural gas wells have a smell added that can drift far from the source.

Fewer Services

In the country, you often need to pay for trash removal service or do it yourself. There may be a designated dump or recycling area in your county or township. A fee may be charged for their use. Some areas still allow paper trash to be burned. Yard waste should be composted if at all possible.

Fire fighting and emergency first aid are often done by volunteers in the country. They wear phones or beepers and leave what they're doing to come to your rescue when called. The equipment may be stored in a central location, or the volunteers may keep it. Response time may be longer than a city fire department response. Ambulances are generally sent out from hospitals or private contracted ambulance services. You may have to pay for fire and emergency runs. In some areas, a fee is charged to the homeowner each time a run is made.

Law enforcement services in the country vary. In some places, county sheriffs or the state police handle calls. Other areas may have dedicated local law enforcement. Some of you are used to long response times from law enforcement in the city. In some country areas, law enforcement time can also be slow.

On the Road Again

At certain times of the year, the roads in some areas are nearly if not totally impassable. Even if your country home is on a paved road, flooding, deep snow, mud, or ice may make it hard to travel.

Some roads are better maintained than others, but all dirt and gravel roads tend to have problems at some time of the year. Potholes and flying gravel take their toil on cars. Count on spending more for mufflers, shocks, and windshields if you live on dirt or gravel roads. Forget washing your car if you travel the roads often. (See Chapter 11 for more about country roads.)

Unwelcome Wildlife

You may have wanted to see the deer and the antelope play at your new country home, but not in your new orchard. And those cute field mice? They're cute in the field, but wait until they come inside your house for the winter. Don't forget about the sea gulls who swoop down to take that cookie out of your kid's hand and scare him to death. Snakes, scorpions, ticks, raccoons, and bears all live in the country. Hopefully, you can learn to co-exist.

You won't be able to clear your country property totally of these critters, but you can reduce damage and encounters. (See Chapter 24 for more on dealing with unwanted critters.)

Sinkhole

Don't feed animals close to your home or buy a home where animals have been fed close by if you like your landscaping and gardening. Animals think a garden is a buffet laid out just for them.

Unexpected Expenses

If you were thinking about changing jobs as well as lifestyles, be aware that country areas may not have as many job opportunities as urban areas. If by moving to the country you have actually cut your living expenses, this may not be a problem. Some skills are easily transported to the country but the pay may be less. Teenagers and older people seeking part-time employment may find it even harder to find jobs.

Trash pickup, road maintenance costs, higher electric bills for running the water pump, increased car maintenance costs, and septic tank pumping may strain your budget. If you need to purchase a riding mower or tractor, a different car or truck to handle road conditions, or other specialized tools, add that to your budget. Commuting long distances also adds to the gas bills.

If you expect to be on a tight budget to afford your country dream, don't forget to take these costs into account.

The Least You Need to Know

- ◆ All family members should know about and discuss your plans to move to the country.

- ◆ Different family units have different considerations when moving to the country. Consider the age of children and whether anyone has special needs.

- ◆ Go in to your new lifestyle with an open mind and learn as much as you about your new location before you move. People who are prepared for changes accept them better.

- ◆ Choose your country location carefully. There are noises, smells, bad roads, and bad neighbors in the country, too.

Part 2

Your Home in the Country

You've made the decision to move to the country, and everyone's in tune. It's time to get busy and find that country home of your dreams. In Part 2, I help you make your dream a reality.

In the following chapters, I serve as your virtual real estate agent and help you find your place, whether that's an existing home or land on which you can build your perfect country home. And then we look at landscaping and other outdoor features you might want at your new country home, sweet home.

Decisions, Decisions

◆ Property taxes

Chapter 3

Finding and Funding Your Place

In This Chapter

- ◆ Making decisions about your new home
- ◆ Looking for your country place
- ◆ Do you need an agent?
- ◆ Narrowing down your wants and needs

You've made the decision with your heart that a move to the country is right for you. Now you need to use your head and go about finding your country place. Even if you inherited Uncle Bob's farm, you have many things to think about.

In this chapter, we look at the financial decisions that come with a move to the country and how to differentiate wants from needs. We also go over the process of finding the perfect country home, including how to pick a good realtor or search on your own.

Decisions, Decisions

You really need to go into this move with a strong plan. Don't just think about the move in your head, though. Get a notebook or start a file in your computer, and keep track of what you find out or decide about the big move to the country. You'll be talking to a lot of people and researching many answers to your questions, and trust me, you won't remember everything. Write it down.

What Can You Afford?

This is probably the most important decision to make about your move. Many people are willing to sacrifice a little to achieve their country living goals, but be very careful not to make your move to the country too much of a financial burden for you. After all, what fun is there in moving to the country if you have to work three jobs to pay for it and can't even afford to take a day off?

Don't get discouraged. If you're willing to be patient and do a lot of research and footwork on your own, you'll likely be able to afford a home in the country. Do be realistic and willing to explore all options. Maybe you need to start small and work up to the place of your dreams, but at least you'll be in the country.

First things first: sit down and make a budget. Write down all your sources of regular income along with your current expenses. Include your current rent or mortgage payment, and be honest about your other expenses. Look at your expenses in comparison with your income. Your first stab at this may make you think you can afford more than you really can. If your current house or rent payment is about all you can afford every month, don't kid yourself that you could afford more when you move, unless your income is also going to change for the better.

> **Rural Rule**
>
> If you're going to get a mortgage, someone at the bank will probably want to go over your income and expenses, too, so keep your numbers handy.

When working on your budget, try to figure in new expenses you may have after your move. This is a little difficult if you haven't even started looking, but it can be a great help when deciding what house payment you can afford. And if you currently rent, there might be many costs you aren't aware of. Here's a list of some costs to consider:

- House insurance
- Property taxes

- Additional costs of commuting to your job

- Heating costs

- Water and sewer costs if you're not on well and septic system

- Trash removal costs

- New maintenance costs, mowing, or snow removal

- Child care expenses, if they will change

When you buy a house, mortgage companies typically pay the cost of house insurance and property taxes and add a certain amount to your monthly house payment to cover it. Some people are shocked when they figure a certain amount for house payments, find a loan that allows them to remain within their budget, and then have $200 a month or more added to cover taxes and insurance! Don't be tempted to take on a loan you'll struggle to pay.

Remember that your house payments also include an interest payment. Interest rates vary depending on your credit rating and what's going on in the economy. And your payment could fluctuate depending on whether you get a fixed interest rate on your loan or a variable one that changes as the market changes.

When you have a rough budget, you'll have a general idea of what you can afford for a house and a monthly payment. This is a beginning point for all the other decisions you need to make.

> **Sinkhole**
>
> Mortgage lenders tell you what they think you can afford to spend on a house. Only you know deep down if you can really be that good with your budget. In the last few years, mortgage companies have approved loans for many people who really couldn't afford them.

Choose Your Location

This is much more fun than a budget. It may also be a no-brainer for you because you might already know where you want to move. Or you might know the general area you need to move to stay within commuting distance, but you need to clarify just exactly where you want to move.

If you need to commute to a job, first decide how much time you're willing to spend commuting every day. The actual distance of the commute may be different than the time it takes to drive it, especially during rush hour. For example, if most of your driving will be done on expressways that rarely have traffic backups, you may be able to move farther from your job. Someone who has to travel on a lot of surface streets that are frequently backed up will spend longer on the trip and may need to stay closer.

Remember that gasoline and maintenance costs increase with miles, as do your chances of being in an accident. Also consider how stressful driving is for you. Those in winter weather areas might find that winter commuting time may double.

When you've decided how much time you're willing to spend commuting, get a good map. The map should have a scale that converts inches to miles. Mark your job location on the map and then draw a circle around your job location covering the distance you are willing to drive. Figure about 50 miles to make an hour of commute time for freeway driving and 40 miles or less for surface streets. If you're willing to drive an hour each way to work, make a circle that includes all areas within 50 or 40 miles of your job site. Hopefully, there's a country home for you within that area.

> **Country Color**
>
> The U.S. Census Bureau found that people living in urban areas actually had longer commute times to work than those in suburban areas. New York and Maryland had the longest commute times. This is time, not distance.

If you're considering a move to another climate, define areas of the country that suit your qualifications. Florida and the deep southeastern states have mild winters but hot, humid summers. Arizona, New Mexico, and some parts of California also have mild winters but less humidity in the summer. Do some research about the various areas you're considering, and if possible, take a trip there. Experiencing Arizona in August gives you a better feel for the climate than a trip in February. And remember that all parts of a state may not have the same climate.

Also keep in mind that some areas are less expensive places to buy property and have lower taxes. Some areas are more prone to natural disasters. Other areas are running out of drinking water.

On the other hand, maybe you're moving to the country and to another state in hopes of finding a better job and economy. In that case, don't forget to factor the climate into your decisions. A new job may not be enough to keep you happy if you can't stand the weather.

What You *Want* Versus What You *Need*

Consider what you and your family want and what you need. They may be two different things. You want a lot of land, but if you aren't intending to raise crops or livestock, you probably only need an acre or two. If you do want to raise livestock, you may need more land. You might want a two-story farmhouse with a big front porch and a big red barn, but you need a sturdy house with room for the family and some kind of outbuildings for storage. You may want a home on a lake with a sandy beach but settle for beach access. You might want a home with a view of the mountains, but you need a home with wheelchair accessibility.

Needs are things you cannot do without. I'm not talking about the basic needs, like indoor plumbing, good water, and electricity that most of us wouldn't consider being without. The needs I'm referring to might vary from family to family, but they're the things you feel must be included in your new home. You might need three bedrooms and two baths. Another family might feel they need a home with a horse barn.

Wants are things you'd love to have but could do without if you must. Maybe you'd like to be on a paved road, but a gravel road is fine, too. You want a big porch, but if the house is nice, you could build a porch later. You'd love to have six bedrooms, but you could make do with three.

Write down all your wants and needs. Hopefully, you've narrowed the place where you're going to begin searching for your new country home to at least a few counties.

Qualifying for a Loan

Wouldn't it be nice to be able to just go out and buy a new home with cash? Most of us don't have that luxury and need to get a mortgage. This can take time and preparation, so as soon as you decide to move to the country and have your lists of wants and needs and some idea of what you can afford, go get qualified for a loan.

If you've never owned a home before, your financial institution might ask that you attend a first-time home buyer's class. These are usually offered through nonprofit institutions and are not trying to sell you a mortgage product. These classes are well worth attending even if you have to pay a

> **Sinkhole**
>
> Be very careful of organizations that guarantee you a loan, promise to repair your credit, or charge high fees. Do not be pressured to get a mortgage through any particular place. Good counseling places are nonprofit and don't actually offer mortgages.

small fee. They walk you through the steps of qualifying for a mortgage, including things you may need to do to repair your credit so you qualify for a lower interest rate. They may also direct you to programs that help first-time buyers afford homes. Your county Extension office may offer classes. To find counseling programs in your area, go to www.hud.gov/buying.

Don't be afraid to talk to several financial institutions about qualifying for a mortgage. Compare plans and rates, and choose one that seems right for you. When you qualify, you aren't getting a mortgage; the financial institution is just telling you that if the property meets their approval, they are willing to fund you up to a certain amount.

Showing that you've qualified for a mortgage makes realty companies much more eager to work with you. And it lets you know exactly where you stand as to how much mortgage money you can get.

Buying Vacant Land

Most mortgage companies won't fund vacant land. Vacant land is usually purchased on a land contract or with a personal loan. When you get ready to build and obtain a mortgage or building loan, the land contract or personal loan is generally paid off by the mortgage company, and the amount is added to your mortgage.

def•i•ni•tion

All **realtors** are licensed to sell real estate, but not all people licensed to sell real estate are realtors. A realtor has joined the National Association of Realtors and pledged to follow a code of ethics.

Rural Rule

If you purchase land and pay on it until you have a substantial amount of equity, it may qualify for a down payment when you're ready to build a home. Check with your lender.

If you're buying vacant land and not using a *realtor*, be sure you have a lawyer look over the paperwork, whether it's a land contract or cash sale. Yes, it will cost something, but I can tell you from experience that the fee is well worth it.

A neighbor approached my husband and me and asked if we wanted to purchase some land adjacent to our property. We decided that we wanted at least half of it and took a second mortgage on our home to pay for it. She said she worked for a real estate company and would have all the paperwork taken care of there. Sounded good, no fees, and she was a neighbor. We paid her cash.

To make a long story short—and instructive—she didn't have a clear title to the land. The real estate company she worked at for a short time—*before she was fired!*—didn't know anything about the sale. We had a title, which was recorded, and we were paying taxes on the land, but there was still a mortgage on it. We were unaware anything was wrong, as was the new owner of the other half of the property, until the original neighbor defaulted on her mortgage. We were surprised and angry when we received notices that the mortgage company was going to sell the property at a sheriff's auction. After a long and expensive battle to obtain a clear title, we finally got it, but only because the mortgage company was gracious enough to split off the property from the original mortgage.

Lesson learned: a lawyer would have checked to see if the title was clear. Other things could also have gone wrong. Always use a lawyer!

Finding a Good Agent

Whether you're buying a house or vacant land, a good realtor can help you immensely. That doesn't mean you should stop looking on your own, but a realtor often has insider information the general public doesn't have. The realty agency he or she works for has a reputation to maintain and generally will have checked to be sure the property offered has a clear title and is otherwise saleable.

A good realtor is often one who "clicks" with you. If a realtor seems friendly and eager to help you, that's probably the one to use. You, as a buyer, are not under contract to a certain realtor. You can go to another realtor if the first one doesn't seem to be that interested or is too busy to help you. But if a realtor is taking a lot of time to help you, it's good manners to let her show you homes exclusively.

> **Country Color**
>
> Some real estate agents aren't interested in showing vacant land because the commission is generally small. But they will often give you directions to vacant property or show you videos. If you live a good distance from where you want to purchase property, finding a realtor who is interested in showing you vacant property is worth the time and trouble.

Let your real estate agent know exactly what your needs and wants are—remember that list you made earlier? Also tell her what price range you can afford. If you see a home or land listed with someone else, take down the address and ask your realtor if she can get permission to show it to you. Most realtors have reciprocal agreements that allow this.

Use a Local Realtor

If you're selling a home in the city, it's tempting to have the same realtor find you a new home in the country. This can work if the country home isn't too far from the old one and the realtor is familiar with the area. But generally you'll want a separate realtor, one who deals with homes in the area where you want to move.

A local realtor knows about the area you're considering and also knows where the homes are located. Maybe she can even give you the scoop on who's getting ready to sell a home. Someone who regularly sells the type of home you're looking for—farm, beachfront, mountain cabin, etc.—likely has a feel for what's a good deal and where you can find those homes.

Consider a Buyer's Agent

No matter how well you like a certain realtor, how caring and interested in you she seems, and how experienced and knowledgeable she appears, never forget one thing: unless you've hired a buyers agent, your realtor's loyalty lies with the person whose property she's selling. That's the law, and that's who is going to pay her commission. She has to balance getting a good price for you with a sale getting less commission.

A buyer's agent works for *you*. You are paying her to find you a home you like. She has no loyalty to the seller and should work hard to get you the lowest price and protect you from fraud and misrepresentation. A buyer's agent is a particularly good choice when you live far from the area where you're searching for a new home. She can weed out some of the homes available according to your needs and wants list so your valuable time is spent only looking at qualifying homes.

> **Rural Rule**
>
> When you use an agent from an established firm, you may not need a lawyer of your own. Agents and realtors are very conscious of the law and their reputations and will do their best to conform to the law and make you a satisfied customer. If you think anything looks suspicious or you want to be extra careful, have your lawyer look over the contract.

Looking Online

Thanks to the Internet, it's easy to sit in comfort and look at property, even in areas far from where you now live. If you're looking at property and homes on the websites of established realtors, you're probably seeing fairly represented homes. It's a good place to start and see what's available in your chosen area and price range.

However, beware of scams and misrepresentations. Never send money to buy land or homes to anyone if you've only seen the property online. Remember two things:

- If it seems too good to be true, it probably is.
- Always use a lawyer!

DIY Home Searches

It never hurts to take a leisurely drive in an area you want to move to and take down addresses and realtor names and phone numbers of homes for sale. Take a camera with you to photograph the properties, recording the location of the property with each picture. You can then review them at your leisure. That sure beats trying to remember what place had the porch and which had the pond!

It's fine to do the searching for a new home yourself, if you have the time. Remember, however, that people who sign up with a realtor to sell their home generally can't or don't want to let you in their homes to look around without their realtor involved.

Sometimes people see a piece of property or a home that seems abandoned and they decide they want to buy it. Sometimes they see an occupied piece of property and want to buy that, too. It never hurts to ask someone if they're interested in selling a home or piece of property. But if they say no, be polite and go away.

> **Country Color**
>
> A *plat book* can tell you who owns a particular piece of property, if it is of certain acreage (the size varies by area). Ask the county clerks office or the county Extension office if they offer such books. They're usually available at local libraries, too. For smaller pieces of land with an address, the county treasurer may be able to tell you who pays the taxes.

Buying from Family and Friends

When word gets out that you're thinking about moving to the country, someone you know might approach you and offer to sell you land. Or you may decide to ask Gramps if you can buy some of his land. Buying from family and friends may seem easy, but it comes with some special pitfalls.

As the story I related earlier in this chapter illustrates, always use a lawyer when purchasing real estate. Your friend or relative might not be trying to fool you, but they might inadvertently do something wrong during the paperwork that could come back to haunt you in a big way. Or they might be unaware of something in the properties paper trail that needs to be fixed so you have clear title. Even if they work in real estate and seem to know what they're doing, consult with a lawyer before closing the sale.

If you're buying on land contract from a family member or friends, who will you pay if that person dies? You may have an informal agreement that both you and the seller honored, but if interest or ownership of the property passes to someone else, that contract may not be recognized. If the land contract is prepared by a lawyer, your interest in the property is protected legally should a question arise. You may avoid family feuds, too.

There are additional pitfalls when buying from family and friends. You might not feel comfortable negotiating a price or requiring a survey be done. And the friend or family member may have unrealistic expectations from you as the purchaser of the land. Does Gramps feel that because he sold you the property you will always be around to help with the chores? Do Uncle Charlie and Aunt Grace think they'll be able to come back for a vacation anytime? Sometimes relatives want the property to remain as they left it and have hurt feelings if you tear down the barn or remodel the house. Or they may never have allowed hunting on the property and your husband is an avid hunter.

It's better to try to anticipate issues that could come up before they become huge problems. You can then decide if you want to buy from a family member or friend or elsewhere, without strings attached.

Buying from Strangers

You may come across a wonderful home or piece of land that's for sale by owner. Some of these owners are delightful people who are experienced in real estate transactions. Others have no clue about what they're doing other than avoiding paying someone a commission. The owner can be pleasantly daffy or mean and crabby, and it's very important that you do not use personality to judge whether or not you should buy their property. It's what they know about the property and selling it that counts.

To buy on your own, without a real estate agent's help, requires some careful homework and planning. You will, of course, use a lawyer to draw up and finalize the actual sales agreement. Here's a list of things you should do:

- ◆ Look at other real estate listings in the area to see what similar pieces of property in the area are selling for.

- Find out the zoning for the area and if there are building restrictions.

- Insist on seeing the results of a recent survey or having a survey done. The property boundary corners should be plainly marked.

- Thoroughly inspect the property. Walk the land and inspect every building.

Take your time, and don't be pressured or sweet-talked into a sale. Be sure the seller knows that your lawyer will inspect any documents before you will sign them. (See Chapters 4 and 5 for additional things to look for in selecting country property.)

Inherited or Gift Property

Inheriting or being given country property sounds like it would be the best possible thing that could happen to someone who wants to live in the country. It can be the answer to your prayers, and everyone will live happily ever after. But there can be pitfalls, too. Inherited or gift property may have abandoned dumpsites that require expensive clean-up, back taxes that will cost you a considerable sum, unusable water, lawsuits and liens involving the property, and numerous other problems. Sometimes a clever and resourceful person can make lemonade out of lemons, but other times, you'll be just as well served to decline the gift.

Country Color

I knew of a young man who wanted to farm, and he was offered some property for a very nominal price, almost a gift. From the road, the property looked nice. He didn't do his homework though, and on the property was a gully that had been used as a public dump. The gully was primarily filled with tires—thousands of them. The township had issued an order that the property be cleaned up within so many months. The young man was able to use clever thinking and hard labor to clean out the gully and eventually was able to use the land. But other people have found out the hard way that things aren't always as they seem.

Sometimes the property would be just fine—for someone else. Maybe you don't want to live 50 miles from a store, in the desert, or right next to Uncle Bob. If you don't want to live there, don't feel bad about selling the place and buying a country home where you do want to live.

You might inherit or be given property that you'd really adore to live on. But the house may require more upkeep or expensive repairs than your salary can afford. The taxes on the property might be more than your current rent payment. You would have to give up your job if you moved there. All are big problems.

Think long and hard about this situation. Sometimes a compromise will allow you to keep the place. Could you sell off part of the property? Could you rent out part of the house? Could your job transfer you to a position in that area? Don't squeeze yourself too tightly financially, but don't be afraid to take a little risk, either.

That Head-Heart Thing

Just because you can imagine sitting on that deck watching the ocean, don't make it impossible for your children to ever go to college. Just because it's so close to the best skiing in the world, don't take the seller's word that the road is always maintained free of charge and you'll never get snowed in. That sweet old lady who's weeping as she tells you she can't afford a survey and she'll send you the deed next week if you just pay her today might not be as sweet and honest as she seems.

Stop. Think. Listen to reason. Trust your instincts if they seldom fail you, but do your research, too. Use a lawyer when it involves the transfer of money and a good chunk of your life to repay a loan.

There is such a thing as overthinking a decision. Don't stall on the tracks, or the train will go right over you. Real estate agents know that buyers sometimes panic at the last minute, or even after the sale is completed. It's called buyer's remorse. Sometimes there's good reason for it; other times it's just because the step is so frightening.

Your move to the country will remain a dream unless you take those first steps then keep on walking all the way home. If you have prepared and planned for this moment, start walking.

The Least You Need to Know

- Clearly and honestly define your wants and needs, and stay focused on that list.

- A good realtor, particularly a buyer's agent, may be immensely helpful in finding the perfect country home.

- Always use a lawyer when purchasing country property without a realtor.

- Use your head *and* your heart. Both are vital factors in the country home–buying equation.

Chapter 4

Purchasing Vacant Land

In This Chapter

◆ Finding the right size property

◆ Zoning ordinances and building restrictions

◆ The importance of water

◆ Getting a survey

◆ Inspecting the property

It's easy to fall in love with a beautiful view. But the view isn't the most important thing to consider when purchasing vacant land. There are many things to consider when looking for country property.

When you go to look at vacant land, you're often on your own. Real estate agents may take you to the property, but they may not know much about the land. Many times you'll be sent to look at the land on your own.

Talking to the owner, especially if he has owned the land for a long time, may help you make vital decisions. Even if the land is for sale by owner, though, he may not be helpful or honest. It's up to you to do the research and take the time to be sure the property is right for you.

Is It the Right Size?

When you go out looking for land, or send a realtor looking for you, you should have some idea of how much you want. If you want horses or other livestock, you'll want enough land to satisfy any zoning ordinances. If you want to be secluded from neighbors, you'll need a bit more property than someone who is fine with seeing a neighbor's house. In the arid Southwest, you'll need a lot more acres to support your horses than in the Midwest or East. If the land is swampy, you'll need enough land to include a dry spot to build a house.

Be flexible when going to look at land. If you're moving to the country for recreational activities and don't care about room to garden or raise animals, a small piece of land backing up to thousands of acres of state land may be just right. If you're set on living in a certain area such as on a lake, you may have to settle for the lot size available.

When many people settle on small parcels in an unimproved area, it can be a strain on nature to support many wells drawing off the same groundwater and many septic systems pumping waste into the soil. If you're buying fewer than 2 acres in a newly subdivided area, use caution. Ask the developer or seller if he can guarantee that wells and septic systems will work properly when the area is fully developed.

How Big Is Too Big?

As long as you can afford the purchase and pay the taxes, there's no such thing as too much land. Land is and always will be valuable. If you buy too much now you can always sell some later. But don't make yourself land poor. It won't help to have a thousand acres if you can't afford to build a house on them.

Land is going up in price, and too big may be what is too much for you to afford. Remember that after you build a home on your land, your property taxes will go up. Property that has road frontage or a drain running through it may be assessed taxes per foot for road improvements or drain clearing. If you're on lake or ocean side property, you may have to pay for beach maintenance.

Maintenance Concerns

In the country, if you have a lot of acres, you don't have to maintain all the land as you would in a small subdivision yard. You can leave some land as meadows and forest. If the land is now cropland, you can let it revert to a meadow or forest, which it will do rather quickly. Planting native trees and shrubs, or creating a pond or wetland, is ecologically sound. Creating 2 acres of lawn is not.

Some pieces of property may have more maintenance concerns. If the property has or needs break walls to keep water from washing away the land, you'll have to maintain them. If the spot for a driveway will pass over marshy land, you'll need to maintain that. If the spot you want is on the side of a mountain, you may need lots of maintenance in rainy weather. If the only clear spot to build a home is way back in the trees, you might be spending a lot of time plowing that driveway in the winter. Many areas of the country are susceptible to wildfire, and you do need to have a clear spot around the house for fire safety. (I discuss this in more detail in Chapter 7.)

Rural Rule

To keep large pieces of land affordable, you can lease some of it for farming or hunting. In some areas, your taxes will be reduced if you put your property into a conservation or farmland trust. In some cases, you can divide the land into parcels and pay higher taxes only on the parcel with the home on it.

On most pieces of property, the only maintenance you really have to do is to clearly mark your boundaries and keep an area around the home clear.

Zoning Ordinances

Almost every township, ward, and/or county has some form of zoning. Zoning determines what can be done on a piece of property within a certain area. This is generally part of a long-term plan for the development of an area.

When buying land, the zoning is an important consideration. You could buy land only to find that you can't build a home on it or that the restrictions for building are so great that it's impractical and too expensive. Other zoning restrictions could limit your enjoyment of the property.

Determining Your Zone

A real estate agent generally has the zoning information in the property description. But realty agents don't make a big profit on vacant land and sometimes spend less time reviewing the listing than with a home sale. A mortgage company generally won't check up on the property because vacant land is seldom, if ever, mortgaged. So if you get serious about a piece of property, it's vital that you check the zoning yourself.

To check the zone, get the tax ID or address of the property and go to the offices of the township, village, or county it's in. Sometimes a map with the zones colored in can help you determine the property's zone. Other times, someone will need to look it up for you. Be sure it's the most current zoning information available, as the zoning may change when property is divided and put up for sale.

The zoning may be listed in a variety of ways. The usual zones are residential, agriculture, business, and manufacturing, but there can be many variations of these categories plus zoning specific to the area, such as mining. Look for residential or agricultural zoning. In some very remote areas, there may be no zoning at all.

Zoning Restrictions

In residential zoning, you need to consider the type of home you're going to put on the land. Some areas require homes of a certain minimum size. Some restrict the use of trailers or modular homes. If you're thinking about a very unusual type of home such as a yurt (a circular or domed tent home), you'll need to be very careful when checking zoning and building restrictions.

In some areas, homes cannot be built on the property unless a certain amount of acreage or road frontage is present. Endangered species on the land, wetlands, or even historic trees may be other causes for restrictions. These may be listed as zoning ordinances or building restrictions. Zoning restrictions also let you know if the property can be divided again if you want to sell some of the property.

Although some residential property allows a certain number of animals with a certain property size, if you want to have horses or other livestock, you'll probably want to look for agricultural zoning.

Sinkhole

Don't assume that because horses are across the street or even on the property now that you can have them after you buy the property. When zoning is changed, people who have livestock are usually allowed to keep them. New buyers won't be allowed.

If you're buying property to build a home and operate a new business, be sure the type of business you want to run is allowed in that zone. Agricultural property generally allows some agriculture-related businesses, but residential zoning may allow no business operations.

Zoning can sometimes be changed or an exemption or modification made, but don't buy property on the assumption that this will happen. It's often an expensive and lengthy process that can cause hard feelings in your new community. It's better to start with property where the zoning suits your needs.

What About Water?

Good land for building a home should have just the right amount and kind of water. Too much or too little water severely impacts your ability to build a home on the land and the value of the property. Sometimes you can see a problem with water when you look at a piece of land, but other times you cannot.

When the property is near any body of water, including small streams, one concern should be flooding. Flood insurance is expensive, and even a small stream can turn into a raging torrent of water when conditions are right. Living by the ocean or on one of the Great Lakes can invite other problems. Ice jams and storms on the lakes are known to flood lakeside property. High tides or storm surges do the same on ocean side property.

When checking property, look for signs that it has flooded in the past. Low-lying areas with few trees and very lush grass and weeds may be a sign. A line of debris washed up to a particular area or signs of damage to tree trunks at a certain point are also telltale signs of flooding. Certain plants like cattails, black ash, willows, and other plants that like wet areas are another sign.

Avoid building on land that regularly floods. If the flooding is limited to very unusual years, you might carefully consider the property and how you can build on it.

Too Much Water

Land that has a high water table is excellent for building a pond but not so good for building a septic system. You can find out how suitable the land is for a septic system by having a *perk test* done. Sometimes the person selling the land will have the perk test done when the property is surveyed. If it's not been done, it's a good idea to have a clause in the sales agreement stating the sale is subject to a good perk test. Some septic systems are engineered to deal with some drainage problems, but they are expensive to build and maintain.

Poor perk tests can also occur when there just isn't enough soil above a bedrock layer. (In Chapter 15, I cover septic drainage in more detail.)

A high water table does more than affect the septic system. It may make a basement in a home impractical. Driveways

def•i•ni•tion

A **perk test** involves digging a hole, filling it with water, and seeing how well it drains. There's a formula to this, so hire a professional to conduct this test.

to the home may become impassable or require frequent repaving or regraveling. Landscaping problems can also occur.

Wetlands are excellent homes for a diverse number of plant and animal species and are vital to filtering, absorbing, and cleaning runoff water. However, they also breed tons of mosquitoes or even pests like alligators and may not be great to have close to your home.

Don't think that you'll just fill in these low spots. Most states now have laws that limit what you can do to wetlands, even on your own land.

Availability of Drinking Water

Some water you *do* want on your property. In fact, if you don't have good drinking water available, the property probably isn't worth building on.

Groundwater availability is more of a problem in some areas than others. If it is a problem, local well drillers and other nearby homeowners will know, so ask around. It isn't as easy to test for good drinking water as it is to do a perk test and check for good drainage. Therefore, you'll need to rely on the experience of others in the area.

If you find out that the area you're considering doesn't always have good wells, you may want to add a clause to the sales agreement stating that a working, safe well is a condition of sale. Even in the best groundwater areas, a well driller sometimes cannot find good water. This is a part of buying and building on vacant land that requires a little faith and hope.

Houses can be built that use cisterns for drinking water. This is much more work and expense, so avoid it if possible. (Find out more about cisterns in Chapter 14.)

Defining the Land

When land is newly subdivided and offered for sale, it's usually just been surveyed and the corners marked. Older pieces, and especially property offered for sale by owner, may not have been surveyed. The seller may state that a survey will be done after the sale and give approximate boundaries until then.

And the Survey Says ...

If the property has a certain feature you definitely want included in your purchase, be sure a survey is done before you buy the property. If you aren't particular and just think the land in general is nice, you can do a survey after the sale.

Your deed will show you bought a certain piece of legally described property, but you'll have no physical sign where the property begins and ends until you get the survey. In the meantime, it's good to have someone show you where the boundaries are. However, it's been my experience that you can't always rely on real estate agents or even owners to know exactly where the boundaries are. You also cannot count on old landmarks, such as fence posts or tree lines. In nearly every case where I bought property, there was a discrepancy in where the boundary was said to be and where it actually was.

When a survey is done, the surveyors generally mark the corners of the piece with a metal rod driven into the ground and then add aboveground stakes with florescent flags. These aboveground stakes disappear quickly, so when you buy your property, find and mark the corners with a good, strong metal post for future reference.

Rural Rule

You absolutely must have a survey done before you begin any improvements on the property.

Are You on the Right Piece?

How do you know when you're on the piece of property that's for sale? This can be tricky. You don't want to walk all over a nice piece of land and fall in love with it only to find that you were supposed to be on the *left* side of the real estate sign when you were on the *right*. So get good directions and ask questions.

When you're serious about buying land, bring a 200-foot or longer tape measure with you—or better yet, borrow a *measuring wheel*. Measuring gives you a better idea of what "200 feet from the NE corner of Section 8" means. You'll also need a legal description that tells you those measurements or some written indication of the size and shape of the land. Here are some land measurement terms you may see:

◆ A *rod* equals 5.5 yards or 16.6 feet.

◆ An *acre* is 43,560 square feet, 4,840 square yards, or 160 square rods.

◆ A *section* is a mile square and contains 640 acres.

◆ A *township* consists of 36 sections.

def•i•ni•tion

A **measuring wheel** looks like a bike wheel with a handle. As you roll it along the ground, it clicks off feet like a pedometer does when you walk. You can sometimes borrow or rent a measuring wheel at your county Extension office or the Soil Conservation and Natural Resources office. If you want to buy one, they cost less than $100 and are handy to have around a country home site.

A square 2-acre piece of land will look much different from a rectangular or oddly shaped 2-acre piece of land. Don't depend on the acreage amount to decide if the property is right for you or even if you can build on it. If it's only 50 feet wide at the road, you may have a 5-acre parcel but not a parcel you can build on if the zoning requires 200 feet of road frontage. Or you could have property that's 200 feet wide along the road but only 50 feet deep—not a choice piece.

Check for Encroachments

An encroachment is any use of the land not by the legal owners. You may notice a fence or shed that seems to be on the property you're interested in. Someone showing you the property could mention "Billy Green has his shed a little over the line, but I told him not to worry."

Encroachments can mean big trouble and must be dealt with before a sale. There are various ways to deal with encroachments. You can insist that all encroachments be removed before a sale. What the encroachment is and how you intend to use the property will help you decide what to do. For example, a fence that's a few inches over the line might not be a problem. A garage that sits on property you want to buy might be a considerable problem.

Country Color

In some areas, a person using land for a certain number of years actually ends up owning it. This is called adverse possession.

If you're inclined to let things be, a lawyer can draw up a legal agreement that the person doing the trespassing has to sign. (Of course, the lawyer will first check to see if the seller still has rights to the land encroached on.) The agreement states that the user of the land knows he is on your property and is using it with your permission and does not seek to own the land. Fees or other stipulations may be added according to the situation.

In all cases of encroachment, it's strongly advisable to consult with a lawyer before making an offer on property. If you've made an offer or bought the property and then discover an encroachment, consult a lawyer at once.

Check for Easements and Lake Access

Easements and accesses are similar to encroachments but usually just require travel on your property to another location off your property. They may also allow you to travel on someone else's property to get to your property or to another location. Utility easements allow utility companies to maintain electric or other services that cross your property. Easements should be part of the legal property description. Frequently there will be a road easement on the front of your property that allows for public travel. Public road or utility easements rarely cause problems. Other types of easements may become problematic.

If someone uses part of your property to get to their land, they need a legal easement. The person selling the land should have that easement put in the legal property description and state exactly what the easement is intended to do. If the public uses part of your land to travel to a beach or boat dock or other destination, that should also be part of the legal description.

Problems arise when you're buying land that you need an easement to access. Don't let the seller tell you that he will always let you use that driveway to reach your home, even if the seller is Uncle Joe—what happens if Uncle Joe dies and his heirs decide they no longer want you to cross the land? Get it in writing, as part of the selling agreement and the deed. And use a lawyer.

Problems also arise when an easement or access road suddenly begins to be used for something not originally intended. Maybe the access to the beach has become a place where boaters are storing their boats all winter. Maybe the driveway to the landlocked house becomes the road to a new subdivision with lots of traffic. Or the owner of the landlocked house has decided to do some gravel mining and huge trucks begin lumbering through your property at all times of the day. Having the size, location, and use of the easement in writing and legally recorded will save you a world of grief later.

Pay attention to the deed and selling agreement of property you're buying. An easement may not be in evidence now or even in use, but if it exists, it may become a problem in the future.

Check for Rights

Your sales agreement, and eventually your deed, should mention if any "rights" to your property have been sold. In some cases, mineral and gas rights, timber rights, water rights, or other rights have been sold. This means that someone else owns the minerals, gas, water, or whatever on that piece of property.

Sinkhole

If someone owns the mineral rights on your property, they also have the right to come in and mine for them, however inconvenient that is for you. And if they have the timber rights, they can come and cut down all the trees. They get all the profit from the sale of what they took from your property.

It's to your advantage to own all the rights to your land. If someone wants to look for oil on your land, for example, you can then lease access to them and control how and where the well is put in—and share the profits.

Walk the Property

If you're looking for easements and measuring a piece of property you're interested in, you are probably walking it. But unless you're considering a huge amount of land, you should attempt to walk every foot of the place. Thick brush or swampy areas may prevent you from accessing some places, but at least you'll know they're there.

Rural Rule

Bring a camera with you and photograph the property. Be sure to label the photos in some way. If you're looking at several pieces of land, this will help you remember things about the property.

You might be surprised at what you will find when you walk a piece of property. From the road, that tree line may look nice, but it could be concealing a gully full of junk. When you attempt to get close to that beach, you might find 50 feet of sucking muck. Or behind that tree line could be a strip mining operation or a factory farm.

If you're lucky, that piece of land that looks rather average from the road will be concealing a spring-fed pond in that grove of trees or offer a breathtaking mountain view just over that little hill. You'll never know unless you walk the land.

Think About Seasonal Changes

When looking at property, consider how it may look at other times of the year. When the leaves fall, do you get a view of 30 junk cars and a rundown barn? Or when the trees leaf out, is your view of the lake gone?

Also consider how good access to the property will be in all kinds of weather. In some remote areas, roads aren't maintained all year round and may be impassable at some times. Even roads that are maintained may flood in the spring or turn into wheel-high mud.

The sun may feel good in February, but how good will it feel in August with no trees and miles of sand around you? The wind off the lake feels wonderful in July, but how will it feel when it's –10 degrees?

It would be ideal if you could visit the land in all seasons, but that probably isn't practical. You'll need to use your imagination and your reasoning skills to determine how the seasons affect the property you're looking at.

How Was the Land Used Before?

We've probably all heard the horror stories of homes built on old landfill sites, so when buying property, consider the land's previous uses. Even if it wasn't a toxic waste dump, building a home over a landfill area isn't wise. The settling of the soil over time may crack foundations, and wells may become polluted from old household waste. And people may continue to dump surprises on you from time to time!

Old farm or ranch land is probably one of the most common sources of new country lots. Most of the time this land is fine, although it may take some landscaping to turn a cornfield into a comfortable home site. But buying old farmland can have some problems. The soil may be heavily contaminated with pesticides used on crops or too salty to grow anything after years of crop irrigation. The land could also have abandoned wells or old basements that are a safety hazard.

If you have a choice of lots carved from an old farm, it might be wise to choose sites away from old homes or barns. You'll be less likely to unearth surprises during home construction. The downside to this is that electricity and phone lines may already be close to the old house site, and you'll pay extra to extend them to your site.

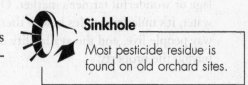

Sinkhole

Most pesticide residue is found on old orchard sites.

When my sister bought some rural property, she was unaware that the long-abandoned farm was a hot spot for hunters. As one irate hunter told her when he was asked to leave, he had "hunted the land for 30 years and wasn't about to stop because [she] bought the place." It is a scary and intimidating thing to see groups of armed men parked in the driveway and spread out across the property despite No Trespassing signs.

If the property appears to be a party spot or is being used as a public beach, boat ramp, hiking trail, or ski slope, you may have more trouble than it's worth trying to change the use of the land and protect your privacy. If you allow the use to continue, you could be liable if a problem occurs.

Talk to the Neighbors

You can learn a lot about a piece of property if you take the time to talk to nearby neighbors. One of the things you might learn is that you don't want to live anywhere near them. More likely, you'll learn some colorful history and maybe something you really should know—such as there's an old mine shaft back there home to thousands of bats.

Ask about the well water and if there have been any problems. Ask about the roads and if you can access them all year. Most people will be helpful, but be aware that some will try to mislead you, either because they want you to buy the land or they don't want you to. Talking to neighbors will give you a feel for how the community views newcomers, too.

Drive the Area

The last thing to do when you're seriously considering buying property is take a tour of the area. Where are the stores, the hospitals, the schools? How far is it to the main roads? Is some industry nearby that could impact your quality of life?

You may find you're close to some wonderful recreational areas or near a quaint village or wonderful farmer's market. Or you could find that although you're near the water, it's miles and miles before there's public access to it. The feel of the area, the way people live, and the availability of certain amenities may change your mind about buying the property.

The Least You Need to Know

- The view is not the only thing to consider when buying land. Views can change with the seasons or hide big problems.

- Be sure to check the deed for zoning and easements. Don't count on the current use of the land or what someone tells you about the property to determine what kind of home, animals, or business you can have.

- When you walk the land, look for problems such as dump sites, party sites, encroachments, and hazards such as abandoned wells.

- Be sure good well water is available, but also be sure there's not too much water that could cause problems for you later.

5

Purchasing Existing Houses and Outbuildings

In This Chapter

- ◆ Inspecting country homes
- ◆ Testing country home systems
- ◆ Checking out existing structures

Buying a home in the country is much like buying a home in the suburbs or city. But there are some special considerations to keep in mind when purchasing a country home. Country homes may have wells and septic systems and other things you're not familiar with; they may have unusual heating systems and outbuildings, and they might not have all the amenities you're used to in the city. If this is the first home you're buying, you may be even more confused or surprised at what you find.

In Chapter 4, we looked at vacant land. Many of the same things that pertain to the land mentioned in Chapter 4 pertain to the land the home you're considering purchasing sits on, too, so in this chapter, we look at the actual home.

Get It Inspected

You have to like the looks of the home and feel safe there. But don't choose a home based on looks alone. A house can look very nice but have serious structural problems. On the other hand, a home may be in need of lots of cleaning and sprucing up but be basically sound and in good working order.

If you're purchasing a home with a mortgage, the mortgage company will probably send a licensed building inspector to check out the home. It wants to be sure the house is worth the money it's loaning you. You'll be told if the mortgage company thinks the house is not worth the price asked. It may give the seller a list of things that need to be fixed, too.

Rural Rule

You'll probably pay for the home inspection, so ask for a copy of the report. Some things the inspector finds during the inspection might not affect the mortgage loan, but knowing about them may give you a bargaining advantage with the seller. You may ask for those things to be repaired or that the selling price be lowered.

If you're buying a house other than with a mortgage, such as with cash or a land contract, always have a professional inspector go over the home. It really will save you money in the long run. You might think you can spot a leaking roof or cracked foundation, but there are many things only a trained and experienced inspector will be able to evaluate.

Most home inspectors are honest and fair. However, there have been cases where realtors or sellers have paid inspectors to give homes good reports when they didn't deserve them. If you have a gut feeling that something isn't right even after the inspector gives his okay, it might be worth it to hire a second inspector.

How's the Water?

The mortgage company will probably order a well test before it approves a mortgage because a bad well drastically lowers the value of a home. If the mortgage company doesn't do this, have the water tested yourself. (See Chapter 14 to learn about testing well water and what to do about well problems.) Test the water for contaminants, and also see how much water pressure the home has and how the water tastes and smells. Ask for a glass of cold water, and taste it. It probably won't taste like city water, but if you can drink it, that's a good sign.

Turn on several taps at the same time, particularly those on an upper floor. Do you get a good flow of water? Poor water pressure can be the result of a faulty or under-size pressure tank or pump or from a well going dry. Pumps and tanks can be replaced much easier than a well. If there seems to be a problem, have a plumber check it out.

Look around the home for signs of other water problems like hard water scale and rust on the fixtures from mineral-rich water. Does the house have a water treatment system? Is it just a softener, or does it filter other things from the water? Suspicious signs of a water problem include large quantities of stored water, taps that don't work, expensive and elaborate filtering systems, and more than one well.

Ask About the Septic System

Country homes handle the disposal of waste from the toilet, sinks, laundry, etc. via the septic system. Some professional inspectors properly inspect the septic tank, but many skip this part as long as the septic system seems to be working. If the tank has been recently pumped and the seller has proof or the system is new, inspection may not be necessary. But there are some things you should check.

Locate the Parts

Have the seller or realtor show you where the septic tank and septic field are located. It's important to know if they're sited properly and accessible because septic tanks need to be pumped out periodically. (See Chapter 15 for information on how the system works.) The suctioning equipment accesses the tank through a lid or a special hookup outside the home. If you don't know where the septic tank is, you risk paving or otherwise covering the access point, which can create a huge problem. The septic tank normally has grass or mulch over it, but the homeowner should be able to point out the site. If in doubt, take a metal probe and feel for the lid.

Have the seller point out the septic field, too. This is where water is absorbed into the soil. Unless it's new, it will probably just look like any other area of the lawn. There should be no pavement over it, no large trees growing near it, and nothing showing aboveground. Some engineered septic systems look like a berm or mound.

The septic system should be located at least 50 feet away from the well. In new homes, this generally isn't a problem, but older homes often have the septic tank too close to the well. If you find this is the case with the home you're considering purchasing, you'll have to monitor your well water very carefully.

Signs of Septic Failure

Unless it's raining heavily, there shouldn't be any wet areas over the septic tank or field. There should be no smell of sewer. Water or very wet soil above the septic tank or field or a strong odor means there's a problem. A failing septic system can be extremely expensive to repair or replace.

Inside the home, flush every toilet and see if they drain quickly. If they don't, it could mean a clogged pipe or that the tank needs pumping. A telltale sign of a poor septic system is a wastebasket full of used toilet paper. Instead of flushing it, the homeowner has opted to keep solids out of a failing septic system. It's nasty and a sign you need to have the tank inspected.

Inspect the Basement or Crawl Space

If the home you're looking at has a basement or cellar, inspect it. Country cellars can be a scary experience. Sometimes they're accessed by a door on the outside of the home; other times, you may have to lift up a trap door somewhere in the house to get under it. And the access stairs might be steep or dimly lit. But take a flashlight and go look anyway.

The basement may simply be a hole in the ground under the house with stone or cement walls and a dirt floor. It may not be tall enough to stand up in. In more recently built homes, it may be a fully finished basement. If the doors are outside the home, be sure they're safe and don't leak. Metal doors are preferable to wood, which can rot away in time.

In the basement, look for a *sump pump*. This could indicate a water problem (but not always; even more modern homes may have a sump pump for times when the basement leaks). Take a look around to see if the walls look like any flooding has occurred in the past or if everything is up off the floor. Ask the seller how often they have trouble with leaks.

def•i•ni•tion

A **sump pump** is a pump, usually in the basement, that pumps leaking water out of a home. It's usually set to come on if water rises to a certain level.

You can check the condition of plumbing pipes and heating conduits under the house. Signs of rotting floors above or sagging beams may be evident. In older homes, the well and pump may be in the basement. Do they seem to be clean and functioning? Look for plumbing leaks and signs of insects and rodents.

If the heating system is in the basement, take a look at it. Are the ducts solid, with no holes or duct tape patches? Does the furnace look old or fairly modern? Are hazardous things stored near the furnace?

There may be a root cellar dug out of the side of the basement. This is where apples and potatoes and other things may have been stored. There may be an old coal bin also. These are not problems if they are cleaned out.

Rural Rule

If a lot of old jars of canned food, old paint, pesticides, junked equipment, etc. are stored in the basement, make it part of the purchase agreement that those things are cleaned out.

In some areas of the country, a colorless, odorless gas called *radon* may seep into basements from naturally occurring deposits. Radon is believed to cause health problems, including cancer. Ask your real estate agent if radon is a problem in the area and if the home has been tested for it. (It's relatively easy to test for it.) There are ways to seal leaks or otherwise remove radon from homes.

Some country homes that don't have basements have a storm shelter underground somewhere close to the house. Inspect it to see if it's still functional.

Special Country Home Precautions

Older country homes may have different problems than older city homes, although some problems are the same. Tighter regulations, regular trash pickup, and different use of the property change the type of problems some homes have. Newer country homes may also have problems that are more common to the country.

Stored Hazardous Wastes

Agricultural use of the land may have led to the homeowners using and storing large amounts of chemicals, fertilizers, and other substances. Farmers can get special licenses to handle chemicals that homeowners don't have access to. These are more likely to be stored in an outbuilding, but some could be stored in the attic or basements of homes. Some chemicals may have been stored on the property for a long time. People put them away and forget about them, or they don't know how to safely dispose of them. If they leak, or children and pets get into them, it can be very dangerous. Even small amounts of some chemicals can be dangerous in the wrong hands.

When inspecting potential country property, check all the outbuildings, barn lofts, basements, crawl spaces, storm cellars, cupboards, and attics for stored pesticides and other chemicals. They can be in bags, bottles, big drums, or even loose piles.

> **Rural Rule** _____
>
> If, after you've bought a home, you discover old chemicals, call your health department or county Extension agency to ask what to do. Many counties have periodic hazardous waste collection days or a place to bring hazardous wastes year round.

Hazardous waste also includes old gasoline and fuel oil tanks that may still contain gas or oil. Sometimes these are buried in the ground, but they may also be aboveground. If the home no longer uses fuel oil for heat, or the gasoline tank is corroded and unusable, the tanks should be removed. The contents can leak and contaminate groundwater, or explosions and fire can result.

Some hazardous waste can be very difficult and expensive to dispose of safely. If you find hazardous waste when inspecting a home to buy, make the owner remove it as a condition of the sale.

Lead Paint

All old homes—country and city alike—were probably painted with lead-based paints at one time. Country homes may have many outbuildings and fences that were also painted. Lead paint becomes a problem when it flakes off and gets into the soil, is breathed in, or is ingested. It would be very hard to remove all the old traces of lead from a country home site. This is just to remind you that the soil around old homes, barns, and buildings may be contaminated, and care should be used when building children's play areas or planting vegetable gardens close to them.

Using old painted lumber for crafts and home improvement projects could also prove to be a problem. This is especially true when sawing the lumber and fine particles get in the air. Old, weathered, paint-free wood should be safe.

Kits are available to test for lead, and many laboratories can also test soil for lead if you need to know.

Pest Inspections

One of the joys of country life is dealing with critters. You are going to have to deal with pests, even if you build a brand-new home. (I discuss them later in Chapter 24.) For now, let's consider the pests that may be currently infesting a home you intend to buy.

One of the worst cases of a missed pest problem I know of concerned a young woman who called me about bats in her newly purchased home. Bats are common in old homes, but this was more than a few bats. *Thousands* of bats filled a part of the home's attic and the void between two walls.

The woman was a single mother with two boys who had used all her savings to put a down payment on a home in the country. She purchased the home in winter, with the help of a real estate company. Bats are inactive in winter, though, so she noticed nothing unusual, other than a slight smell in one upper floor room. In early spring, when she had moved in and the bats were waking up, the problem hit her head on. The bats were not in the living space, but the attic had 3 feet of bat droppings—which began to smell quite ripe as the weather warmed! The sound of the bats squeaking, scratching, and rustling kept the family from sleeping at night, too.

An inspection by a pest company revealed that bat urine was degrading the home's wiring. The company estimated that 3,000 to 5,000 bats were present! It would take thousands of dollars to remove the droppings, tear out walls to clean, rewire parts of the home, and put up excluders to keep the bats out.

You can bet the previous owners knew about this problem but chose not to tell the buyer. The real estate company may or may not have been aware of the problem; that's up to a court to decide. But the buyer didn't do a good inspection, and she learned a sad and horrible lesson.

Check every room, all attics, basements, and crawl spaces for signs of pests. Strange noises or smells may alert you to the presence of pests. Be suspicious if a seller doesn't want you to go in attics or basements or certain rooms. Open the doors of closets and cabinets. Look for chewed areas and holes. Do you see droppings anywhere? Look for things the homeowner may be doing to combat a problem, such as putting out rat bait or having an ultrasonic device running in the attic. (Read Chapter 24 for more signs of pest presence.)

> **Sinkhole**
>
> A few bats in a home may be hard to spot, as will a few mice or even rats. A few of anything can generally be dealt with without a lot of expense and danger. It's when the pest population gets large that you want to run.

Animals like raccoons and squirrels are cute, but they're also very destructive and should be kept out of homes. These animals can be hard to get rid of if they've been around a while. Bats are great for the environment outside your home, but your house may be condemned if the population grows large inside. Bats can carry rabies and other diseases.

Signs of insect problems such as termites may be hard to detect. In areas where termites are common, the mortgage lender might require a termite inspection. A flea infestation in a home may result in you getting bites around your ankles.

Pests in outbuildings aren't as important unless they've reached very high numbers. A skunk under the porch can seem like a bad thing, but it's a temporary problem that can be fixed. Woodchucks under the shed or possums in the barn can also be kept under control.

A good home inspector will spot pest problems. A good, honest real estate company will have pest problems reported on the disclosure. If you get a chance to talk to the sellers, ask about pest problems.

Real Estate Disclosures

Most real estate companies have sellers fill out a disclosure form that asks them to report any serious problems in the home or on the property they're selling that would not be obvious on inspection. If the seller knows of a problem and doesn't disclose it, he or she can be subject to legal action.

This disclosure is open to all kinds of interpretation. The sellers have to know of the problem—that can be proved if they ever consulted someone, had the problem worked on, etc. If they say they never went in the attic and saw the bats or say they never smelled or heard them, they might get away with it.

If a buyer had free access to a house and didn't inspect it and the court rules that an ordinary person could have spotted the problem, the buyer may not have any grounds for complaint. If you can't physically inspect the home, or feel embarrassed about doing it, hire someone to do it.

The Fixer-Upper

Many people believe the best way to find the country place of their dreams is to find a rundown home and restore it. This can be less expensive in the short term, but it could possibly cost you much more in the long run. Or it might be the charm of an old place, or its sentimental value, that turns you into a handyman. Either way, be sure you carefully consider what you're about to undertake if contemplating a fixer-upper. Fixing up an old home can be a lesson in patience, humility, endurance, and stress management.

If you can live in the home, and you have the time and skills, it's probably a good match for you. If, on the other hand, the place cannot safely be lived in, you have to squeeze work on it in between caring for your other home and a job, and you have little experience in home improvement, you may be getting in over your head.

At least be sure the basic structure is still sound and the well and septic systems work or are fixable. Running water and a leak-free roof make living in a home improvement project bearable.

> **Rural Rule** _____
>
> While you're checking out the house, ask about Internet accessibility, TV reception, and cable availability, if those items are important to you. High-speed Internet connections may not be available in some parts of the country, and cable TV might not reach to your potential country home. Satellite dishes are available for both Internet and television just about everywhere now, but they can be costly.

Examine Existing Structures

When you look at country property, you may find all kinds of outbuildings. Take the time to look them over and find out what they were used for. This can give you insight as to the history and use of the property.

Barns, Defined

Barns in the South and West tend to be long and narrow one-story structures. In the far North, barns may have steep roofs to shed snow better. Big, hip-roofed barns are mid-western and eastern landmarks. Most of these were built before the 1940s, but if they were well-cared-for, they may still be in good shape. Starting in the 1960s, pole barns were often made with steel or aluminum sides attached to wood poles in the ground. They are extremely popular today and come in all sizes and shapes.

A long building with rows of narrow stalls usually made of metal or wooden rails, cement floors, and with whitewashed walls, is a milking parlor. Another small building might be attached or close by. This is the milk room where milk was stored until it was picked up.

Country Color
Generally hay was stored in the top of the barn, called the *mow* or *loft*, and animals or equipment occupied the lower part. Sometimes barns were built into a hill so a wagon could unload at the top floor on one side and animals or equipment could enter the bottom from the other side.

Chicken houses usually have nests and roosts built inside and often have east-facing windows. Small sheds could be everything from tack rooms to shops. There may be a smoke house, which might still smell good and look smoked inside. Corn cribs are round or rectangular cages of wood slats or wire that once held corn on the ear. Silos are tall, towerlike structures of brick or metal that once held grain or silage, which is green matter that is fermented. And you might even find an old outhouse. You'll know what that is when you open the door.

Can That Barn Be Saved?

That perilously leaning barn isn't doomed to fall. Such structures can be straightened. In almost every rural area, you can find someone who specializes in evaluating and restoring old barns. This person can check out your barn and tell you if it can be saved and at what expense.

When looking yourself, the most important factor in a barn's health is whether water has been kept out with a good roof. If the roof has kept most of the timber framing rot free, the side boards can be replaced. If the roof is caving in, chances are the barn can't be saved.

Barn wood has become quite valuable. The old weathered boards are often used in rustic home décor. If the barn isn't worth saving, you may want to use the wood in your home makeover or sell it to someone who does rustic decorating or crafts. And because it can be expensive to take down a huge barn that's dangerously falling apart, you may be able to trade the labor for the lumber.

Junk, Old Cars, and Machinery

Some old farms become dumping grounds for junk cars, old farm machinery of every description, etc. If the seller doesn't want to clean up, you have to decide whether you want to buy the junk and take on the cleaning.

Scrap metal is valuable, and an ad in the paper offering free metal if you pick it up may have the place junk-free in no time. Old farm machinery is often bought for landscape ornaments, sometimes at high prices. So don't automatically overlook a property because of the junk or out-of-control landscaping. You might be able to negotiate a bargain with a seller if you're willing to do the cleanup.

> **Sinkhole**
>
> You may want to require in your sales agreement that any cars that require a title to be removed are removed before the home is sold. A stolen car or some other problem could turn up.

The Least You Need to Know

- ◆ A professional inspection is a wise move. You may not be familiar with some country home systems.

- ◆ Be sure the well and septic system work. These are vital to your happiness and your health.

- ◆ Pests and hazardous wastes can make your home unlivable or cost you a lot of money, so check carefully for them.

- ◆ Use caution when choosing a fixer-upper. Sometimes the finished product will cost more than a new home. Of course, the charm or sentimental value may be worth it to you.

6

Building on Country Property

In This Chapter

♦ Check ordinances and laws first

♦ Is going green for you?

♦ Locating your home on your lot

♦ Living on your land while building

Building a home anywhere can be a headache, with delays and other problems to be expected. The good news about building a home in the country is that you often have more options than you would when building a house in an urban area.

This chapter won't tell you how to build a home or be your own contractor. Instead, it gives you an overview of how to choose a site for your home and discusses some of the decisions and planning you need to build your dream home in the country.

Check Before You Build

Before you even begin the plans for your home, check with the local building code department for any building restrictions on your property because even the most isolated areas may have building restrictions. Some may require that your house be set back a certain distance from the road or from property lines; others might require a minimum square footage. Certain types of homes may be banned, or certain types of roofing may be required.

If you're hiring a builder, he'll probably check all these things, but if you're going to be the contractor for your home or build it yourself, you'll need a copy of the building code for your property.

Choose Local Builders

If you hire a builder from the area where your home will be, he will probably be familiar with the local building codes, where to go to get permits, who to see about problems, and many other quirks of the local area.

> **Sinkhole**
>
> Some rural builders may be a little less flexible or knowledgeable in building homes that aren't common in the area or that require lots of new technology. Standard building materials may be locally available but not high-tech or innovative items.

But just because he's from your new community doesn't mean you don't need to do the usual background checks and get references. Ask the builder if he can show you homes in the area he's built. If you can, talk to the owners of those homes and see if they were happy with the work.

If you're planning a highly technical home or want to use new energy-saving devices, unusual heating and cooling systems, or new building materials, ask the contractors if they feel they have the skills and equipment to work on those types of homes.

Building It Yourself

There are two ways to build your own home. One is to be the contractor, hiring and supervising crews needed for each step of the construction. This sounds easy but can become a nightmare. You have to coordinate when supplies will be delivered, when crews can work, and the order in which they need to work. If one crew gets behind schedule, other crews may not be able to work when needed.

The other way to build is to actually do it yourself—lifting the beams, smoothing the cement, nailing the nails. This is hard work. You can do it bit by bit on weekends, but a better way is to devote several weeks to building, to at least get the home shell up. Some people build their own homes to save money, but for most, it's probably because they want to do it, to do it their way and know exactly what went into the home.

In all but the most isolated areas, there will be building codes you need to become very familiar with. You need to find out what types of permits are needed and where to get them. You need to develop a list of local suppliers for things you'll need during construction. And almost every location requires that you submit blueprints to a building code authority to get a building permit. Remember that someone will inspect the home before you are allowed to live in it, so always follow building codes. Plan to spend more money than you estimated, and give yourself lots of time.

If you've never built a home before, you'll need lots of background preparation. Read all you can and find out the minute details for every step of the process. Buy some good tools, and know where to rent the ones you can't afford. Make lots of friends who have time on their hands and sturdy backs.

There are ways you can save money on construction without building the entire house yourself. You could do the land prep, removing trees, leveling land, and putting in the driveway. You could finish the inside. Most people need to hire at least some outside help. You will need someone to put in the well and septic field. You may need someone to excavate a basement.

> **Country Color**
>
> If you're building a kit or pre-packaged home, the blueprint is usually included. If not, you probably need to have someone help you with this.

> **Sinkhole**
>
> Before doing the plumbing, electrical work, or heating and cooling installation, check with your building code authority. A licensed plumber or electrician might have to do the work to meet your building code requirements.

"Building" Other Types of Homes

If you don't have the skills or money to build your own home, consider a modular home or trailer. Modular homes come prebuilt in pieces that are fitted together on your land. Tri-levels and two-story models are available now, with all kinds of exterior choices and floor plans. You generally have choices in the style and furnishings of the home, but you might not be able to customize them quite as much as traditionally built homes.

Most modular homes can be mortgaged, and most areas allow them to be put on your property. They're not allowed in some areas, however. Also consider whether you can even get a modular home onto your property. If the lot is hilly or heavily wooded, it may be impossible to get the large pieces of your home where you need them to be.

Trailers have come a long way. Today, there are only small differences in some of the larger trailers and modular homes. Double-wide trailers on land are sometimes mortgaged; single-wide trailers generally don't qualify for mortgages. In some areas, trailers aren't considered a permanent home. Check your zoning ordinances carefully. If they are allowed, there may be several restrictions, such as a pitched roof, foundation, and other modifications.

Building Green

Building green means you're building a home that suits the climate and that incorporates as many Earth-friendly or energy-saving systems as you can afford. Green homes may be a little more expensive in the beginning but often pay for themselves many times over in energy savings over time.

Built to Suit the Land

You want your home to look right on your property, but you also want it to take advantage of the area's natural features and climate. Adobe homes are very effective in hot, dry climates but would be very unsuitable for cold and wet areas. An adobe home would also look out of place in the woods of Upper Michigan, as would a Swiss Chalet in the Arizona desert.

Rural Rule

If you have a certain style of home in mind, try to picture it on your property. Sometimes country property is almost a blank slate, freshly carved out of farmland with few trees or other distinguishing features. Older homes in the area can give you a feel for the local style.

If you want to use certain energy-saving features in your home, your lot and the climate of the area have a lot to do with how effectively those systems work. Solar panels can provide most of the energy a home needs in sunny, mild areas, but they're not as effective in cold areas where days are often cloudy and short when energy is needed most.

If you want an earth-sheltered home, having a natural hill to build into is much easier than creating one in a cornfield. You don't want a high water table either, if part of your living space will be below ground. To use passive solar heat storage, the sun must be able to enter the home from the south and west and not be blocked by trees or other features.

Conserve Energy

The cost to heat, cool, light, and run our homes is only going to increase. Everything you can do to save energy during the construction of your home is better for your wallet and better for the planet. Sometimes the energy-saving option costs more, but it's worth it in the long run.

Consider the size of the home you want to build. Do you really need that much space? High ceilings are very much in style, but they waste a lot of energy. If you think large walls of glass are necessary, get highly insulated glass. Get the maximum insulation in ceilings and walls. Get every energy-saving appliance you can afford.

Plan your home so it takes advantage of sunlight and prevailing winds. Proper landscaping, or taking advantage of natural land features such as tree lines, saves energy, too. In cold areas, deciduous trees shade and cool the house if they're on the west and south, but when the leaves fall, they allow sunshine to warm the house in winter. Tree lines buffer winds that can be destructive in winter or summer.

> **Country Color**
>
> Emergency backup systems come in handy. Solar panels can provide backup electric power. They work best in areas that have more sunny than cloudy days. Wind turbines are another source of alternative power, but they're expensive and difficult to install. Generators are probably the most common way to provide backup power, although the cost of gasoline can get pricey.

Geothermal Systems

Geothermal heating and cooling systems are not only easy on the environment, but they're easy on your wallet, too. Geothermal systems are ideal for country property and are one of the best energy-saving purchases you can make. A geothermal system uses renewable energy—the stored power of the sun—and very little electricity compared to even the highest-rated conventional energy-saving systems.

Geothermal systems use a series of pipes filled with water that are buried throughout your yard below the frost line. To read more about geothermal heating systems, go to Chapter 16. Or check out Rural Home Heating at www1.eere.energy.gov/geothermal.

Rural Rule _____

Geothermal heating and cooling systems are more expensive than conventional systems. However, when added to the mortgage when building a new home, the additional cost is immediately covered by the decrease in utility bills—often 60 percent lower than a conventional system.

Living On-Site During Construction

In some areas, you may be allowed to live on your land in a temporary trailer or even a tent while your home is being built. You often have to get a permit, and it usually has a time limit. Sometimes it's your only option, but there are disadvantages to doing this.

You are able to keep an eye on the construction process and guard your new home, but it can get very uncomfortable and the noise and mess of construction can be very stressful. Set up camp a little way from the action so you don't get in the way, but stay close enough to hook up to the water and electricity if possible.

It's always an advantage to get the well in and the electricity to the home site while building, but sometimes things don't happen that way. Be sure to plan those things if you're going to camp there. Occasionally, you may be able to hook up to the septic system, but usually you need to rent a portable toilet or build an outhouse, which you may be sharing with the builders.

If you have children, you must supervise them carefully so they don't get in the way or be harmed during construction.

If you're not allowed to live on land while building or if you prefer to be farther from the action, try to find a campground nearby, where you'll likely have hookups to water, sewer, and electricity. Hot showers and recreational activities are often available, too. Some campgrounds rent trailers or cabins.

Locating Your Home on Your Lot

When you build on a lot, you often can choose where on the lot you'd like your house located. If your lot size is fairly small—an acre or less—you might not have that many options for where to place your home. If you have more land, you probably have more choices.

Sometimes the land dictates where you put the home. A home should be built on a fairly level site. The septic field needs a level area, too. If the lot is heavily wooded, you might need to remove some trees. If the land is very rolling, you might need to level a spot. If it's swampy in the front, you may have to go farther back on your property to find a good site.

Think about centering your home on the lot if you can, at least in relation to the side boundaries. Even if no homes are near you now, there may be in the future, and by centering your home, you'll have some buffer space should the neighbors decide to build close to their boundaries.

It's nice to be way back off the road … except in winter when there's 2 feet of snow between the road and your house. A home at the top of a hill is wonderful … until you have to walk up that hill because it's too icy to get a car up it. A driveway that twists and turns seems very scenic … until the propane delivery truck can't get to your home. The main electric and phone lines generally run along the roadsides, so the farther from the road your home is, the more it costs to run these lines to your home. If you have children, they may have to wait for the school bus out of sight of the house. Sometimes it's nice for no one to be able to see the house from the road, but if your house catches fire when you aren't home, who will notice and call the fire department? And burglars often strike secluded country homes.

So what's a good distance to set the house from the road? It depends on the type of road and how much traffic it has. A hundred feet off the road makes a pretty good buffer from traffic, especially with the right landscaping. That distance won't make the driveway and utility hookups terribly expensive.

It's nice to have a lot of space in back of the home for private activities, also. If the view is better in the back, think of having the home "face" that way and put the backside facing the road.

Sinkhole

Police and other emergency response teams may have a hard time locating homes far from the road. If you build far off the road, be sure your driveway is well marked at the road, with an address clearly visible.

Consider Your Driveway

Think about where you place your home in relation to how hard it will be to get to it in all kinds of weather. Also factor in how much it will cost to construct and maintain the driveway. Can builders even get to the spot where you want your home built? How about people making deliveries in large trucks?

The average driveway is 10 feet wide, with more space at turns or curves. You probably need a culvert at the road; local ordinances can tell you what kind and how big. Every time you have to place another culvert or bridge over a low spot, that adds to your costs. Just to make a simple gravel driveway is quite expensive, both in materials and labor.

If you're thinking about placing your home far off the road, get an estimate for what driveways of that length with various types of material cost. Most modern driveways use a tough barrier fabric under the base material to prevent the material from sinking into the ground. If your soil is suitable, the driveway base can be made of 4 to 6 inches of soil from the property, with 2 or 3 inches of crushed rock or gravel on top. If you're going to pave the driveway, the base needs to be almost the same as putting in a gravel drive, with the paving material extra.

If the soil isn't good for constructing a drive, you'll need additional soil brought in. Heavy clay, sand, and peat do not make good driveways without amendments. If the driveway is long, you may encounter different types of soil along the way.

Country Color

The type of material used for driveways varies from location to location. Most areas have some materials that are cheaper because they're locally available.

Driveways should exit at the main road where someone traveling the road can see you pulling out and you can see oncoming traffic. You may want to install a turnaround at the house or road if traffic is heavy on the main road so cars don't have to back out.

Can You Get Water?

One of the most important considerations in planning where to site a home is the availability of drinking water. Before you begin any actual building, have the well drilled. It'll be easier to get the drilling rig in close to where the house is planned without it having to navigate construction, trucks, or equipment. If you don't find good water close to the proposed home site, you may be able to move the site to where water is found.

The well driller will also be able to tell you if your well location is too close to a neighbor's septic field or some other source of pollution that might affect your water. Try to keep the well away from driveways and garages so there's less chance of damage to the aboveground parts.

An underground line runs from the well to the house. You won't want to build over this line or have driveways, sidewalks, or parking over it, so plan accordingly.

A Spot for the Septic

You'll need a fairly level area for the septic field and at least 50 feet between the well and the septic tank or field in most areas. How much space and what type of septic field you will need depends on your soil drainage. (See Chapter 15 for more information.)

You won't be able to plant trees over the septic field or build over it or the tank. Driveways should not go over the field or tank, but the tank must be accessible for pumping. Plan for all these things when choosing a site for the house.

Other Considerations

You generally pay per foot from the main power line to your home. Depending on the distance, one or a number of new poles will need to be put in, which you have to pay for. Phone lines and sometimes cable lines usually follow the electric line's path, although it may be run separately.

In many areas, electric and phone lines are run underground. You won't be able to build over or run a driveway over these buried lines. Aboveground lines and any meters installed must remain accessible for servicing.

When you're making site plans, include an area for a propane tank or fuel oil tank. It's nicer if they're concealed a bit, but they must be accessible for filling. Propane tanks can be farther from the house and the lines run underground. You can't build over these lines, either.

> **Rural Rule**
>
> Thanks to cell phones, land lines aren't as vital today, but some areas still might not have good cell coverage. If you can't get good cell reception and no phone lines are available, consider a radio tower for communication.

Check Out This View! Wait ...

A beautiful view increases the value of your home and makes it more worthwhile to live there. Remember that views can change. This is especially true if you're one of the first to build on newly subdivided land. Your view may be wonderful ... until the new neighbor builds a pole barn right outside your window.

If the person who sold you the property doesn't own the property you like to view, he or she can't guarantee it will always remain the same. Recently, our newspaper told of some very upset people who had built homes with a view of a beautiful wooded area. Then the owner of the woods decided to log it all out. He had every legal right to do it, and he knew nothing about what had been told to property buyers.

Consider Your Neighbors

Country neighbors can be miles away or almost as close as in the city. You probably don't have to worry about those far away from you. But if you're within a few hundred feet of a neighbor, what you do affects them, and what they do affects you.

You might not even know the neighbor yet, but you can be certain they're wondering what you're going to build on your property. Some people are pretty easygoing and won't give a hoot, but others will watch your every move to be sure you don't do something they think is wrong. So obey the laws and follow the rules.

Your Viewpoint

You may only be thinking about how you can catch a glimpse of the ocean from your bedroom window when you decide where to place your home. You may not take into consideration that when you build there, your garage will be right in front of the view from your neighbor's living room. Yes, you bought the property, and you do have the right to build where you want, but ....

Or maybe you have to place your home on your property so your deck looks out over the neighbor's old-car graveyard. Does he have to clean it up so you don't have to look at it?

Or you need to drain some land so the driveway won't sink in muck so you have a ditch dug that drains the water away—right toward a farmer's wheat field. You'd like to have a pond, so you dam up the creek that runs through your property—the same creek your neighbor uses to fill his pond.

Stop and think about the neighbors around you and not just what's good for you.

Your Neighbor's Viewpoint

Your neighbors might have lived on their property for 40 years, enjoying the quiet and looking out over a beautiful valley. Now here you come along and build this big, two-story house between their house and their view of the valley. And your boys are riding up and down the road on their noisy motor bikes all hours of the day and night. They may know legally you have the right to buy land and build on it, but understand that they'll probably have a hard time dealing with the changes after all these years.

Your neighbors may have legitimate worries such as if you put your septic field there, will their well be polluted? Or will the changes in grade you made flood their property? Listen to their concerns and make changes in your home plans in the early stages if possible. If there's no way to change the plans and experts have assured you that there won't be a problem, politely explain that to your neighbors.

On the other hand, if the neighbors seem to have unreasonable expectations of you, like "I have always let my cattle graze there and I am going to continue to let them do so," or "We don't want a trailer there," you may have to take a firm stand and help them realize that things do change.

> **Rural Rule**
>
> Although you have the right to buy land and build anywhere you want on it, try to consider the neighbors when you site your home. Don't expect your neighbors to change their lifestyle just because you moved in next door. If you don't want to look at old cars, don't put windows there; instead, build a berm or plant trees there.

The Least You Need to Know

- Home sites need level land for the home and septic system. Having to level land is expensive, so avoid it if possible.

- Don't make a final decision on where to site a home until you've found water.

- Long distances from the road may cause problems. Everything you put in—drives, electric lines, etc.—will be more expensive.

- Begin your life in the country without resentment by considering the neighbors when placing your house, if at all possible.

7

Landscaping Your Country Home

In This Chapter

◆ Evaluating your landscaping

◆ Planning it out

◆ Lawn decisions

◆ Making it your own

Landscaping isn't just flowers, shrubs, and trees; it's also driveways, porches, decks, patios, and anything you do to your outside space. Landscaping sets the tone for your home, whether it's formal, informal, southwestern, eastern seacoast, etc. Your landscaping should complement the architecture of your home and suit your climate.

If you bought an existing country home, it might already be landscaped and you only need to adjust what's there to suit your needs. If, on the other hand, you built your home in a subdivided cornfield, you may have serious landscaping to do. In this chapter, I give you some tips on evaluating existing landscapes and for starting from scratch.

What You Have and What You Want

Landscaping is one place where most homeowners can do some or all the work themselves, and how much time you have to spend on landscape upkeep and how well you like to work outside have a big impact on the landscaping you should choose. If you make the right choices, you can have a nicely landscaped home that won't need huge amounts of time to maintain. How much money you have to spend also has some impact, but if you're willing to do the labor and patient enough to let things grow into their space, you can usually achieve the type of landscaping you want on any budget.

> **Country Color**
>
> For lots more information on choosing a style of landscaping and the particular plants that work well in your area, consider taking a class such as the Master Gardener program, available in almost every state through your county Extension office. Many colleges and adult education programs also have landscaping and gardening classes.

Landscaping adds value to a home. You may have chosen this home over another because it had mature trees, a wonderful perennial border, a nice grape arbor, or some other landscaping feature. Or maybe you bought a country home knowing the landscaping was a mess and hoping you could fix it. It may seem like a monumental task, but some of the most beautiful gardens have been created out of chaos.

What You Have

The first step in either fixing, adding, or maintaining landscaping is to find out what you have and do some basic measuring. Then you can make decisions on what to add or remove from what exists.

Get a notebook and a pad of graph paper to begin your landscape evaluation. Assign a length to each square such as 1 square equals 1 foot. Measure the length and width of your house, including any porches and decks. Note what direction the house faces. Measure the distance to any outbuildings and also any buildings you'll landscape around. Measure the distance from the house to all the boundaries of your property, and record the distance to the road edge. Measure the width and length of all drives, sidewalks, and paths. Record all these measurements and then draw your basic home grounds to scale on the graph paper. You don't have to include natural areas in your property drawing.

Now identify the plants you already have on the property. Take samples of the leaves, stems, flowers, and seeds or fruit. You can also take close-up photos of the plants.

Number your samples to correspond to numbers on your landscape drawing. To identify the plants, use good plant reference books, go online to garden sites, or take the photos and samples to a nursery or to your county Extension office. After you've identified them, you can choose what to keep or eliminate.

Rural Rule

Keep your drawing and the measurements you took. They'll be very helpful later, such as when you want to install a fence. As you add new plants or landscaping, update your notebook and map, along with the date. Also remove from your map and notes anything you removed from your landscape.

Give It Some Time

If you buy your home in the fall or winter, you might have to wait until spring or summer to see what existing landscaping you have to work with. Landscapes can change dramatically through the seasons. If some landscaping is in place, it might be wise to just sit back and observe your landscaping through a whole year of seasons. You may find several delightful surprises as things pop up through the year. If you're not familiar with gardening in the zone your new home is in, you might think that some things are weeds or just the opposite, that things you tried to grow in your last garden are pests here.

Also wait on the landscaping if you have a lot of fix-ups or finishing to do to your home. If the roof needs to be torn off and replaced, don't work on landscaping immediately adjacent to the home until it's finished. If you need to remove junk, old cars, or clear out heavy brush, get those things done first.

Waiting also enables you to see how much light you have in different areas, which changes through the seasons. It also lets you see where any drainage problems are or if you'll have any heavy damage from deer or other pests.

If you must plant something that first season, pop in some annuals or a few potted plants. Annuals don't cost that much and won't return the next year anyway. Potted plants can be moved out of harm's way or to where they look better.

Identify Problems

Next, identify where you may have landscape problems. Look for trees that appear to be leaning, dead or dying vines that have lifted areas of the roof or crept under siding, or trees and vines touching power lines. Also check for wires, strings, ties, etc.

Sinkhole _____

If your new home was landscaped by the builder, don't assume experts chose and installed the plants. Landscaping is typically done by subcontractors; some are good, and some are not.

left on the plants. Burlap showing above the ground around a plant wicks water away from the roots. Any type of pot, including peat, left on a plant should be removed. Trees planted within 10 feet from buildings and shrubs planted within 3 feet should be moved.

In your notebook, write down what problem areas you see. You might want to note whether you think you can deal with the problem or if you'll need to hire someone to help.

Making a Landscape Plan

Using the notes and maps you made about your property and existing landscape will help you make decisions for your new landscape. A plan will keep you from forgetting that certain things need to be moved or that your spouse wants a redbud tree instead of a maple.

One of the most important concepts in landscaping is right plant, right place, or choosing species of plants that will thrive in your conditions. Find out the growing zone you are in, determine your light exposure and the type of soil, and you can develop a list of plants for every situation.

Consider Your Needs

Landscape designers like to break the landscape into "rooms." As you think about your landscape, consider what different parts of your property will be used for and decide on what types of plants, paths, or surfaces you need to have to allow that use.

If one part of your yard will be for outdoor entertaining, for example, you'll want a flat surface, probably paved, and electricity nearby. You'll want plants that are colorful but not too messy and that don't attract bees to the area. For a children's play area, you'll need a hard surface or tough grass surface depending on what your children play. You'll want plants that aren't poisonous and that don't have thorns. You may want to see this area from the house or make it secluded, depending on the age of your children. For the front and other entrances, design landscaping that complements the home and adds visual interest. You may want to screen some areas of the property, shade some areas, or stop the wind.

Planning for the Future

Something else to consider when planning your landscape is how the land will be used in the future. If you think that in a few years you'll want to put an addition on the house or add a garage or barn, don't plant a tree where those things would be placed. Be sure there's enough space between the house and landscaping for a driveway to the planned garage or barn.

And remember to plan for the adult size of plants when you're planting those tiny seedlings. One of the most common landscape blunders is to plant trees and shrubs too close to houses or walks and driveways or plant them too close together. Things may look a little sparse for a few years as plants mature but will look much nicer and be healthier farther down the line if planted properly.

Windbreaks and conservation plantings of tiny tree seedlings are a place where crowding in a few years is to be expected. They look so small that people plant them far too close together. These trees should be planted 10 feet apart, minimum.

Prioritizing Your Needs Versus Wants

As you're making your landscape plan, you'll probably have a budget to consider, so you'll need to decide which are the most important landscape projects and do those first. Decide what you really need compared to what you want. If you're in the middle of an empty field, you probably need some trees and shrubs. These take time to grow, so they're a good thing to spend your time and money on first.

When determining your landscaping priorities, make a 1-year, 5-year, and 10-year schedule. In the first year, you may have money and time to put in a play area for the kids but the big perennial bed will have to wait until next year. If your plans were to plant apple trees 3 years from now, but you see a wonderful bargain on apple trees, you can at least refer to your plans to see where the orchard is supposed to be. This keeps the landscape from developing willy-nilly as you find things in your budget to plant but forgot or didn't plan where to plant them.

Rural Rule _____

If you're on a tight budget, take advantage of gift plants or good bargains as they come along and develop a holding bed. This can be in an out-of-the-way place, where you plant those bargains until you can move them to their proper home. Don't worry about color clashes or form and shape here. This is just the plant waiting room.

Soil Test

One very important preparation for landscaping is a soil test. The test will tell you the pH of your soil—how acidic or alkaline it is and the percentage of potassium and phosphorus. It will probably list the soil texture and may add other notes depending on the lab. Do a soil test when you first acquire property to get a baseline, and repeat the test every 3 or 4 years or if you have a problem.

You can collect the soil for the test yourself and send it off to a professional lab to be tested. It's generally inexpensive, and labs generally provide recommendations for improving the soil if needed. Almost all county Extension offices offer soil testing. Soil conservation offices and farm service offices also offer testing. Many private labs do soil testing, too. The lab you select will instruct you on how it wants the sample collected.

Knowing about your soil is important in selecting plants, knowing how to fertilize plants, and understanding why some plants may not be doing well where they are.

> **Country Color**
>
> Some plants are fussy about soil pH. Some prefer acidic soil, and others neutral or alkaline. Most prefer a pH range of 6.5 to 7.5. Neutral pH is 7, lower is acidic, and higher is alkaline.

Water Conservation Issues

Water is rapidly becoming an important issue in many areas of the country. Some areas even have rules regarding the type of landscaping that can be used and the use of water for landscaping. If you live in an area where water is scarce, try using landscaping that doesn't require as much water. Even if you have your own well, extensive landscape watering may not be allowed. If water is scarce in your area, try diverting gray water from the home to areas outside that need water. Gray water is water from anywhere but the toilet.

Landscaping with plants native to your area is generally a good way to conserve water, as these plants are used to surviving the local conditions. They will need some extra water to get established, but after that, they should only need occasional watering.

How Much Lawn Do You Need?

Lawn care uses more pesticides per acre than farmland. Mowing and tending lawns uses tremendous amounts of fossil fuels and water. Because you have a lot of land does not mean you need a lot of lawn. Lawns look nice around the home and between flowerbeds. They cool the air and add oxygen and are good for playing on. However, in many areas in the United States, lawns really have to be babied to do well. They consume more energy and time than is logical. They waste water and other natural resources.

In areas where wildfires are common, a home should have 30 to 50 feet of clear land such as lawn around it. Most other homes should have some clear space around them, but 30 feet of lawn is usually enough. Most people want more lawn than that, but more than 100 feet of lawn in any area is not environmentally sound.

> **Country Color**
>
> The use of lawns comes mainly from old European roots. It was a sign of wealth and privilege to have empty space around a home that wasn't used for food crops or pasture.

You may have 150 feet of bare land between your house and the road, but it doesn't have to be lawn. You might want to consider a row of trees and shrubs close to the road to buffer noise and screen your home from view. Or put in an orchard, garden beds, pasture, paddocks, or even a vegetable garden to use some of that property.

Meadows Versus Lawns

Many people have meadows rather than lawns in the country. Similar to a lawn, a meadow consists of low-growing native plants. You can have a combination of meadow and lawn by keeping the area closest to your home nice and letting areas farther out develop naturally except for occasional mowing.

One type of meadow uses what's already growing naturally. You just mow it to about 5 to 6 inches two or three times a year to keep shrubs and invasive plants from taking over. Mowing actually helps grasses and other desirable plants spread and thicken the stand. No fertilization or weed killers are used.

Another type of meadow is the one most people dream of—the one studded with pretty wildflowers. Those meadows are not easy to obtain. They require starting out with bare, tilled soil and sowing a seed mix formulated for your area. Results vary tremendously, and over time most of these revert to the first type of meadow.

Renovating Old Lawns

How do you fix an old, neglected lawn? There are two ways. One is to tear out everything and start over. (I talk more about that in the next section.) The second is a plan that will take a few seasons, depending on the lawn's current condition.

First get a soil sample done and tell the lab you'll be planting lawn grass. It'll give you recommendations for the nutrients to add. Ask at your county Extension office or a good garden shop about the types of grasses that do well in your area, and buy the best grass seed you can afford. Check the label for the percentage of weed seed, annual seed, and junk included.

Renovation works best if you begin in early spring or fall. Remove as many broad leaved weeds as possible by applying a broad leaved weed killer or pulling by hand. Then in a week or so, apply the fertilizer recommended in the soil test results and water it in. If you didn't get a soil test, use a fertilizer for lawns without weed killers or crabgrass preventer.

Remove *thatch* with a de-thatching blade or by hand, and go over the old lawn to gently loosen the soil. Concentrate on bare spots. Then re-seed at about half the rate recommended for seeding a new lawn.

Keep new grass well watered until it's up and growing well. Wait to trim new grass until it's at least $3^1/_2$ inches long but not much more, and only cut it back to 3 inches. Fertilize again in late spring and early fall. Don't mow grass shorter than $2^1/_2$ inches, and keep it watered during dry spells for a thick, healthy lawn.

def•i•ni•tion

Thatch is an accumulation of dead grass leaves and other vegetation. It's not harmful unless it builds up to more than a couple inches but should be removed before re-seeding so the seeds have contact with the soil.

Starting New Lawns

As with renovating a lawn, begin with a soil test. If the home is new, part of the lawn area may be covered with subsoil from excavating the basement, septic, etc. This will not grow a good lawn, so add 3 or 4 inches of good topsoil. If you've ripped out old lawn or pasture, till the soil and then rake it smooth. Remove all rocks and debris, and try to level the surface. Work in the fertilizer recommended by your soil test, or use a good lawn fertilizer without weed killers or insecticides.

There are several ways to start a new lawn. One is by *sod*—strips of already-growing lawn that you lay down on the prepared soil. You can also use *plugs*, or small sections of grass or individual plants that you literally plug in or plant across your area. Only a few types of grass are grown this way, primarily in the south.

Then there are seeding methods. *Broadcast seeding* is simply distributing seeds evenly by hand or spreader across the lawn. Chopped straw or other mulch may be applied over the seeds. *Hydroseeding* is done by professionals and involves spraying a mixture of seed, water, and mulch over an area. There are also *mats* that are implanted with grass seed and laid down over soil.

Seeding is best done in early spring or fall. The seed must be kept moist until it germinates, which may mean watering every day. Don't mow the new lawn until it is about 4 inches high, and only remove 1 inch.

What About Trees and Shrubs?

The old saying is that you don't plant trees for yourself; you plant them for the future. It does take a while for trees to grow, although if you put some trees in the right spot, you'll be amazed at how fast they grow.

How important planting trees are in the scheme of your landscaping probably depends on your country home site. If you bought a home with no trees near it or just built a home on a subdivided field, you'll want to plant trees. Trees add value to just about any landscape. Not only are they valuable for their appearance, but they cool the air around them, block the wind, and provide homes and food for wildlife.

In your landscape plan, trees should have priority because they do take time to grow. For trees and some shrubs, larger is not necessarily better when it comes to choosing a size to plant. Some trees do not transplant well after they have reached only a few feet in size. Trees that lose their leaves are best planted when they're dormant, and evergreens are best when planted in early spring. Avoid planting any trees and shrub when it's hot and dry.

It's become commonplace to move large trees on to a home site using a big machine called a tree spade. These expensive trees require a lot of care if they are to survive. They must be kept well watered throughout the first year and checked frequently for signs of insect and disease problems brought in by stress.

Choosing the Right Plants

Before purchasing trees and shrubs, consult with knowledgeable people in your area or good reference materials about what species of trees grow well in your area. Most people know that palms won't grow in Wisconsin, but many don't know that plants like apple trees and blue spruce are unhappy in Florida.

Besides how hardy they are, you also need to decide what you want the trees to do—give shade, highlight a garden spot, give fruit, provide a privacy screen or windbreak, or provide timber or homes for wildlife. You should also find out the size and shape of mature tree or shrubs so you can decide which will suit your needs. If they are fruiting trees or bushes, do they need a pollinator? To get holly berries, for instance, you need a male and female plant on the property.

Sinkhole

Beware of trees and shrubs that are considered invasive because they seed or sucker themselves a little too freely and out-compete native or more desirable species. Your state may also have a ban on some types of trees and shrubs, such as ash trees. The emerald ash borer is spreading across the country, killing ash trees by the thousands.

Many rural counties have tree sales sponsored by the soil conservation district, the Department of Natural Resources, or other agencies that provide seedling trees at a low cost. It's very tempting to overbuy or buy too many of one species when the price is so attractive. But remember, these are very small trees for the most part, and planting a thousand trees is much harder than buying them.

Diversity in the type of plant species you use is very important. If you plant all one species of trees or shrubs in a windbreak, hedge, or conservation planting, you risk losing them all if a pest or disease comes along. Animals and birds prefer diversity in plantings also. Different types of trees and shrubs mature at different rates in a mixed planting. Fast-growing trees and shrubs provide protection for some other species. Diversity in planting is the best way to mimic succession, the natural way land rejuvenates itself.

Planting Trees and Shrubs

There's an old saying about planting a $10 tree in a $100 hole. But you don't have to spend more than a little time and effort to correctly plant a tree or shrub.

First, dig a hole somewhat wider than the root ball but not much deeper. For potted trees and shrubs, take off all the pot, including peat pots, which don't dissolve fast enough in most soil. For balled and burlapped trees and shrubs, set the plant in the hole and cut away as much of the burlap as you can. If the plants have a wire cage, cut enough wires to slip it off. Remove all strings, wires, and other ties both above and below ground. The top of the root ball or soil from the pot should be even with the ground. For bare root trees, look for a dark mark on the trunk that indicates where the soil level was before.

Research has shown that trees and shrubs put out good root systems and recover from transplanting much faster if the hole is backfilled with the soil that came out of it. Do not add topsoil, peat, compost, or any other additives. Do not put fertilizer in the hole.

After backfilling the hole, water the tree or shrub very well. Don't tamp down the soil around the plant; let the water settle the soil. Add mulch, but don't let the mulch directly touch the trunk or base of the plant. Don't overmulch; 3 or 4 inches is plenty.

If you're planting hundreds of small seedlings, the planting procedure is generally much different. With a shovel or a special tree spade (you can often rent these from where you bought the trees), make a deep slice in the ground. Pull the soil back slightly, insert the seedling roots, and let the soil fall back in place.

Outdoor Lighting

It's a strange thing, but one of the first things many people new to the country do is put up a big mercury vapor pole lamp that turns on at dusk. The intense blackness of a country night scares them. To city people, darkness equals danger. These lamps have their place, but be sure you have a switch that's easy to get to so you can turn them off because there's nothing nicer than looking at the sky on a clear country night. Without the glow of thousands of lights, you can see things you never saw before. Meteor showers, the Space Shuttle, even the northern lights if you live in the northern United States. It's beautiful and inspiring.

Lights you can turn on at night to go to the barn or to another building are good to have. A small light where you turn off the road onto your drive can be very helpful and prevent accidents. Some people like to have low-voltage lighting along paths and in patio areas.

But don't overdo the lighting. Darkness doesn't equal danger in the country, and light pollution affects the planet and the animals and plants that inhabit it.

The Least You Need to Know

- ◆ Evaluating what you have already is the first step in planning or revamping your landscaping.

- ◆ A plan helps you develop a neat and orderly landscape. No one remembers everything, and a plan keeps you from wasting time and money.

- ◆ Start with a soil test. You'll be able to make better decisions on what to plant on your land.

- ◆ Lots of lawn is not ecologically sound. Lawns use chemicals, gasoline, and our precious time.

- ◆ Diversity is important. If you have a preponderance of one species in your landscape, one pest could wipe out everything.

Chapter 8

Country Ponds

In This Chapter

♦ Laws concerning ponds

♦ Where to build your pond

♦ Pond maintenance

♦ Let's go fishing!

Ponds are popular. Some country properties already have ponds, wetlands, or even a lake on them, and if your property does, you might need more information on how to maintain it. If your country property doesn't have one already, you might want to build one. But how practical is it on your land or for your lifestyle?

Country ponds can be used for swimming, fishing, watering livestock, attracting wildlife, or holding water for irrigation or fire fighting. Ponds improve the value of property—if they are constructed properly and don't become a muddy hole in the ground.

Pond Laws

In every state, laws protect *ponds* and *wetlands*, and most states also have regulations about creating new ones. Before you rent a backhoe to dig your pond, check your state and local regulations to see what you can do and if you need a permit to do it.

def•i•ni•tion

For our purposes in this chapter, **pond** refers to a large, earth-bottom pond used for recreation or conservation, not small garden ponds. **Wetlands** are transition areas such as swamps, bogs, marshes, or fens where water is close to or at the surface of the land at least seasonally. Wetlands are extremely valuable because they filter storm runoff, protect land from erosion, and are the nursery or home of thousands of animal and plant species.

Ponds Already on Your Property

Even if a wetland is totally within your property boundaries, the Environmental Protection Agency (EPA) or state and local laws may prevent you from altering it. When you buy property, you can't assume you're going to be able to fill in a swampy spot or dig it out to make a pond.

In some areas, you'll need a permit to alter wetlands, and that might require you to have a professional draw up a site plan and inspect your pond. Do not try to skip this stage; the fines can be very steep, and the work you'll need to do to correct any mistakes can be very expensive. Do your homework, and be sure all the legal angles are covered before turning the swamp into a pond or damming the creek to make a larger pond. You may also want to talk to your neighbors to see if anyone has strong feelings about what you intend to do and take that into consideration.

Creating a New Pond

Creating a new pond on your property doesn't usually come along with as many legal issues as altering an existing one, but many areas do have laws requiring permits before constructing any kind of pond. In areas where homes are fairly close together and uninvited guests such as children have access to your pond, you might want to consult with your home insurance company before building a pond. On the other hand, home insurance rates may actually drop when you put in a pond if the water can be used to put out a structure fire.

Ponds are constructed in two primary ways: damming and digging. Damming can mean diverting water from a small creek or other natural waterway or enclosing a valley or low spot so it collects water from the surrounding area. A dug pond starts on flat land and tries to get to the water table or a spring, or it may also collect runoff water. I discuss this more later.

The important thing about pond building is to determine if a pond is suitable for your property, where the best site is, and what type of pond you should construct. It's okay to ask for help making these decisions.

Where to Get Help with Your Pond

You'll probably not get any government help to build a small pond for swimming, but in some states, you may get help to construct ecologically sound wetlands or ponds. Check with your state Department of Natural Resources, Federal Conservation District or U.S. Fish and Wildlife Service, or county Extension office.

After a knowledgeable person has evaluated your property and helped you plan your pond, you may be confident enough to rent a bulldozer and go at it. But not every guy with a bulldozer can build a good pond, and paying a professional to do the job may save you money in the long run. If you can't get the pond to hold water, or worse yet it holds too much water and then collapses, you'll have a muddy, expensive nightmare on your hands.

> **Country Color**
>
> Check out www.epa.gov/owow/wetlands/facts/contents.html for links to facts about wetlands and state and local programs.

You might have several pond construction firms in your area. Ask neighbors with ponds, a farm supply store, or other local businesses for recommendations. When you have had professional help designing and building the pond and all governmental permits and inspections are handled properly, if something does go wrong you are fairly well covered. This is particularly important with dammed ponds. If you design and execute your own plan for a pond, and millions of gallons of water break through and flood the neighbor's home, you are also in deep water.

Picking the Right Spot for Your Pond

Finding the right spot for your pond is crucial. Yes, theoretically you could build a pond anywhere, with enough money and time, but most of us have to conserve at least one of those things. Some country properties will have several suitable sites to locate a pond. Some won't have any.

How Much Space Do You Need?

If you have less than an acre of property, you probably don't have room for a pond. But even people with more land may have problems finding enough surface space.

Ponds need at least $1/2$ acre of surface area to be practical. You'll need room around the pond to move equipment, store soil, and otherwise construct the pond.

Larger ponds require more upkeep and more water to fill them and keep them filled. It's better to have a smaller but deeper pond than a shallow pond with a lot of surface area. All ponds should be at least 6 to 8 feet deep through much of the pond area.

The average farm pond surface area is about $1/2$ acre, which is about 75 by 200 feet. If that pond is at least 6 feet deep, it will hold more than 1 million gallons of water. If that water is to be gathered primarily as runoff from surrounding land, you'll need 5 to 10 acres (for a $1/2$-acre pond), of surrounding land that drains into the pond, depending on climate and other factors.

> **Sinkhole**
>
> Avoid filling your pond with surface runoff that comes from agricultural land, areas where animals are concentrated, roadways, and other areas where the runoff may carry pollutants.

The drainage area doesn't have to be all your property, but you can see that problems could arise when several neighbors who each own 2 acres want to build ponds. All ponds that depend on runoff will have seasonal fluctuations in depth, but if many ponds share the surface runoff, some may go dry at times.

More About Land

If your pond taps into groundwater seeps or springs, you'll need less surface area to collect water. If you hit a good spring, you might actually want to divert water from running into the pond. When a strong spring is uncovered and the pond tends to overflow, that water needs somewhere to go. It can't go to the neighbor's property unless he wants the water there. It can't be diverted to a natural body of water unless you have permission from local authorities. You need to plan for an overflow area that will handle all the water coming out of your pond at its highest peak.

It's really hard to divert water from a natural creek or stream and create a good pond, even if you get permission. You might think it's ideal to have a strong source of free water for your pond, but this type of pond creates many headaches. It's probably the most expensive type of pond to build.

For a pond that has a constant outflow, you need a good way to channel that outflow that can handle the flow at its highest rate. Even a small creek can become a raging river after a heavy rain. An earthen dam will quickly crumble if it has a strong flow over the top. You need a series of overflow drain pipes that are properly engineered or a concrete spillway to handle the flow.

You may also need some land to "borrow" the clay subsoil from if you're making a dammed pond. Because the excavated area is smaller, there's less clay subsoil for the dam and pond sides. The topsoil from the borrow area should be returned there, and some of the topsoil from the ravine or gully could be used to fill the area where the subsoil was removed.

Dug ponds often have trees and brush removed and may have more soil from the hole than is needed to make the banks. These materials have to go somewhere.

Will It Hold Water?

It doesn't matter how much land you have if you can't find a spot that holds water. If you're in an arid area with sandy, gravel-filled soil, your dreams of a pond might not be realistic.

For the best water-holding soil, you need a good amount of clay. When you look at the soil, you're not considering the top layer, about the first 3 feet. You want to see what's underneath.

To be sure you have a good area for a pond, you'll generally need to dig test holes. These can be about 3 feet wide and 6 feet deep. If you hit water when digging, you probably have a good site. As long as there's a good amount of clay under that soil, you have a chance. Remember that soil can change drastically from place to place, even on a few acres, so if the first site isn't suitable, try another.

When you're looking for a good spot for your pond, look for low spots or areas that hold water after a heavy rain. Ravines and gullies may make good places to dam runoff water. In old farm fields, areas that were left to grow up to brush and trees are often wet spots and may have a spring or groundwater close to the surface.

What about using a well to fill your pond? It can be done, but it's extremely expensive

Rural Rule

If the soil on your property is only marginally suitable for holding water, you might be able to import bentonite, a natural substance that expands when wet to make a watertight liner. This can be expensive and is not practical in all areas.

to run a well to fill a pond or keep it full. It'll also take a long time to fill even a small pond. Don't even consider using your home well for that purpose.

Other Site Considerations

If a pond is to add value to your property, it has to blend into the natural features of the property and function as intended. Generally, ponds don't look good when they're 25 feet in front of the house, although many people plunk them there when other places won't work.

Families with small children may want to site the pond a little farther from the house for safety reasons. If part of the point for constructing a pond is to use the water for fire fighting or emergency water for livestock or crops, it must be accessible for those uses.

Don't place a pond uphill from your home, neighbors' homes, or public roads. If a dam or bank gives out, millions of gallons of water could quickly flood and cause serious damage.

Keep ponds away from septic tanks and fields. Don't put ponds under power lines, and keep them away from public trails for hiking, horseback riding, or off-road vehicle use.

Ponds can be considered an attractive nuisance. Even though you don't want trespassers to use them, you could be liable if they are harmed in or around your pond.

What's the Purpose of Your Pond?

The purpose of your pond might help you make decisions on size, depth, and shape. You can construct a pond in the right soil in just about any shape you want. A pond that's at least twice as long as it is wide is more visibly appealing.

If swimming is the primary purpose of the pond, you might not want to add fish. You'll want to discourage wild waterfowl and domestic ducks and geese from using the pond, too. You'll probably want to treat the pond with a dye to control algae growth. A pond for swimming should have a shallow end and a gentle slope to the deeper part. Banks should also slope gently so they're easy to climb; clay walls can be very slippery.

Ponds primarily for fishing should have a deep area and a shallow area. Steep sides help prevent predation from wading birds and other animals. Ducks and other waterfowl are fine after the fish have grown to a good size. Some natural vegetation should be encouraged, such as cattails, but it should be kept in control so the whole pond doesn't fill in.

In cold climates, ponds that will have fish and other aquatic animals need to be deep enough that they don't freeze solid and have a good level of unfrozen water left beneath the ice. Fish and other animals' metabolism slow down in cold water, but they still need some oxygen.

If the pond is to attract wildlife, a shallow area with an accessible shoreline is best. If wildlife ponds are not stocked with fish, they can be relatively shallow, about 6 feet or so. Let natural vegetation grow, but keep invasive species in check.

If ponds are used to water livestock, either a shallow area should be fenced to limit access or the water should be piped to a trough. Large animals can pollute the pond, ruin the banks, and destroy vegetation that prevents erosion.

> **Country Color**
>
> Ponds can have dual or multiple uses, and larger ponds more easily support multiple uses. Often a swimming pond evolves to a fishing pond or wildlife pond.

Don't Forget the Drain

While you're planning your pond, be sure to plan a drain near the bottom of it. A drain is constructed of a 6- to 8-inch-diameter pipe that runs under the pond bank and allows water to flow to a lower location. (You must also plan where all this water will go to if you drain the pond.) Drains allow you to fix problems with banks, silt buildup, or leaks and control unwanted fish and weeds. Drains must be installed very carefully with collars around them and sealed well so water doesn't leak out of the pond by running along the outside of the pipe.

You can plan drains only for emergencies or so water can be periodically removed to fill stock tanks or harvest fish, for example. Ponds can also be drained with pumps, but this is more expensive.

Playing in the Dirt

Some people look forward to digging their own pond, but if you're not experienced with a bulldozer, you might want to hire someone who is. There are many steep banks and other hazards when excavating a pond. Depending on what size the pond is and what has to be done to stabilize the soil banks, pond construction can take from 2 days to 2 weeks.

When the dozer operator begins to strip the ground in the pond site, be sure the topsoil that's removed is stored somewhere until the pond excavation is finished. It can be brought back later and spread on the sides of the pond where you need vegetation to grow and prevent erosion. Plants won't grow well in the subsoil brought up from the pond basin.

Rural Rule

If you're going to dig your pond yourself, spend a lot of time researching and planning the type of pond you're considering. You might want to watch or help someone else dig a pond first.

After the soil is pushed to where it needs to go, the bottom and sides of the pond are tamped and compacted. The slope of the banks, the amount of compacting, and many other details are determined by the site characteristics.

Your pond may begin filling before it's even finished, and that's a good sign. Most ponds take several months to fill. Wildlife will begin populating the pond as soon as it begins filling.

Planting Around a Pond

Planting around a pond is not something you can wait to do later. The banks must be stabilized immediately so they don't erode. Grass roots hold soil and keep rain and wind from carrying it away. That topsoil you saved must be carefully spread on the outside and top of banks. Then grass should be planted as soon as possible. Grass and other vegetation also filter water coming toward the pond, collecting silt and other debris. Leave the grass and vegetation a little long near pond edges. Mow the banks several times a year to keep unwanted trees and brush from growing.

Rural Rule

Ask your county Extension office or soil conservation office what kind of grass is best in your area.

Ground covers, ornamental plants, and some shrubs can be planted around ponds. Be careful about planting trees too close to the pond, though. The roots may invade banks and cause a leaking point. Trees also use a lot of water, drawing it up from the pond and evaporating it into the air as well as holding it within the tree.

You can plant a few carefully selected trees a short distance from the pond, but never plant trees on dam tops or sides. Set trees back from the pond edge by 10 or more feet. You may want to site trees on the east or north sides of a pond, where leaves are a little less likely to blow into the pond.

Evergreens are good to plant near ponds, as are small trees such as crabapples and redbuds. Avoid water-loving species such as poplar, sassafras, cypress, birch, and willow, whose roots will quickly find the water and may reproduce vigorously. If you must have one weeping willow near your pond, place it far back from the pond banks and watch for "babies."

If you're planning the pond for wildlife, you can let natural vegetation fill in as long as you keep invasive plants and trees in check. Remember that nature works in succession, and in nature, small ponds often quickly become swamps or bogs, with little open water.

Controlling Rooted Water Plants

If the pond is to be used for swimming, keep the water free of plants. If you quickly pull out rooted or floating water plants, they won't have time to spread. Use a dye in the water to keep plants that grow underwater out of the pond. It'll reduce the sunlight they need to live.

If you have a pond where plant growth is already out of hand, you have some work ahead of you. The safest thing to do is to get in there and pull, cut, and rake them out. If you have a large pond, that may be very hard to do. Chemicals can kill aquatic plants, but some also kill any fish or animals in the pond, so use these chemicals very carefully. For guidance with this problem, contact your county Extension office.

If your pond has a drain, you can drain the pond, pull and remove weeds, and start fresh. Remember, with chemical fixes, all plants will be killed. If you drain the pond, you can save plants you want such as water lilies or leave plants like cattails in one corner of the pond. The plants will survive being without water for several days.

If you have fish in your pond, don't be too quick to remove all plants. Plants provide cover and shade, places to spawn, and hunting grounds for small critters that fish love to eat. You'll want to control plants though, so you can get a fishing line in there without snagging it.

> **Country Color**
>
> Draining is best done in early fall, when water levels are probably already at their lowest. It may take hours or days to drain the pond, depending on a number of factors. It may take some time for the pond to refill, too.

Controlling Algae

Algae are the usually green growth that covers the tops of some ponds. Many people commonly refer to algae as *scum*. Algae need sunlight and calm water to grow.

A heavy load of algae on the water's surface means the water has lots of nutrients in it. This can be because of runoff that's carrying lawn or crop fertilizers into the pond, or it can be from natural causes. Algae can crop up and then disappear quickly, or it can persist.

Green algae won't hurt you, although some types of algae that occasionally get into ponds can. Swimming in algae is unpleasant, and for ponds used for swimming, you'll want to control it. You can put dyes into pond water to shade the top layer and prevent algae growth. These must be put in early in the spring, or they can be poured on ice, and may need to be refreshed after heavy rains or late in the season. They are harmless to frogs and other aquatic life and won't harm swimmers or pets drinking the water.

> **Country Color**
>
> Barley straw submerged into a pond has long been used to prevent algae, although there's no scientific research to prove that it's effective.

Strong water movement through a fountain or an aerator can also help prevent algae. Some pond fountains use solar panels for power, avoiding the need for a source of electricity. Wind aerators are also available, but if the wind is strong, you probably won't have algae.

If algae are very persistent, something needs to be adjusted. If the pond collects runoff water, it might be picking up too many nutrients from lawns, cropland, or animal areas. Stop using fertilizer near the pond, and try to divert water that carries waste away from the pond.

Too many domestic or wild ducks or geese on a small pond may encourage algae. They also cause bacterial contamination. Feeding fish in the pond too heavily may also cause it. Shallow water tends to have more algae. Adding catfish or goldfish doesn't help with this problem.

Got Fish?

Before stocking a new pond with fish, give it several months to a year to settle and begin a natural community. If you're thinking about stocking an existing pond, you need to determine if it contains fish already.

You might want to have the water tested, especially if there doesn't seem to be much aquatic life in the pond. Minerals and gases may come into a pond with spring water, and all kinds of chemicals can come into ponds with runoff water. If frogs, water insects, and plants are scarce or nonexistent in a pond that's been filled for a while, fish probably won't live there either.

Buy your fish for stocking from a hatchery. Don't go out and catch fish to put in your pond because wild fish can carry disease and parasites. Check with your local farm store to see who sells fish in your area. Often orders for stocking fish are taken one or more times a year and a truck delivers the fish to the store, where you can pick them up.

Check to see if you have a hatchery nearby. It will usually sell fish that are good for your area, and it can answer any questions you might have, too. Some mail-order companies sell fish, but you will generally need a large order to get fish this way. Also check with your local DNR office; they sometimes offer fish for sale.

Rural Rule

If fish are in your pond but they're not desirable for fishing, such as goldfish, you may want to drain the pond or use chemicals to kill them. The Department of Natural Resources, your county Extension office, or any large fish hatchery nearby can advise you on what chemicals to use and how long to wait before re-stocking.

What Fish to Use

Ponds are usually stocked with some game fish like small-mouth bass and some pan fish like sunfish or bluegill. The pan fish are food for the game fish and are stocked in larger numbers. Minnows are often added to this mixture as food for both other types of fish. Fish that don't do well in most ponds are pike, salmon, and trout.

Don't overstock your pond. Fish that are crowded are stunted and more prone to disease. For a pond with a surface area of $1/2$ acre, about 50 game fish to 250 pan fish and maybe a few channel catfish would be ideal. Your fish will reproduce if they are happy.

Sinkhole

Don't put goldfish, koi, or carp in your pond if you want to fish in it. These fish will quickly overpopulate your pond and displace the game fish.

Feeding Your Fish

In a pond where natural conditions haven't had a chance to get established, feeding your stocked fish may get them off to a better start. You can buy pond fish food in large bags in the same stores that sell chicken or horse feed. These are usually pellets that float.

Some people continue to feed pond fish long after they need to simply because they like to. They think it makes the fish larger and stronger. But don't provide too much food because it will cause water problems.

And don't feed fish in the winter. In cold weather, fish eat very little, and the decomposing food robs the water of oxygen.

Controlling Your Fish Population

In a $1/2$-acre pond with a good ecosystem, you could harvest, or cull, around 10 pounds of bass and 40 to 50 pounds of pan fish a year. You must keep the pan fish numbers in control, or all the fish will be stunted. If you don't want to eat the fish, you can throw the culls to the chickens or cats. You can also use them as garden fertilizer.

People have different ideas about culling. Some keep the big ones and throw the little ones back; others put the big ones back to grow bigger. The important thing is to reduce numbers. If you stock the pond for fishing, someone needs to fish! Kids love to catch fish, so let them do some of the culling.

Shared Lakeside or Pond Property

If you're moving to property that shares a lake with other people, you have some of the concerns of pond or lake owners that own the entire water feature, but you have many other concerns.

You generally cannot add anything to shared lakes or property without getting permission from all who have rights on the lake. That includes weed killers, dyes, and even fish. And if the lake is connected to other bodies of water by a canal, river, stream, etc. it also comes under the control of the EPA and other government agencies. You need a permit to do just about anything. You probably need to get a permit to make a dock, build a break wall, or repair the beach. Ask other homeowners who controls the activities on the lake, a homeowners' association, a government branch, or all of these groups.

On small lakes, motorized boats may be banned, or there may be a *no wake* rule. There may be hours of the day when boating is not allowed. Hopefully, you'll have investigated all these things before you bought the property.

Don't maintain your lawn all the way to the water's edge. Leave some longer vegetation for at least 2 to 3 feet before the water or beach edge to slow runoff and filter out pollutants. You can landscape this with low groundcovers, ornamental grasses, or other plants. A porous path that doesn't channel runoff directly to the lake can be used, too. Try mulch.

def•i•ni•tion

No wake means boats must move slowly and not cause waves. This helps wildlife living in the water and also helps curtail erosion. (But mostly isn't a human nuisance and safety issue.)

People who have lakeside property should be very careful of all fertilizers and other chemicals used near the lake because they are a big source of surface water pollution. It should go without saying, but it's illegal to discharge any sewage into lakes.

In most places, people traveling on the water have the right to cross your property. They can wade by offshore or float by. This has caused many headaches for people who live near public beaches. People are not supposed to come up on your beach or use your dock, but it happens—sometimes intentionally, sometimes accidentally—where boundaries aren't clear. It can be an occasional problem or a major nuisance. Many lawsuits have been waged over this issue, and the legal rights are very muddied in most areas water travel is still allowed.

Pond Safety Considerations

Kids and animals are drawn to ponds. In the good old days, if a child slipped off to swim in a farm pond and was hurt, the pond owner generally wasn't blamed, but times have changed. Today, it's safer to be a "meanie" and chase kids away from your pond. Don't allow unsupervised playing in and around the pond. Teens and even adults can drown or get hurt, too. A fence and posted "no trespassing" signs helps a bit, but be watchful and don't let a habit get started.

Supervise your children around the pond, and practice what to do if a pond emergency arises. Someone in the pond owner's family is more likely to drown in the pond than a stranger.

Pets and farm animals can also be harmed around ponds. An animal walking on thin ice may fall through and drown, or animals may get stuck in mud or panic trying to climb up slippery banks. Dogs sometimes drown when chasing ducks or geese. Fence in the pond areas where livestock or pets may roam.

On each end of your pond, anchor a stout post in the ground. To the post, tie a strong rope with a flotation device like a ring to the other end. The rope should reach at least half the pond. Use this rope and flotation device to help a struggling person or wrap it around a rescuer's waist so he or she can get back to shore. If the pond is too large for ropes to be effective, keep a boat on shore.

Owners of lakeside property should also discourage trespassers and keep safety devices near the shore.

The Least You Need to Know

- ◆ Laws might determine if you can build a pond on your property.

- ◆ When planning your pond site, choose an area that will yield or hold water.

- ◆ Ponds require maintenance. Be sure you have the time and the money to maintain your pond before you build one.

- ◆ Stocked ponds need to be fished.

- ◆ With a pond comes safety concerns. You're responsible for what happens in and around your pond.

Part 3

Adjusting to the Country

You made it! You're living your dream out in the country. But are you getting overwhelmed with all the new things you need to know? Feeling a little lost in the new community? You've turned to the right place. In Part 3, I help you adjust to your new home and help you explore how you can fit into your new community. And if your children are having trouble adjusting to "life on the farm," I've dedicated an entire chapter to helping them see what you see.

Chapter 9

Your New Country Community

In This Chapter

- ♦ Becoming part of the neighborhood
- ♦ Getting to know your new community
- ♦ Commuting to a job
- ♦ Resolving neighbor disputes

You've moved to the country, but you're not out there alone. It's time for you to get to know your neighbors and join your new community. In this chapter, I present some ideas to ease the transition.

Being a Good Country Neighbor

People who move to the country describe all kinds of experiences with neighbors, from good to bad. People are people, whether in the city or country, and they like to be treated politely and honestly. There may be some people who have been in the country a long time and have preconceived ideas about people who move from the city. They may fear you'll want to change how they live, and that you'll complain about their animals and their homes.

As soon as you're settled in—or maybe sooner, if you bought land in the area and are building—go meet your neighbors. If they're farmers, respect the fact that some times of the year are very busy for them, usually planting and harvest time. If they're relocated city folk like you, they may have long commutes and a lot to do when they get home, so weekends may be a better time to introduce yourself. Country people tend to go to bed earlier (I realize this is a generalization, but see if you don't move your bedtime up after a while in the country), and they can be suspicious of people who show up late in the evening.

If you see your neighbors sitting on their porch or if it's a Sunday afternoon, go introduce yourself. If you sense it's a bad time, make your introduction short and sweet. They probably have a pretty good idea of who you are, but introduce yourself and tell them where you live. Invite them to stop by your home if you truly don't mind. Asking for advice is a good ice breaker. For example, ask them where the best hardware store or best local restaurant is. If you can sincerely complement something, do it, for example, "I love that lilac bush in your front yard. It's so beautiful." Just don't be fake or insulting.

You may not have to go to your new neighbors; they may come to you. In some areas, everyone for miles around may stop by to say howdy. It may be inconvenient and yes, they are curious, but grin and bear it. Being polite and friendly will serve you well later. Offer refreshments, especially if the visitor brought you something. You can encourage visitors by sitting outside on a nice day and giving a friendly wave as people pass by. Some may take the opportunity to stop and chat.

Whatever you do, don't judge people by their clothing. After all, the nicest person for miles around may be wearing torn overalls and smell like a cow barn, and the meanest gossip may be dressed like a *Country Living* magazine model.

Be sure your new neighbors are really neighbors, not some strangers looking to case your home. Ask them where they live. If you feel uneasy, try to get a license number, and be sure you get a first and last name. And never let anyone go in your home alone.

> **Sinkhole**
>
> Not every country neighbor is a good guy. People are people, no matter where they live. As in other areas, some people in the country are ready to cheat you, steal from you, and otherwise make your life miserable. Don't divulge secrets too fast, such as when you work; don't flirt; and don't put yourself in compromising situations.

Keep It Local

One of the best ways to meet your neighbors is to shop where they shop, dine where they dine, use the same plumber they use, etc. All communities benefit when money is spent locally, and your neighbors will appreciate you helping the community.

The stores may be smaller and things may cost a bit more, but it's worth it. You'll probably get a lot more help in the small-town hardware store than at the monster hardware store miles away, and you may meet a neighbor while you're at it. You may not be able to find a sushi bar or even a martini in town, but Rosie's Diner may serve up the best breakfast you ever had. If you like the bar scene, every country area has some kind of watering hole. Buy a round, and you'll probably make some fast friends.

One of the best places to get to know people is at the local farmers' market or flea market. Every area has one somewhere, and you'll probably find plenty of neighbors and some bargains to boot. There's lots of mingling and friendly banter at these places, and you're sure to learn how to "dicker" for your purchases.

Listen to Advice

While you're out and about in your new community, you'll probably discover that everyone likes to give advice to the newcomers. Pay attention and at least listen to what's said without saying something dismissive. Not every country neighbor you meet is as wise as the hills, but they may know more than you do about certain things, especially if they've lived in the area a long time.

Nearly everyone is flattered when you ask them for advice, so that's a good way to connect with new neighbors. Just don't make a pest of yourself by asking for advice on every little thing.

Obey the Laws, Respect the Customs

There's the law of the land, which everyone generally follows, and there are customs unique to certain areas. These might not be official laws, but they may as well be.

Some customs may be based on experience or something else factual, such as an unpleasant consequence if you do something. For example, someone tells you no one uses Burden Road after November. You decide that because Burden Road is closer to where you want to go, you'll use it. You get halfway down Burden Road and get stuck in the mud. Now you understand why no one uses that road after November ....

Other customs just may be pleasant things a lot of people in the area like to do. Maybe everyone gathers at Dilly Creek on the first Sunday in June for a picnic, or everyone sleds down Maybe Hill after the first big snowstorm. These are fun times you may want to join in on. Hopefully someone will clue you in on when and where they take place.

If everyone takes their shoes off when they go in the corner café, take yours off, too. If all the stores in town are closed on Sunday, don't open a store there and stay open Sundays. If school lets out every May 1 to celebrate May Day, don't complain that the kids don't need another day off.

Let's go back to obeying the law for a moment. Many people think that when they move to the country they may be able to get away with things that are illegal. Growing certain plants is one example. Others feel that hunting or fishing laws shouldn't apply or road laws such as speeding are not valid. In most country areas today, such things may be enforced even more strongly than in urban areas. The country should not be used as a place to hide from the law or break the rules when you feel like it or when you think no one is looking.

Control Your Dog

People who move to the country so Buster can run free are being bad dog owners as well as bad neighbors. Your dog may run free only on your property, not the whole countryside. You will make enemies very fast if your dog continuously harasses your neighbor's livestock or wildlife or destroys their property.

Dogs don't understand where the boundary lines end, and 2 acres or even 10 acres is easy for a dog to quickly run across. People who put their dogs outside without supervision and without a fence are being irresponsible. If your dog scares a horse someone is riding or attacks a walker, you are liable if anyone is injured. If your dog kills livestock, it may be shot and you will still have to pay for the animals killed or injured, sometimes up to three times the actual value.

It's also not safe for dogs to run free. They can be killed by cars, shot, caught in traps, kicked by horses, or stomped by cows. They may eat poison left for pest animals or dead animals that will make them very ill. They can drown or get lost or become dinner for large predators. (I talk more about dogs in the country in Chapter 22.)

Control Your Kids

Kids new to the country can go a little wild, too. Children should be taught to leave animals alone and not to touch or feed them without permission. They should stay out of crop fields or pastures, close any gates they open, and stay away from farm machinery parked in fields. If your children have off-road vehicles, dirt bikes, snowmobiles, etc., teach them that they must stay off other people's property. It may look like empty land, but someone owns it.

Every year the agriculture agent in our county is called out to assess damage kids have done in farm fields—some of which can add up to thousands of dollars in crop losses. For example, some boys rode their four-wheelers around in a field they thought was just covered with grass. The grass was actually wheat, and their damage cost the farmer thousands of dollars. In another case, some girls who liked horses brought a neighbor's horses some sweet feed they found in a barn. The horses weren't used to the feed, ate too much, and became extremely ill, costing hundreds of dollars in vet bills. If your kids were the culprits in these cases, guess who is going to pay for replacement wheat or the vet bills? You are.

The main thing to remember with children and pets who are unfamiliar with so much freedom is to use common sense and keep watch over them. A little supervision goes a long way in keeping your kids and animals safe and your neighbors happy. (In Chapter 10, I talk more about helping your children adjust to the country.)

Rural Rule

Many people won't mind children crossing their property or even playing in their woods as long as they don't cause any damage, but get permission first.

Lend a Helping Hand

Country people help each other out. If you see someone stranded on a back road, stop. If your neighbor is chasing loose cows, ask if you can help. If an elderly or disabled neighbor can't clear snow from the drive and you have a new snow plow you're dying to use, clear his or her drive. Or maybe ask the older lady up the road if she needs a ride to town.

You may hesitate to help someone chase cows, for example, if you've never rounded up cows before, but that's why you ask how you can help. If the person chasing the cows asks you to do a certain task, such as "swing the gate open when I say now," follow his directions. If you don't understand what he wants, ask for clarification.

Sinkhole _____

Don't try to help if you aren't sure that what you're going to do will be helpful. I was once leading our wayward sheep home with a bucket of grain, and they had settled into following me single file. We were almost to the gate when a new neighbor came down the road behind us and honked his horn, scattering my sheep everywhere. He thought he would scare them back into the pen for me.

If someone is gone and you notice that their boat is coming loose from the dock, tie it up. If you see a neighbor's horse is loose and he's unaware of it, let him know or catch the horse. If you're driving by and see a neighbor struggling to unload his truck and you're strong and able, stop and help. Someday someone will help you in return.

Becoming Part of the Community

Your community may be thousands of acres in a western state or 50 acres of rural homes near a small town. A community is not defined by legal boundaries but by people who share the same environment and have interests in common.

You can actually have several communities. For example, you may have a work community and a home community. It's the home community we're talking about here.

Join In

Become part of your community by joining it. Could you become a volunteer firefighter or emergency response team member? Is there a Lion's Club, a women's garden club, or a local bowling league you can join? When you become part of a club or service group, you meet new people who also live in your community, and they get to know you. Nothing feels more like home than having someone know your name at the grocery store.

If you're religious, join a faith community in your area. Most country areas, no matter how small, have several churches, and most welcome new members. Churches sponsor many rural activities and may be the meeting place for other types of social activities.

This is your community now. Attend community meetings. Go to meetings requested at schools. Support local activities like parades or firework shows by simply showing up. Attend local theater productions or church musicals. Mingle, greet, and talk to your fellow community members.

If there's no way you can become a volunteer firefighter, how about helping plan the farm bureau picnic or the school play? Can you teach Sunday school or coach a T-ball team? If you have special skills such as legal, medical, bookkeeping, or engineering, is there a way you can use those skills to help out the community?

Country Color

After you've moved, you might need to reregister in your new community. Find out where you vote on local and state elections, register in your new location, and make a point to vote. Community leaders will be at the voting place in many cases, and if you haven't met them you can introduce yourself.

Read All About It

Consider subscribing to your local newspaper. Many small papers don't keep up on state and national news, so you may want to subscribe to a larger newspaper also (or check out the online version). Small papers can seem a bit corny at first, but keep reading. You'll get local ads and sales, along with other important information from your hometown paper. Stories about people you don't yet know may inspire you to meet them. You'll get the flavor of your community from reading what important news in your area is. If it's the price of farm commodities, fishing, the opening of a new store, the ski conditions, or the high school band uniforms, you'll learn what's going on in your new community. Plus, you might get to meet your paper delivery person sometime!

It's refreshing to read the police report section and find that police responded to cows in the road, a missing garden ornament, or a broken window instead of three shootings and a bank robbery in a week. When there's real crime in the country, the small town paper will be the first to let you know what to watch for, probably in lots of detail.

Commuting

For many people, one of the hardest parts of living in the country is the long commute to their job in the city. You leave early and get home late. In good weather, when things are going well for you, it might seem like a breeze, but when the weather is horrible or you're under a lot of stress, that drive can be a real pain.

Rural Rule _____

> If you live in an area that experiences extreme winter weather, you need to have a backup plan if the roads get really bad while you're at work or driving home. Do you have a friend or relative in the city with whom you could spend the night? Is there a reasonable hotel or motel along the route? Can you sleep at the office?

When you first start making the commute, find out where all the emergency stops are—*before* you need them. Where can you get gas, go to the restroom, buy milk, get a flat fixed, even stop for the night if conditions are really rough? Have backup plans and find out if stores and gas stations on your way are closed on certain days or during certain hours.

If you've never fixed a flat, have someone show you how to do it. You may also want to know how to check and add oil and how to check tire pressure and add air.

Your Commute Kit

It's helpful to have a commute kit in your car. It doesn't have to be official, but it should contain things you might need.

Always carry a set of backup comfortable clothes, especially shoes and socks. If you have to walk for help, you won't want heels or dress shoes.

Carry an appropriate car emergency kit for the type of weather and terrain you have to drive through. (I talk more about emergency kits in Chapter 13.) Keep your car well maintained, and be sure you have a spare tire—and that it's properly inflated! An emergency jump-start machine and a tire inflator that runs on a cigarette lighter are also handy to have.

A cell phone is a must-have for long commutes, but be sure you have service through as much of your route as possible. Know where you have trouble getting a signal, and know who to call for help along your route because it won't always be 911. Some areas don't have 911 services. You may pass through several different emergency help providers, depending on how long your commute is.

Until you're very familiar with the area, keep a map or maps in your car that show all the local surface streets and back roads you might have to use as a

Rural Rule _____

> In some rural areas, it can take road service a long time to reach you. Check with your service provider in advance of a problem to see how service works in your commute area.

detour. If you have the time, you might want to drive an alternate route occasionally so you're familiar with it. Spend a little time studying the maps so you have an idea what to do if one route isn't passable.

If you can afford it, a GPS system may be helpful. But just be aware that GPS directions in rural areas may not be as accurate as in urban areas.

Drive Safe

The more miles you spend on the road, the greater your chances of having an accident. Don't increase the risk by trying to multitask on the road. Listening to music or an audio book is fine. Putting on makeup or reading your reports is not.

Use your cell phone only when you're stopped. Research has shown that driving and talking on a cell phone affects your concentration and reaction time as badly as having a few drinks and driving. Even hands-free models affect driver performance because you're not fully concentrating on the road and on driving. Just checking for messages is a distraction, and texting is a good way to end up running into a tree.

Don't drive when you're too sleepy. This is one of the greatest challenges for many long-distance commuters. If you find yourself nodding get off the road, get something to drink, stretch, or if you must, stop your car and take a short nap. Be sure you get enough sleep—if you have to, train yourself to go to bed early enough so you wake up refreshed.

Know when to call it a day. If the snow is too deep, the roads too icy or flooded, know when to say "I can't do it." Warn your boss that the weather or road conditions may be vastly different where you are from where the office is located. When you move to the country, accept the fact that you may be stuck at home because of weather more frequently than you would be in the city.

Animal Encounters

When driving on rural roads, you may encounter deer. Deer are more active at dawn and dusk but can pop out anytime. The rutting season, in late fall, is the peak time for car-deer accidents, but that's not the only time deer cross the road. In some areas, elk, antelope, or even moose can also be a problem.

When you see one deer, you can often expect more to follow. If one crosses in front of you, slow down and watch the sides of the road for more. If deer appear before you, hit the brakes but don't swerve. You're more likely to be injured if you lose control of your car or go into oncoming traffic rather than hitting the deer head-on.

If you hit a deer, stop as soon as you safely can. Pull off the road, and put on your flashers. Inspect your car for damage. In most states, you are legally obligated to report the accident. States and counties vary as to what happens next. In many cases, you can proceed on your way if the car is drivable. To collect insurance payments for damage to the car, you may need a police report.

Some states allow you to pick up the deer and take it home for the meat. Most people won't want the carcass. If you can safely move a dead deer off the road—and if you can stomach the task—do so. If not, notify police that it is a road hazard. If the deer is injured and unable to move, call for a police officer or animal warden.

If you should hit a large farm animal, you should probably stay at the scene until police arrive. In most cases, the owner of the animal is liable for any damages, but someone will need to locate the owner. A police report will need to be filled out, too.

If you hit a pet animal, you should try to find the owner, especially if it is still alive. If you can't, contact the police.

Carpooling

In some areas, many country people commute to the same city for work, and you might be able to carpool. This saves wear and tear on your car and gives you a break from driving, as well as someone to talk to on the long drive. Many areas have designated parking spots where people can meet to carpool.

Ask at the local store or a police station or other government office if carpool lots exist in your area. If they do, maybe drive there in the morning and see if you can find a match. You can also advertise on a bulletin board or in the local paper for someone driving your way at the same hours.

When Neighbors Don't Get Along

What if you moved to the country and one of your neighbors seems to really dislike you? Or what if you find you can't stand your neighbor? Distance does help, but sometimes even a good bit of distance between neighbors doesn't keep feuds from developing. Sometimes a new country dweller feels he's being harassed, or sometimes he can't understand why he's being ignored and given the cold shoulder. If you're being harassed, taunted, or teased, or if your property is being damaged, something is wrong. Perhaps you are resented because you bought property that someone else wanted. You may be perceived as the bringer of unwanted changes, or maybe you caused some problems, perhaps without knowing it.

The very first thing in any kind of dispute is to talk with the opposing party. If you're worried about what might happen, take a neutral person with you to talk to your neighbor. Ask another friendly neighbor, the county supervisor, or a preacher in the community to go with you to the harassing neighbor and find out what's bothering him.

Rural Rule

Try to resolve problems as soon as you notice them. Don't let them fester for months or let built-up feelings explode into a fist fight.

When you're new, you're more likely to be given a break about understanding things about the community, but as time goes on, people will expect you to understand more.

Talking may be the only thing that's needed. After the two of you have discussed the problems, they may suddenly be resolved. If you're serious about fitting into the new community, be willing to compromise on some issues. You should also expect that some concessions will be extended to you.

Sometimes a person who seems unfriendly or won't talk to you is just like that with everyone, and you did nothing wrong and should accept it. If a person is busy and not inclined to talk much anyway, you won't get them to chat about the new bird you just saw. Try again another time, or just give a friendly greeting when you see the person and let them open up to you.

If you're moving to a community where the Amish, Mennonites, or other religious groups live, or where there are many immigrants, the people may not know how to speak with you, or in the case of religious orders, may be asked not to talk freely with you. Respect those wishes. Be polite and friendly, but don't treat them as a curiosity.

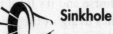

Sinkhole

Treat an Amish buggy tied up outside the grocery just as you would someone's car parked there. Would you let your kids climb in and out of someone's car?

Remember, you are not a tourist here, you are a member of the same community. You may see these people many times. Don't ask questions like "Do you have to wear that dress when it's this hot?" or "What part of Mexico did you come from?" Don't take pictures without permission or talk about people as if they are scenery. As these people see and meet you in the community, they will be more likely to talk to you when they're comfortable.

Unrealistic Expectations

A woman once called our Extension office to complain about her neighbor's farm. She said it was a source of flies that were all over her house. She asked us what she could do to force him to get rid of the flies. After questioning, it was found that her neighbor's barnyard was at least 300 feet away from her house. He kept a few steers and a horse out on pasture. There were no visible manure piles. The neighbor wasn't responsible for the fly problem. Flies and other bugs are part of the country, and the neighbor's farm was an unlikely source of the problem. So the lady needed to solve her own fly problem.

If you checked out the neighborhood before you moved in, you should have been aware of any farm operations nearby, any neighbors with animals, and other things that could potentially annoy you. It's unrealistic to expect everyone to alter their lifestyles to suit you.

Roosters crow, boat launches get noisy sometimes, cows moo, children squeal sliding down a toboggan run, harvesting might run into the night, pigs smell, and the woods might be filled with hunters in November. All these things are normal country living.

On the other hand, sometimes the neighbors have unrealistic expectations of you, too. Just because no kids have lived nearby for 10 years doesn't mean you have to keep yours quiet all day. Just because the previous owner of your home let the neighbor use his dock to tie up a boat doesn't mean you have to continue to let him. You don't have to put up with cows eating your garden, your beach being used as a public access, or your driveway being used as the local necking spot.

If you want a horse and it's legal there, get your horse. If you want a rooster and it crows, well that's living in the country. When I moved to the country I really wanted farm animals. We moved in with 2 goats and 10 chickens, purchased just before the move. It was "way in the boonies" country, and others in the neighborhood had animals. Surprising to me was the fact that our nearest neighbor was very unhappy with us moving in animals, although she had lived in the area most of her life. She didn't want to smell or hear them.

We checked the zoning, and it favored us. We tried to keep everything neat and as far from her property as possible, but because having animals was the reason we moved here, that was as far as the compromise went. She moved out in a year or so, and the new neighbors were quite content with the animals. They even talked us into raising some pigs.

The Right to Farm Law

In many areas, the right to farm law protects anyone who is in a zoned agricultural district, with no restricting local ordinances, who wants to pursue farming with normal, accepted farming practices. That doesn't mean the farm operation has to be in place when you move there. This is something to remember when purchasing land zoned agricultural without other restrictions.

If the farm operation is in the proper zoning, it could begin or expand at any time. If the farmer follows accepted practices for that kind of farming, he is pretty well protected. He can spray crops; bring workers to the field to harvest crops; raise animals; properly store manure, grain, or other substances; operate machinery, etc., all as he sees fit. He can cut down trees to make pasture, build barns that block views, and many other things.

Don't Force Change, Model It

You've moved into your country community, and you're beginning to see some things you think need changed. Maybe no one has flowers in the front of their houses. So plant beautiful flower beds in front of yours. You can almost bet that someone else in the neighborhood will soon be planting flowers and it will spread to others. Maybe you can offer extra plants to anyone who tells you how nice your yard looks.

Paint your fences and tidy up any junk in your yard, but don't go to a community meeting and propose ordinances that require everyone to paint their fences. Fix up your boat dock and clean up your stretch of beach. Go to your child's school and offer to monitor the playground a few days a week. Pull the weeds in front of the library.

Soon everyone will be helping you and not complaining about a meddling newcomer. After you're seen as a helpful person who wants things to be improved for the better for everyone, you can start proposing other changes. Keep your requests low key, and be patient as the proposed change gets mulled over. This will get your suggested changes implemented much faster than if you demand that something be done.

The Least You Need to Know

- ◆ You have to join the community to feel part of it.

- ◆ Buying locally and using local services helps you *and* your community.

- ◆ Manage your long commute by avoiding risky behavior and being prepared for emergencies.

- ◆ Both old and new country residents can have unrealistic expectations.

10

Helping Kids Adjust to Country Life

In This Chapter

- ◆ Different-age kids have different concerns
- ◆ Making the transition to the country easier
- ◆ New country rules and customs
- ◆ A whole new set of safety concerns

You and your partner might long to move to the country and live a simpler life, but maybe your children don't share that same dream. They might fear new experiences and worry about being out of place. And every child will approach a move to the country differently. When I was a child, for example, I begged my parents to move to the country so I could have a horse. When my husband and I were considering moving to the country, our sons begged us not to. They didn't want to leave their friends.

Do children have a better life in the country? That depends on many things, but the country does have a lot to offer. If their parents are happy in the country and see it as a better way of life, most kids will, too, even if they do miss some aspects of city living. Fortunately, some kids love the idea of a country move. But they may also have trouble adjusting if their expectations aren't met. In this chapter, I help you help your kids adjust to country living.

Helping Kids of All Ages Adjust

The age a child is when she moves to the country affects how she settles into country living. Toddlers will adjust easily, preteens will take it a little harder, and teens usually have the hardest time—unless they've been the ones lobbying for the country move.

But even if a teen secretly is enjoying the move, she's bound by the rules of teenhood to make it seem as if the world is ending! Some teens, however, will truly have a hard time adjusting.

Country Color

If you have a special needs child, there's a wide variation in how she'll adjust, depending on her personality and previous experiences. If routine is very important to her, it may take a while before she establishes a new routine and feels comfortable in your new home. Other special needs children will embrace a country lifestyle, loving the freedom to play outside and be with animals.

Play Dates and Other Ways to Keep Small Children Busy

One of the concerns parents of small children have when they move to the country is who their children will play with if neighbor homes are far apart and siblings are few or much different in age. If your child is going to daycare while you work, she'll have plenty of interaction with other children there. School-age children will be with other children at least during the school year.

Beyond that, you might have to get creative and organize play outings for your young child, just as many parents do in the city. Some neighbors may love to trade babysitting days with you—you take the kids one day, and they take them the next. Rural libraries may have story hours for toddlers, and churches often have activities for older children. Some children don't mind playing by themselves or with pets. If you have nieces, nephews, or other relatives nearby who can occasionally spend time with your kids, invite them over.

There are probably other children your child's age somewhere near you (unless you really moved off the grid!), and children usually seem to find each other—on a bus ride, on the playground, etc. If your child does find a friend, meet the parents and arrange transportation so the kids can play at least a few days a week.

4-H, FFA, and Sports

At any age, involve your kids in community activities whenever possible. Let them join 4-H, FFA (Future Farmers of America), or a sports team in the area. 4-H and FFA have a wide range of activities available for kids, from computers to cows, from designing clothes to growing tomatoes. These organizations screen volunteers carefully and often offer college scholarships.

In many rural areas, FFA or 4-H is an important part of the community. The county fair is the premier social event of the year. Many rural teens find friendships, develop lifelong skills, and make money for college from their FFA or 4-H project—an animal that won grand champion or reserve grand champion status at the fair may sell for thousands of dollars at auction.

If your child doesn't want to raise large animals, she could raise rabbits or chickens or participate in creative writing, photography, crafts, sewing, performance arts, shooting sports, computer design, growing herbs, bread making, or a wide range of other projects.

Sports are often big in the country. Everyone turns out to watch the football team or baseball team. If your child enjoys sports, get her signed up on a team.

Remember, too, that these teams always need coaches, and coaching is a good way for you to get involved in the community as well as your child.

> **Country Color**
>
> 4-H programs are administered through your county Extension office. FFA programs are usually associated with a high school that teaches agriculture or with your local Farm Bureau.

Teens Missing City Friends

Not all teens will be upset by a move to the country. Some will see it as a way to make a fresh start. If they attended a school with many safety threats to worry about, for example, they may enjoy a smaller school in a safe area where their personal safety isn't as much of a concern.

Other teens, however, will be very upset leaving friends behind. Even if they've experienced moves before, they may worry that this move to the country will throw them into an alien crowd that who share none of their interests.

Sometimes the child who is a little unconventional either in thoughts or looks may have more difficulty adjusting. On the other hand, sometimes she may have an instant cult following. The Internet makes it easy for country kids to keep up with trends. Your kids may find that their new friends are not so different after all.

If the move isn't too far away, assure your teen that her friends can visit—unless the friends are one of the reasons you're moving. As time goes on, most teens will make new friends.

New School Concerns

No matter what age your child, the best way to prepare her for a move to the country is to include her in all preparations. It might also help to gather information relevant to her. For example, find out the name of her new school, what classes she can take, what sports she can play, what art or drama offerings she can get involved in, etc.— *before* she starts the new school. Knowledge and planning always help anyone go into a new situation with more confidence.

Talk to her about riding a bus if that will be a new experience. If you know the bus ride will be a long one, prepare her beforehand. Tell her to go to the restroom before getting on the bus, use the time on the bus to do homework, and for goodness sake, don't miss the bus!

Younger children (and even older ones, although they won't admit it) often have concerns about what will happen if they get ill or another emergency arises while they're at school. This will be especially important if both parents are away from home during the school day and a long commute is involved. You need to have plans in place for this kind of emergency, and your child needs to know them. If she misses the bus, who does she call and how does she make the call? If she gets ill at school and needs to come home, who will pick her up? What are the plans for days off school or days when school lets out early?

Staying Behind to Finish a Grade

Sometimes helping a child adjust to a new community means not coming to the new community right away. If your move is in the middle of a school year, or the teen is about to begin her senior year, maybe the right thing to do is let her stay behind with a friend or relative to finish the school year.

This is a tough decision and not to be entered into lightly. You must trust the person your child will stay with, and you must be sure this is the right thing for your child. Consulting with a school counselor or a family counselor might be in order.

Be Involved

It's always important to be involved in your child's school and know what's going on in her life. When you're trying to help her adjust to a new community, it's especially important.

If your children are in grade school, you'll probably want to go with them on their first day. And these youngsters generally don't mind Mom or Dad popping in to visit the school. Kids in junior high, middle, or high school often don't share those feelings. Visit the school anyway, but just try not to embarrass them.

Be sure your child's school and daycare provider know how to get in touch with you. If you have a long commute between work and where your child is, be sure the school or caretaker knows that. Try to have a backup person to call if you can't make it right away. Many country schools are used to parents who commute long distances.

Rural Rule

If your child seems to be having a hard time adjusting to her new school, ask questions in a way that invites conversation. Often talking while engaged in another activity such as cooking together, working in the barn, etc. makes it easier for a child to talk to you. Being alone in a car together often starts the words flowing, too.

Should You Homeschool?

When people move to the country, they may choose a lifestyle that includes homeschooling their children. This is a wonderful goal, but not all families are good candidates for homeschooling. One parent needs to be home full-time. That parent must like teaching and be very disciplined. Homeschooling is *not* letting your kids study only a few times a week when they want to; it's a scheduled lesson plan and a set of goals.

If you're moving to a very isolated area, homeschooling may be a matter of necessity, but in most areas, it will be a choice. Consider your older children's feelings when thinking about homeschooling. You should also consult with the school district in your area to see if there are any regulations you will need to follow.

In some areas, parents who homeschool their children must register the children and provide a lesson plan, or the children must take standardized tests from time to time. Homeschooling parents should also seek out other homeschooling parents in their area. The children could meet for sports or field trips and get some socialization.

For a summary of your state's laws about home schooling and a brief explanation of federal laws on home schooling, check the Home School Legal Defense Association website at www.hslda.org/laws.

Rural Rule

If you're thinking of going the homeschooling route, many homeschooling sites online offer advice and tell where you can purchase supplies. And homeschooling.about.com has a list of homeschooling support groups by state.

The teaching parent of homeschooled children must keep his or her own learning current, be able to help the children with all levels of learning, and be able to make a plan and stick to it. The teacher-parent should consider the teaching a full-time job in addition to all his or her other household chores.

If you didn't like school, if you get easily sidetracked from one job, and if you tend to be very unorganized, homeschooling may prove to be a difficult challenge for you—and your children.

Country Chores and Responsibilities

One way parents can keep their children occupied in the country is to give them chores and responsibilities appropriate for their age and abilities. Older children can do things like set the table or get dinner started and take care of pets after school until you get home, especially if you have a long commute. Children can also help with household chores such as vacuuming, washing and drying dishes, and doing the laundry.

If the children want animals, be sure they are able to do most of the care for them. If the family has adopted a more self-sufficient lifestyle that includes farm animals, allow older children to feed and care for them after proper training and restrictions.

Moving to the country may mean increased yard work from what you were used to in the city. Children can help here, too. Older children can mow the lawn, and younger children can rake leaves or shovel snow.

Sinkhole

Children should not use any kind of machinery until they've been thoroughly trained and are old enough to control the machinery. Riding mowers and tractors are very tempting to children, but only responsible kids who are big enough to reach the controls should use the machines, especially when you're not there to supervise. And teach your children to never use these tools for pleasure, such as a joy ride down the road.

New Country Rules and Expectations

If the move to the country will alter your household rules, decide what the new rules will be and discuss them with your children. Explain the reasons for the rules, and the kids will be more likely to follow them. For example, your new commute may mean you won't be home when the kids get off the bus. Who will have a house key? What are they to do until you get home?

Your new community might have other rules your children should be aware of. For example, if the beaches all run together but it's considered trespassing to go beyond your boundaries, point out the boundaries to your children and make the point that they stay within them.

You may have new expectations of your children after your move. If you're commuting and coming home late, you may tell your children that you expect certain chores and homework to be done when you get home. If the children have pets or riding horses, they should assume most of the care if they're able. But you may also have a rule that there is to be no horseback riding until you're home.

Even if one or both parents are home with the children at all times, there will be new rules and expectations with the new home. Explain clearly, repeat often, decide on a penalty for breaking a rule or not meeting expectations—and actually enforce those rules and expectations.

New Safety Concerns

In the country, your child may be more likely to have an accident. It's very important that as a parent, you understand the risks your children may be exposed to and plan to minimize them. Explain the rules for safety, and take steps to keep your children from accidentally hurting themselves—or others.

Kids can be counted on to sneak off to do something without letting you know where they're going, often because they're not supposed to be doing it. They're also the ones most likely to get lost or injured.

Know Where They Are

Make a deal with your kids: if they're allowed to go somewhere, they have to tell an adult where they're going. If they decide to do something they're not supposed to do, have an emergency plan. (Believe me; most kids go places they're not supposed to go.)

Put an old mailbox somewhere a short distance from the house, where you won't be tempted to idly check it. Keep a note pad and pen inside, and tell your kids to leave a note inside, telling you where they're going, no matter what. Promise you won't look at the note unless you suspect something's wrong. If they get back safely, they can destroy the note, and you won't have to know anything about it.

If the children turn up missing, you can check that box to get an idea where to start looking for them. It's not good that they disobey you, but knowing where they are is most important.

Safety on the Road

Children can't become involved in the community unless they can get to where the action is. In the country, there's often no way to walk to where the child needs to be and there's also no public transportation. That means Mom, Dad, or someone else needs to be the chauffer.

One way to give your kids access to the community is to let them drive. Country teens are often allowed to drive earlier and more frequently than city teenagers, because everything is farther apart and many parents feel country roads pose less risk to new drivers. If your child is new to driving, let her drive with you for a while on country roads so she gets used to gravel and dirt roads, wildlife, and other road hazards, before going solo. Point out danger spots like steep hills and curves, one-lane bridges, and low areas that wash out.

Rural Rule

In remote areas, a driver—teen or otherwise—should always have a cell phone in case of an emergency.

Teens have a higher rate of accidents, and that rate increases with the amount of time they spend driving. In the country, teens often feel they're less likely to get caught if they break rules and that back roads are safe. Unfortunately, inexperience with driving and things like speeding on a back road are recipes for disaster.

When I was commuting to and from a job in the city I often noticed teens speeding in the morning to make it to school on time. Be sure your teens leave plenty of time to get to school or other places. Insist that they don't use the cell phone while driving. Restrict driving after dark. Make them stay home when the roads are bad because back roads are often much worse than main roads.

Safety Off the Road

A move to the country often involves the acquisition of machinery such as riding mowers and tractors and recreational vehicles such as all-terrain vehicles, dirt bikes, snowmobiles, and boats. People seem to be a little more lenient about allowing children to use such equipment in the country, and that can be a safety issue.

Mowers and tractors are not toys or personal transportation and should not be used as such. Children must be given the safety rules and made to follow them. Tolerate no horseplay or riders when using tractors or mowers; always turn off the engine before adjusting or removing anything; and be careful on slopes, where the vehicle could roll over.

Children should take safety classes before operating any off-road recreational vehicles and boats, and they should be closely supervised until you know they can operate the item safely. They must be old enough and strong enough to reach the controls and steer the machine. They should also wear long pants and shoes when operating these machines and have properly fitting helmets, life jackets, or other safety devices—and be made to wear them. And always follow the law and the vehicle manufacturer's recommendations regarding the age of drivers.

> **Sinkhole** _____
>
> Recreational vehicles pose special risks because children are supposed to be having fun on them. But too often, children are allowed on these vehicles when they're too small to safely reach the controls, can't see over the hood, and aren't wearing the proper safety equipment such as helmets that fit correctly.

Even when they can operate the machines better than the average adult, children often use less caution than adults. Teach them that country roads may be less traveled, but that it only takes one car to hurt or even kill them. They must obey traffic rules and ride on roads only if it's legal to do so. They must be especially cautious about crossing roads at a corner, coming up over hills, and on curves. If children ride off-road, they must respect other people's property and not ride on neighbors' land without permission. They should tell you where they are going. They must never chase or injure wildlife or farm animals. They should not wear headphones and should not carry riders. They should be home before dusk.

Even if they're just going to waste gas cutting circles on your property or on the lake, children can still be injured. Be sure they don't build unsafe jumps, try to leap ditches, or create other unsafe conditions. They should always wear safety equipment, at home or not.

If you don't want your child riding certain vehicles when you're not around, you might have to hide the keys. This may be wise in any case, as even good kids can be peer pressured into doing unsafe things by friends, or friends may take the vehicle themselves.

Getting Lost

If you move near many acres of woods, desert, or other undeveloped land, be aware that children can easily get lost in these places. I know from experience that children can be playing in the backyard one minute and lost the next.

Rural Rule

Toddlers can get lost on just a few acres of rough land. If you live next to undeveloped land, you may want to fence a play area in your yard for young children.

Instruct your children to always tell you if they are going for a walk … but expect that they won't if there's a place they like to visit that you don't want them to go to. Make them realize that if you know where they are and they don't return in a reasonable amount of time, you'll know where to find them to rescue them.

Talk to your children about what to do if they get lost. As soon as they realize they are lost they should stop, find a tree or rock, sit down next to it, and wait for help. They should yell "Help!" loudly every few minutes. You may want to add other instructions for the weather and conditions in your area.

Teaching your children how to tell the direction from the sun and teaching them to mark a trail as they explore unfamiliar areas may help keep them from getting lost. Don't assume your kids won't ever go into the woods or desert alone or with friends because you warned them not to. A story about lost treasure or a missing dog may send them right out into the wilderness.

Drowning

Water areas, whether permanent or caused by flooding, are very alluring to children and are, therefore, a big risk. If you live near any body of water and have young children, a fence is a must, either around the water or around your children. It doesn't take a lot of water to drown a small child. Even something like a watering trough can be dangerous. Don't forget about seasonal water in ditches or low areas as well.

All children should be warned about playing in and around water. Children who have access to ocean beaches should be warned about the tides stranding them in places if they forget about time.

Slippery banks and unsafe ice are two ways a lot of children get into the water without actually wanting to be there. Tell your kids to not play on the edge or banks of water because they could fall in. Teach your children to stay off the ice until an adult has tested it and to get off at once if they see or hear it cracking.

Children should not swim in creeks, rivers, lakes, or ponds without adult supervision. That said, you can count on it happening if you live near such a swimming spot, so warn kids about undertows, swift water, and diving into places where they don't know the water depth.

Hunting Season

In many country areas, there are a number of hunting seasons. Walking in the woods in those seasons could be hazardous, even for adults. Even your own woods may not be safe; hunters have been known to trespass and to shoot from the roadside. In hunting season, either stay out of the woods or at least wear bright orange clothing.

Warn your children not to tease, try to fool, or confront hunters. Strangers in the woods mean you turn around and go home and tell someone. Also caution your kids not to climb into tree stands they find in the woods.

Be aware that in some areas *poaching* is very common. Anytime in the woods is dangerous in those areas, especially if children are crawling around, hiding, or playing in other ways that may mimic animals. If the children go into the woods to play, they should wear bright orange, go in groups, and tell you beforehand.

Get a list of opening and closing dates for hunting seasons in your state by contacting your state Department of Natural Resources. Hunting season calendars are also available in most places that sell hunting licenses.

def•i•ni•tion

Poaching is shooting or otherwise killing animals outside a legal hunting season or without a license.

Farm Animals

In most country areas, children are far more likely to be hurt by a domestic farm animal than a wild animal, and children who aren't familiar with large animals are most at risk. Even if your family doesn't have large animals, your children may encounter them at neighbors' or friends' houses.

Teach your children never to enter fields, pastures, pens, or stalls unless the owner of the animals has told them it's safe to do so. Never try to handle babies when Mom is near. And never handle animals or feed them over a fence. Feeding animals may harm or even kill them if you don't know what you're doing. It can also cause pushing and fighting among animals that will harm a child. Children should never tease animals. A fence that holds a happy animal may not contain an angry one.

Children should never chase or deliberately scare animals. Not only is this cruel, but the animals could run through a fence or hurt themselves. Cows may not produce as much milk, baby animals can be trampled, animals may abort—all kinds of problems can occur. The owner will have every right to ask that you reimburse him for damages, which can be considerable.

Cows may look gentle grazing in a field, but those 1,000-pound animals can be quite aggressive if they want to be. I'm not talking about bulls either. Cows with calves can be very dangerous. A cow can run faster than a child and isn't frightened easily if she's angry. *Steers* often like to play rough with small animals, which a child might be considered.

Some horses will attack strangers in a pasture or other enclosure. Horses may also come up to you in a friendly manner and then bite or kick you if you don't know how to handle them. Even if they aren't trying to hurt the child, their jostling and fighting with each other could.

Pigs are also dangerous. They have teeth as sharp as a large dog's and aren't afraid to use them. If they get out, they'll generally run away, but if confined, they may attack someone who scares them or just looks like fun to chase.

Even animals such as sheep and goats have times when they're not safe to be around. In mating season or when small babies are around, these animals can be dangerous. My husband was knocked down and injured by a *ram*—and one who was actually smaller than most rams. This ram would attack at any time of the year without warning.

def•i•ni•tion

Steers are castrated male cattle, generally raised for meat. **Rams** are adult male sheep.

You might think it only happens in cartoons, but even roosters can be dangerous to small children. Roosters develop long, sharp claws called spurs on their legs as they get older. These are used to fight with other roosters or attack predators. Most roosters respect humans, but every once in a while you get a mean one who attacks anything that moves.

Geese, ducks, and swans can also be quite nasty and scary to children, although I doubt they could kill a child or do lasting harm. They are most aggressive in mating season.

Wild Animals

In most country areas, wildlife won't be a life-threatening problem. An encounter with a skunk may seem horrible but generally will resolve without permanent harm. However, in a few areas, you might have wildlife you should protect your children from.

One of the most hazardous wildlife species are the big cats—panthers and cougars. They may actually stalk and kill humans. In recent years, some areas of the country have seen these big cats move in close to homes. If you know of big cat sightings in your area, watch your children closely when they're outside.

Wolves and coyotes rarely attack humans or even come near them. Even in the woods your children are probably safe. However, if children come upon wolves, coyotes, or wild dogs, they should never corner them, attempt to pick up young, or try to help wounded animals or those who seem ill.

Bears occasionally kill humans, but they, too, tend to avoid humans, even small ones. When walking in woods where bears are known to live, make lots of noise and you'll probably never see one. Never feed bears, and keep your trash and animal feed where they can't get to it. Never try to handle bear cubs or come between them and Mom.

Wild pigs are also extremely dangerous, and have become more common in recent years, but they usually avoid humans. When they're very hungry, they may stalk or run after a human. If there are wild pigs in your area, children should play in the woods or near water with great caution.

If a child is bitten by a wild animal, contact your doctor or take the child to a hospital at once. If the animal cannot be found or identified, your child will need rabies-preventative shots. These aren't as painful as they used to be and may save your child's life.

Sinkhole

Any wild animal, even cute baby raccoons, can kill a child if the child gets rabies from handling it. Teach children to leave wildlife alone. Babies usually have a mom hiding somewhere nearby. Animals that should be wild and are acting too tame or acting sick should be avoided at all costs. Tell children to get away from them and notify an adult.

Snakes and Other Reptiles

Snakes are another hazard for children playing outside. The majority of snakes are not poisonous and won't kill you even if they bite you. Learn to identify the poisonous snakes in your area. If anyone is bitten by a snake and the wound is painful or swelling, go to the doctor or hospital at once.

In tropical areas of the country like southern Florida and the Gulf area, alligators can be a problem and could harm a child. They will be near water or in shallow water, so keep children away from any water areas known to have alligators. A fence will help keep alligators away from children.

The Least You Need to Know

♦ Depending on their age and other factors, children differ in how well they adjust to country life.

♦ Keeping children informed and busy helps them adjust.

♦ Attempt homeschooling only if you're organized, like learning, and are a full-time, stay-at-home parent.

♦ Living in the country presents new safety concerns for children. Be sure you and your children know what they are and how to avoid danger.

Things Are Different Here

In This Chapter

♦ Local government

♦ Who to call for help

♦ Housekeeping in the country

♦ Country roads

City folk who are used to stores being open 24 hours and Sundays often get a rude shock when they move to the country. They may also be surprised to learn the county supervisor's office is his kitchen and—wonders of wonders—there's no line at the post office!

Stores still do close in small communities on Sundays, and they may also close at 5 P.M. or earlier in the evening than city people are used to. Some places even close for lunch. You need to do a little research about store hours in town before you need something at 9 P.M. and find nothing open.

Things May Move Slower

Small village or township government and services might be slower than what you were used to in the city. It may take 2 weeks to get in touch with the township supervisor to see if you need a permit for something. He may then take 2 weeks to give you an answer or get the permit back to you because he's harvesting wheat. Or you may call a repair person to work on your boat. He asks what you use the boat for, and you tell him just for pleasure. A fisherman calls the repairman the next day just as he's leaving for your house and he decides to fix another boat that provides a man his livelihood first. Maybe you call an Amish farrier to trim your horse's hooves. He tells you he'll be out in a day or two, depending on weather. All these things make sense to the people providing services.

The flip side to this is that county service people usually respond quickly when there's a true emergency. They're also more flexible with hours. The line at the post office in small villages and townships is generally one or two people max or even nonexistent. You get to know the people who provide services, and they get to know you. Red tape in the township office is usually much less, too.

Meet Your Country Government

When you move to your country home, it's important to know the name of your township or village officials and how to get in touch with them.

In some townships, the township officials may be part-time and paid only for the time they spend on township or village business. In some areas, there is no township hall, the officers conduct business from their own homes, and they're not paid. In larger areas, there may be full-time employees in an office building, usually called the township hall or village hall.

What Township Are You In?

It's important to know not only where your township or village government office is but also what township you live in. Your deed or other paperwork associated with your home purchase or building will have the name of the township, village, or town you live in. Don't be surprised if your mailing address shows a different city or township. (Your mailing address just reflects where the post office is that delivers your mail.)

You need to know your school district for your income taxes. School districts in rural areas may include parts of two or more counties and numerous townships.

You also need to know your township so you know where to vote. Often you go to a local school, fire hall, township hall, or other location, but your township office can tell you for sure.

All the "layers" can get confusing. For example, I have a township government that works from home. I vote at the fire hall in another township. My mailing address is from a small town in another county. My school district is another small town in a different county. I pay some taxes to the county that hosts the school district, and I vote on school issues in that town. It can be a lot to keep track of!

Township Offices and Officials

If your township or village operates from an office, its open-for-business hours are probably posted on the door or window. If there's a major event such as a parade, summer festival, even a large funeral, it may close. Hours may also vary by season. It always pays to call ahead to see if it's open.

County township and village offices and the post office may close for lunch. Find out when the lunch break is at the various government offices you may need to visit.

If your township or village officials work out of their homes, expect to leave a message and have someone call you back. Be courteous, and unless you're told differently, call about business during the weekdays and not on weekends.

Try to be understanding of small township or village officials who are sometimes unpaid. Give yourself plenty of time before you need to buy a permit, pay a fee or taxes, or get an answer. Don't wait until the last minute and expect instant service.

> **Country Color**
>
> Most townships and villages have periodic meetings, and citizens can generally attend if they have questions or complaints about township or village government.

Volunteer Fire and Emergency Services

In the country, services like fire fighting, ambulances, and emergency responders are often handled by volunteers. Sometimes they get paid for each run they make, but many times these wonderful folks are providing a volunteer service to their community. These emergency responders often buy their own uniforms and safety gear and pay for their own training.

There's usually a central place where calls for help are sent and which notifies the volunteers by radio or beeper. Often these people are working, sleeping, or eating when calls come in and drop everything to come to your aid. The equipment may be in a central location that they have to drive to first, or volunteers may have the equipment at their home or in their car.

Most states now have laws that dictate how much training and equipment volunteer emergency responders must have. A wise use of money from the Homeland Protection Agency has been to establish or improve emergency services in some communities.

Be sure your address is easy to find in the dark and your driveway is well marked. Many emergency response groups sell luminescent signs you can place at the end of your driveway. If your mailbox is across the road or down the road, be sure your address is at the driveway entrance, too, so emergency response teams can find you quickly.

Who Do You Call?

One of the first things you should do when you move into your new country home—or even before you move—is to find out who you call in case of an emergency. Don't assume it's 911 because there are still some places that don't use 911 or use other systems. For example, you might have to call the county sheriff.

Help may take a little longer to reach you in the country. Call for emergency help as soon as you notice a problem, and have plans in place to handle emergencies as best you can on your own until help arrives. (I discuss emergency preparedness more in Chapter 13.)

Will You Be Charged?

In most areas, you pay taxes to provide emergency services, but in other areas, the taxes may not be enough to cover the cost of emergency services and you're charged for emergency runs. Homeowner policies may cover fire runs, and some medical insurance plans cover the ambulance and emergency medical services.

Rural Rule

If you always wanted to be a firefighter, here's your chance. Anyone with medical, fire, or police training is especially needed in communities that rely on volunteer emergency responders. It's a way to become part of the community.

A fire run just to put out a field fire started because you were burning some trash may cost thousands of dollars, so be careful. Even if you didn't call the fire department, your neighbor might have. But guess who pays the bill anyway—you. It may be worth it to pay a little extra on your home insurance if it covers these bills.

If you're a commuter, be aware that if you require emergency services in areas you travel through, you might be charged, especially if you don't pay taxes in that area. Check with your auto insurance company to see if your policy covers such charges.

"This Is Some Weather We're Having, Huh?"

If your country move also involves a big change in climate, you must know how to deal with the weather in your new location. People who've always lived in a warm, sunny place and move to a cold area have a harder time adjusting than those moving from a colder area to a warmer one. However, you can make some simple adjustments in either case, with the right tools.

If the area where you've moved has heavy winter snows, you'll need a way to clear your driveway—a shovel, a snow thrower, a snowblade on a tractor or truck, or the phone number of someone you can call to do it for you. If you have older children, you might be able to buy several snow shovels (and some cocoa for afterward) and let them go play in the snow.

Your car may need special attention in the coldest areas. A local auto shop can tell you if special oil or battery heaters are necessary and can give you advice on things like antifreeze and windshield wiper fluid. You'll need a window scraper and snow brush for your car. You may also want to carry a snow shovel and some salt in your car, too.

If you moved to a warm, humid area or a hot, dry one from a cooler area, there are also equipment and tools to be changed. Even if you never had an air conditioner in Minnesota, you may need one in Georgia or Arizona. You may also want an air conditioned car. Dehumidifiers may also be needed in humid areas.

> **Rural Rule**
>
> If you've moved to a very remote area and you travel roads that may not be well maintained, you may need to consider the type of vehicle you're driving. A four-wheel-drive vehicle may be necessary to get around at some periods of the year.

Keeping a Country Home

It surprises many people what adjustments need to be made in general housekeeping when you move to the country. Country homes have many surprises waiting for city folk, especially if you're moving into an older home.

Critters Galore

There's the critter problem. (I discuss critter control in more detail in Chapter 24.) Let's just say that when you move closer to nature, you may get closer than you bargained for.

If it isn't wildlife, it will be new pets and livestock coming to share your space. If you allow your kids to have a pony, there will be manure tracked into the house. If you get a big dog, he may leave some hair behind.

Mud Season

Then there's that time of year, usually between winter and spring, called *mud season*. Country people in most climates learn to deal with mud, thanks to muddy roads—sometimes axle deep, muddy driveways, and muddy kitchen floors. No matter what type of walkway you put in and what rules you devise to stop the spread, mud will invade your home.

> **Sinkhole**
>
> Mud season is worse for housekeepers if anyone in the home takes care of outside animals or gardens. A doggie door is great most of the year, but in mud season it turns into a nightmare of muddy tracks. Small boys and dogs equal a major mud mess.

To help deal with the mud, place a boot cleaner just outside the door. You can choose from a variety of styles, from simple bars you scrape the boot or shoe over, to brushes mounted so you can scrub your soles and the sides of your footwear. Inside the door, place a bench you can rest on to take off muddy footwear, a tray to hold them, and clean slippers to put on before you go any farther into the house.

Dust and More Dust

As soon as the mud goes away, in comes dust season. A dirt road will soon have the house covered in a layer of dust, inside and out. The soil may also blow off desert areas or plowed fields. Even if you live far from the road and try to keep windows closed, dust will find a way in. It comes in the cracks of even well-sealed houses.

Air conditioning helps, because the windows aren't open as much. Air cleaners don't help much unless they're the very efficient and expensive ones.

The only real way to deal with dust is to dust. Wash curtains often, and don't keep too many knickknacks around—unless you have lots of kids to assign dusting chores to!

In some areas, road crews put down chloride or other solutions on roads to try and keep dust down. This works … for a while.

Flies and Mosquitoes

Flies and mosquitoes may be worse in country areas. There are different kinds of flies and not all of them feed on animals or manure. Some flies, like biting black flies, actually come from water or even from earthworms, like cluster flies, which are worm parasites.

Many, many products are available for controlling common house and stable flies. Fly control means keeping manure piles away from homes, spraying livestock with fly protection, and keeping garbage picked up.

Some flies, like black flies and deer flies, are hard to control and can make doing things outside almost impossible in areas where they live in high populations. They breed in water, and the water can be a mile or more away, but you'll still see them around your yard. They bite, and it hurts. Mosquito repellent helps only a little. Learn to cover your body with long sleeves and pants.

Mosquitoes are worse in country areas because mosquitoes need water to breed, and there's usually standing water somewhere in the country, be it a pond, swamp, horse trough, or roadside ditch. There's also more tall vegetation in the country, and that's just the spot adult mosquitoes like to rest during the day.

Some counties or townships spray for mosquitoes, which seems to help a little. You can do your part by eliminating standing water close to your home that collects in trash, tires, low spots, and plugged gutters. Empty your bird baths and animal water every other day or so.

Other types of water can be treated with mosquito larvacides containing BT (*Bacillus thuringis*, a bacterium that parasitizes mosquito larva and kills them but doesn't affect other animals). This is harmless to children, pets, and almost every other creature; it targets only the larvae of mosquitoes and some other water insects.

Trash Removal

In the city, you probably disposed of trash in a Dumpster or put it out by the curb and the city collected it. Many city areas have elaborate recycling programs and residents sort their trash and deposit it in separate bins. Your taxes pay for the service.

In the country, trash removal is usually the homeowner's responsibility. Some country areas may have regular trash collection paid for out of taxes, but most do not.

Paying for Pickup

In many country areas, you can pay for trash collection. It's much like city trash collection.

Look for trash removal trucks in the area to get a name of the service to call, or ask a neighbor for the number. If more than one trash collection provider works in the area, you may want to ask neighbors which they prefer and compare prices.

Taking Care of It Yourself

A personal landfill isn't the best decision, but there are ways you can handle your own trash disposal. You can sort your trash, and if burning is allowed in your area, you can burn your paper trash. Check local ordinances first and get a proper burning barrel if you're going to do this. Most plastics will also burn. Yes, this will pollute the air to some extent.

Food scraps should go to a compost pile or to the chickens, if you have them. If you can't burn trash, some paper products will also decompose in a compost pile. Wash out cans and bottles. This keeps flies and animals from getting into them. Remove both ends of cans and flatten them.

Call your county government to find a landfill or recycling center where you can take the cans, bottles, and larger items like old mattresses. There may be a charge for this, or it may be free for county residents. If the cans and bottles are clean, they can be stored in covered trash cans until you have time to make a trip to the landfill or recycling center.

> **Sinkhole**
>
> Things like batteries and old pesticides are considered hazardous waste and many trash removal companies won't collect them and many landfills won't accept them. Call your county health department or county Extension office to find out if there are hazardous waste disposal days, when these things are collected.

Composting

Composting is a wonderful way to dispose of many types of household wastes. Country property usually has a spot where compost piles won't be a problem. This should be away from your home and your neighbors' homes and in a sunny area if possible. Often compost piles are close to the garden, where the finished product can be used to improve soil and garden waste can be quickly added.

You can buy a fancy compost bin or tumbler you see in stores and catalogs. These work best for small amounts of waste. Or you can build your own compost bin from old pallets or a circle of wire. Or your compost pile can be simply that—a pile.

All compost piles work better if they are of an equal mixture of juicy, moist items, or "greens," and dry matter, or "browns." Piles that are turned will rot faster—and that's what you want to happen. The piles need to be moistened in dry weather or climates, but in climates where it's very wet they may actually need to be covered.

Sinkhole

Do not dispose of pet waste in a compost pile that will be used for gardens. Pets often have parasites or disease that can be passed to humans who handle the compost. Some compost piles will get hot enough to kill disease or pest organisms during decomposition, but it's hard to tell when that has happened. You can dig a hole for this type of waste and cover it with soil. Livestock manure is safe to put in a compost pile. There's a small chance of disease if fresh manure is used directly on food gardens, but virtually none from composted livestock manure.

The smaller the pieces in the compost pile the faster it will rot, so chopping weeds and garden waste, shredding paper, etc. makes it decompose faster. Large branches, chunks of wood, and whole folded newspapers and magazines will take a long time, maybe years, to decompose.

Here's a quick list of what to include in a compost pile:

Browns	**Greens**
Livestock or poultry bedding	Livestock manure
Dry leaves	Grass clippings
Sawdust	Vegetable or fruit peels
Eggshells	Spoiled fruit/vegetables
Coffee grounds	Table scraps—but not meat
Straw or hay	Weeds and prunings
Shredded paper	

Meat scraps will attract animals to a compost pile and may smell more but will decompose. Grease, however, tends to impede decomposition. If you have chickens, they will take care of a lot of table scraps and unwanted fruits and vegetables. This will make your pile less attractive to animals.

Country Color

Most compost piles will have little smell. But too-wet piles or piles with lots of meat scraps will sometimes smell more.

Glossy, colored paper may have lead in the ink and should be disposed of elsewhere. Colored paper that is not glossy is fine to add to the compost because it's usually made with soy-based ink. Most plastics should not go into the compost pile, but some of the new bio-degradable plastics made of cornstarch will decompose. They are generally marked as such.

Traveling Country Roads

Country roads may take you home, but they may jar every tooth out of your head along the way! Country roads can be very scenic, but they can also be very dangerous.

Country roads run the gamut from paved to two dirt ruts in the ground. Some are private roads, some are county roads, and some are state and federal roads. Some country roads aren't maintained in all seasons and may become impassable. Others regularly become impassable due to snow, flooding, or mud slides.

Some country roads may be private roads, and the homeowners on the road either take turns caring for the road or pay someone to do it. Hopefully you'll know this before you move into your home so it won't come as a shock when someone comes to collect money to grade the road.

Country roads may be less well patrolled by law enforcement, and knowing this, people tend to do what they want on them. Speed limits may not be posted, so you must travel the speed that's safe for the conditions. Some states also have maximum speed limits on such roads.

Weeds and trees grow up and obstruct vision; cows wander onto the roads; and people use the roads for walking, horseback riding, and biking. Be especially wary when coming up over a hill or going around a curve, where you can't see what lies ahead. Slow down at crossroads, even if there's no stop sign, and don't ever blow through stop signs because you believe no one ever travels the road. Watch for hidden driveways and farmers driving machinery out of fields. Also watch for one-lane areas over bridges.

When coming up behind horseback riders or horse-drawn vehicles, do not blow your horn and do not speed pass them. Wait until they have acknowledged you and pulled the horses over before you slowly pass them. Blowing your horn at horses or speeding by them may cause them to panic and throw their riders or run. Teach children not to yell at the horses or throw things at them. Horse-drawn vehicles are supposed to obey all traffic laws and must have a slow-moving-vehicle symbol attached to the back. They have the same rights on the roads as a car.

Dirt and Gravel Roads

Different types of materials are used in different parts of the country to construct roads, usually what's available locally and suits the terrain.

A washboard road, one full of regular ruts crossing it, is hard on you and hard on your car. Country people who live on dirt roads know they'll be replacing mufflers and shocks much more frequently than those who live on paved roads.

After the road is graded, be careful of soft shoulders, where the surface is loose. This can pull your car off the road.

After snow has been graded off a dirt road, it leaves a smooth layer that often melts during the day and refreezes at night into a very slick surface. Water on top of that can make the road treacherous.

Rural Rule

Speeding up *a little* may actually smooth out the ride on a washboard road, but don't go too fast, or the ruts may make you lose control of your car.

Gravel and chip-stone roads have their own hazards. People who travel gravel roads frequently also need their windshields repaired frequently. Speeding on a gravel road is a good way to end up in a ditch, and loose gravel can cause the car to slide if you have to stop quickly.

Slow-Moving Vehicles

In addition to horse-drawn vehicles, other slow-moving vehicles traverse country roads. In farming country, you'll often come upon slow-moving farm machinery. Remember, farmers have the same rights to use the roads as you do, and they're driving those slow machines to make a living.

Most farm implement drivers will pull over when they can and let traffic pass. If you are on a paved road behind a slow-moving vehicle and there are traffic passing lines or no passing signs, you must obey them, even if the vehicle is slow. Be very careful passing these machines on dirt roads where your vision is obstructed by the farm implement or on hills or curves.

All farm machinery should have slow-moving vehicle signs (a bright orange triangle) on the back, flashing lights, and headlights after dark. Sometimes another vehicle will follow

Rural Rule

If you commute, allow yourself extra travel time during planting and harvest times. That way, if you come upon slow farm machinery, you won't be so impatient and take unnecessary risks.

the farm implement with its flashing lights on. When you see these signs ahead, slow down, or you'll be on the machine in no time.

Some new farm machinery is very large and may take up both lanes or have pieces that protrude into the other lane. Be extremely careful when passing these. Also be careful passing overloaded hay or crop wagons, and leave plenty of room between you and the wagon in case something falls off.

Animal Hazards

When you see deer-crossing signs, pay attention and stay alert. But deer don't just cross at the signs—boy, wouldn't that make it easy!? Be alert at dawn and dusk especially, but remember deer can appear any time of the day or night. Good areas for deer crossings are between farm fields and wooded land or fields and water sources.

In some areas, antelope, moose, or elk may also be problems. Large farm animals can wander onto roads, too. (See Chapter 10 for what to do if you hit an animal on the road.) Small animals are common on country roads, too. Don't try to kill things like opossums and armadillos, but don't kill yourself swerving to miss them.

If you drive country roads, sooner or later you're going to hit a rabbit, skunk, or some other small animal. Don't feel too guilty. Many large animals and birds of prey feed on road kill; in fact, some depend on it. And without cars to control their numbers, we would be overrun with species like opossums and rabbits.

Snow and Mud

When you're traveling a country road with open fields on both sides—and during a snow storm—you have a problem. You may not be able to see where the road ends and the field begins. Blowing and drifting snow may obscure landmarks, even mailboxes. Deep drifts on the roads may prove impassable. Take note of where snow drifts so you can be extra cautious when you approach these areas. In a storm, you may run into these drifts before you know it. Also be alert for small sheets of windblown snow that cross the road and cause a slippery area.

When commuting, plan alternate routes. Some roads may not be as prone to drifting, especially roads lined with trees that act as a windbreak. If you get off the road or are stuck, call for help and tie something brightly colored to your door handle and antenna so other cars or emergency vehicles can see you.

At some times of the year, mud can be as much of a problem as snow. Different types of roads handle water better than others. Sometimes the problem only happens in early spring when the ground is still frozen; in other cases, it happens every time it rains.

Stay off soft, muddy roads as much as possible. Every car or truck that gets through leaves a deeper rut for the next one to deal with. If you're scraping the bottom of your car, stop before you pull off something important. If the ground freezes at night, the road might be more passable then.

Rural Rule _____

After many years in the country, I have found the best way to deal with winter storms and the roads is to just stay home!

Deep Ditches

In some areas, particularly in crop growing areas, large, deep ditches might border the road. Sometimes these are full of water on one or both sides of the road. Sometimes these ditches are so deep that a car that runs off the road may not be seen for days. Your car can be ruined if you go into a deep ditch—not to mention you could be hurt.

Be very careful if you have to pull off the road in an unfamiliar area because sometimes brush and weeds obscure the depth of the ditch. If you go into a ditch and can't get out, leave your lights on, put them on bright to raise the beam, and blow your horn whenever you hear traffic.

Missing Road Signs

One of the most frustrating things about country roads is often the lack of signs, which either get stolen or knocked down. Sometimes they were never put up in the first place.

To find your way, keep a map that lists local streets—right down to two-lane roads—in your car. If you're forced to take an unexpected detour or trying to find a street, the map will help you.

A compass in the car can also be helpful. Many country roads are laid out along section lines and fall about a mile apart, but you can't always count on that. Look for roads that are marked and use the map and compass to plot your route.

The new navigation systems can be very helpful, but they sometimes don't cover rural areas completely, and Internet map searches may also come up short in rural areas or just be very wrong.

Rural Rule

To find a detailed map listing local streets, try checking where sporting goods or licenses are sold. Hunters and fishermen often need such maps. Your local library or tax assessor's office may also have one you can copy or buy.

As you'll probably soon discover, sometimes a country road is known locally by one name and listed on maps or on street signs as something else. When getting directions from locals, ask them if the roads have any other names or turn into other named roads. This can save you a world of grief and a lot of time.

You'll no doubt run into the country person who gives directions by landmarks. They tell you to go up the road to the big red barn, turn right, and go down to Darcy's farm, turn right, ... etc. When faced with this type of cartographer, pull out your trusty map and ask him to show you the way. He might mumble "City folk ..." under his breath before he shows you on the map, but it's better to ask questions now than spend an hour driving on rutted back roads.

A phone number is also helpful for a destination you're trying to find, if you carry a cell phone.

The Least You Need to Know

♦ Local government may have irregular hours or even work out of their homes.

♦ Emergency services may be run by volunteers, and there may be a charge for the service.

♦ Country living requires some different housekeeping techniques.

♦ Country roads can be difficult to travel at some times of the year.

Chapter 12

Enjoying Outdoor Activities

In This Chapter

- ◆ Hunting on your land property
- ◆ Fishing, boating, and other water sports
- ◆ Getting off-road with horses and bikes
- ◆ Enjoying winter sports
- ◆ Recreational safety

Many people move to the country so they can spend more time in the great outdoors. Whether you're a hunter, bird watcher, or white-water rafter, it's nice to be close to the action. In this chapter, I discuss the outdoor recreational opportunities available in the country.

If you have children, try to get them interested in outside activities, especially if they're suffering from city-homesickness. Being in the country makes it easier to get them to do something physical outdoors. You may have to go with them, at least at first, but it will be worth it. Participating in outdoor activities together is a wonderful way to bring the family closer together. And research has shown that children who spend time outside in a natural setting are less stressed, more creative, and healthier than children who rarely go outside.

Hunting

Hunting is one of America's favorite outdoor activities and pumps a lot of money into country communities every year. If you've been hunting for years and driving long distances to a hunting area, you might have moved to the country so you can get more hunting time.

Hunting on your own land, where you've managed the conditions for wildlife, have scouted the area, and know your prey's habits, can be very rewarding. You'll want to be a good caretaker for your property and know how to attract game animals. (I cover that in Chapter 25.)

The federal government regulates hunting to some extent, but your state Department of Natural Resources (DNR) is the primary source of rules and regulations for hunting in your state. If you've been hunting for a while, you're probably familiar with some of your state's hunting laws. If you've moved to a new state or you're a homeowner who doesn't hunt, you may want to pick up a copy of your state's hunting and fishing laws. Even people who don't hunt or fish may need to know about the regulations to protect their rights or to inform a guest.

Local governments may also have laws about hunting. These generally involve areas where hunting isn't allowed for various reasons.

Hunting on Your Property

A hunter once walked into our Extension office bragging about just buying 40 acres, where he was going to build a house and "hunt every single day if I want to." If the laws in the area say that's okay, that's okay. But some people don't realize that the fish and game laws apply to private property in almost every area. You own the land, but the government owns the game animals, and you might not be able to hunt every single day if you want to.

Hunting seasons apply to private land as well as public property. It's illegal to hunt out of season, even on your own land. You still have to have a license, and you have to obey the limits and tag if required.

Even if it's hunting season, you have a license, and you're on your land, you may not be able to hunt. If you bought 2 acres in a country development, chances are you can't hunt there. Hunting laws state how far you must be from a building or road before you can discharge a gun. Most rural areas have such laws because it just isn't safe. Sometimes bow hunting is allowed, but check to see before getting your bow. Of course, if there are no laws and no one has moved into those other 2-acre lots, you may be able to hunt.

Country Color

Limits are the legal number of animals or fish you can kill, either by day or by season. In some areas, you're required to place a tag you get from game authorities on animals you kill. This is registered to you and helps officials keep track of what game was taken. You may also be required to take animals to a check in point for examination. And in some areas, you can get special permits to kill nuisance animals out of season. They can sometimes be given to others to hunt on your land, too.

Remember when hunting or target shooting on your property that a bullet can travel a long way if it misses its mark. Don't shoot toward buildings or roads. When target practicing, be sure there's a large area behind the target to catch stray bullets. It can be a dirt bank, pile of straw bales, or another soft surface.

If you really want to hunt in your backyard, you must either purchase a lot of land or land that is remote from other homes. Another good way to be able to hunt close to home is to live near a state hunting area or rent land from a nearby landowner for hunting. Many farmers are happy to allow hunting on their land if they are asked.

Posting Your Land

Even if you enjoy hunting, you'll want to regulate hunting on your property. If you're going to hunt in your woods and fields, you want to know who else is out there. *Posting your land* means putting up No Trespassing or No Hunting signs. This is also some protection if someone wanders onto your land and is injured.

Hunting goods stores and other stores in rural areas carry the signs, or you can make them yourself. They are usually in a bright color and come in different sizes and materials. If you're posting a large area, you can even buy plastic signs on a roll.

Most people attach the signs to posts or trees using a staple gun or a hammer and nail. You may also need posts of some kind to use in open areas and something to drive in the post like a sledgehammer. Put the signs about 10 feet apart, at a man's chest height or higher if there's a lot of brush. Post the signs along the road edges of property, at boundaries between property, and at the edges of any trails or waterways that go through the property. If private roads or

Rural Rule

Before you buy signs, check your state and local laws for any regulations about size and placement of the signs, or wording that makes them a legal warning to trespassers or hunters. Some areas may require that your name and phone number be on the signs.

trails go into your property, you may want to put up a chain or gate across it with your signs attached. If you notice areas that have been used in the past as camps, or where there are tree stands, post signs there, too.

You'll probably have to replace some of the signs every year. If the area is a favorite with hunters, you may have problems at first with hunters ripping down the signs or simply ignoring them. If you want to control your property, you need to periodically patrol it, especially during hunting season.

Even if the land is posted, be cautious about going into the woods and fields during hunting season, and keep livestock and pets confined. Wear bright orange when you patrol your property so you can be seen, and don't try to sneak up on people.

If you find trespassers, the best thing to do is ask them to leave. Remember, you are approaching people armed with weapons, so be careful. If they give you a hard time, walk away—it isn't worth a life. If you see where their cars are parked, you can take down the license place numbers and call law enforcement.

Conservation officers probably won't respond unless the hunters are illegally hunting out of season. You have to count on regular law enforcement, which may put these calls on a low-priority basis. If cars are parked on your property, not the road right of way, you could have them towed.

Hunting Safety

Hunting safety is the same on your property as it is anywhere else. Hunters tend to be a little less cautious on their own property, though. Always wear bright orange because you never know when a trespasser will be near. Wear proper clothing for the weather, too.

Just because you're 500 feet from your back door doesn't mean you can't have a heart attack, shoot yourself, or fall out of a tree stand. Take a cell phone with you into the woods, try never to hunt alone, and tell someone where you're going. Be very cautious with tree stands, and always use a safety harness. And always know what you're shooting at before you shoot.

Fishing

Fishing is a wonderful sport that gets you outside—and allows you to catch dinner. Unlike hunting, you can enjoy fishing even on small pieces of property close to neighbors. You can stock your own pond and control your fishing, or enjoy fishing in waters that touch your property (with the necessary permission, of course).

In Chapter 8, I briefly discussed stocking a pond. Pond fishing is great to get new-comers "hooked" on fishing. The pond owner will have a good feel for when the fish are biting and what they want to bite on his or her own property.

Fishing on Your Property

If you have a pond or lake on your property, no public water flows in or out of it, and you've stocked it with fish, you can probably fish to your heart's content. If you have a lot with access to a lake that's open to the public, state fishing laws probably apply. Oceanside property is subject to state and or federal fishing laws. If a river or creek runs through your property, it may provide some dandy fishing, but you'll probably need a fishing license, can only fish during the proper seasons, and must follow state fishing rules.

Be aware that in most places people can use a waterway just like a public road. They can come down the river on a boat or wade downstream and anchor or stand offshore to fish, but they can't legally come on your bank. Post your bank with No Trespassing signs if you don't want people stopping on it.

What if you divert water from a stream, creek, or lake into a pond on your property, or you discharge water from your stocked pond into another waterway? You may have to have a license to fish, or follow certain rules regarding both stocking and fishing. Check with your local DNR.

Ice Fishing

Stocked ponds rarely provide good ice fishing unless they're very deep natural ponds or small lakes. The fish in smaller ponds are generally down on the bottom sleeping away the winter and not species that feed much in winter.

If you're on a large lake that freezes over, you may have some good ice fishing. Depending on the species and conditions, you could spend winter and summer fishing close to home. You will need something to cut a hole in the ice and ice fishing equipment.

Be very careful when ice fishing. You can drown on a small pond on your property when you fall through the ice as quickly as on a large lake many miles away. Carry something you can use to grab onto ice to pull yourself out of the water. This could be a big screwdriver or special hook devices you can buy.

Be sure the ice is safe before you go on it. This is especially important at the beginning and end of the season. If you see or hear the ice cracking, get off at once.

Water Sports

You may have moved to your country home because you wanted to be closer to the water or live on it. Or maybe you decided after you moved that being on the water would be fun.

Whether you're interested in boating, rafting, canoeing, or swimming, you and your family can spend lots of enjoyable time on the water.

Rafts, Canoes, and Other Boats

Rafting and canoeing are a dreamy way to spend a summer afternoon, drifting or slowly paddling downstream. (Just don't go too far because you have to paddle back home!) If you like white-water rafting, you'll probably want your country home to be near a large river. Most country homeowners will be doing gentler rafting or canoeing down country rivers and streams.

Boats come in all sizes, from row boats to large yachts. If you have a small pond, obviously you don't need a yacht or large motor boat. But if you moved close to the Great Lakes or the ocean, a large boat may be your choice. Sailboats also do better on larger lakes.

Rafts and canoes are fairly inexpensive, don't require docks or special trailers, and are easy to store. Boats require some equipment. For example, if you're not on the water, you need a trailer to get the boat there. You'll also need safety equipment, which includes life jackets and anchors, a radio for weather reports and to call for help, emergency flares or lights, and a first-aid kit.

Country Color

If you live where winter weather makes boating unpleasant or impossible, you'll need somewhere to store your boat in the off season. You can put small boats in a garage or pole barn or cover them with boat covers. Larger boats may require special buildings—perfect if you have the space on your property to build. Some people rent storage space for large boats near the water. Check your homeowner's insurance to see if your boat is covered while it's in storage.

Docks

If you're right on the water and you have anything but a small rowboat, sailboat, or canoe, you'll need a dock to get in and out of the boat on the water. Docks can be strictly utilitarian, to get in and out of the boat and to tie it to, or they can serve as recreational sites. Some people use docks for sunbathing, swimming, and parties.

Unless you own all the property surrounding a pond or lake, don't assume you can build a dock legally. Lakefront and oceanside property may have many restrictions on what kind and size dock can be built. You may own that little piece of shore, but because your dock may affect the environment and others using the water, you might not be able to build, or build what you want. Check local laws before you proceed too far with your dock plans.

The size and type of your dock depend on your needs and what you're allowed to build. On a small pond or lake on your property, the dock can be a simple affair of wood and plastic barrels used as floats or as elaborate as you can design. If you're handy with tools, building a simple dock isn't much different from building a deck. On a large body of water, you might want to hire a professional to build your dock. It must be engineered to withstand the worst conditions in the area and may require equipment the average homeowner doesn't have.

Docks are usually anchored on the shore and extend into the water to where it's deep enough to float your boat. Docks can be floating or anchored at the water side, depending on the lake floor. They can be made of wood, aluminum, steel, or the newer plastic wood materials.

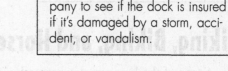

Sinkhole

Docks can be a considerable expense. Check with your homeowner's insurance company to see if the dock is insured if it's damaged by a storm, accident, or vandalism.

Docks may need a lift—powered for large boats or hand turned for small boats—to get them out of the water in storms. The dock also needs bumpers to keep the boat from being damaged as it approaches the dock and something to tie a boat to.

A nonslip surface and handrails make a dock safer, especially if it will have recreational use. A ladder might make it easier for swimmers to get in and out of the water, too.

Swimming

If you live on waterfront property, swimming may be a big part of your outdoor recreational activities. And don't forget swimming pools—many country homes have them.

On any beach or by a pool, have appropriate safety equipment available. On large bodies of water this may mean a small boat. Float rings and a rope attached to a firmly anchored post are a must. If you have small children, you might want a fence between them and the water.

In some areas, the law might require that ponds or pools be fenced. It may make for a better insurance rate as well.

Teach everyone not to dive off docks, off boats, or off the bank unless they know the water is deep enough that they won't hit their head. Remind swimmers that it's better to jump in feet first. And remember that the water level can change throughout the season.

When you live on waterfront property, you may have to post it for trespassing and monitor the use of the beach. People can walk by your beach in the water, but they have no legal right to use the beach area.

> **Country Color**
>
> If you just need a pool for kids to splash in or to cool off after a hard day of work, consider a "farmer pool." Farm stores carry huge livestock drinking tanks, in metal or plastic, that can be 8 feet or more across and about 18 inches deep. They are very sturdy and hold up through years of use.

A swimming pool in the country is fun, but filling it is not. Filling a pool with your water pump will take a long time and is hard on the pump. Most people opt to have water for the pool trucked in. You can keep it topped off with your well water.

In dry areas, swimming pools may attract wildlife that can sometimes fall in and drown or require rescue. A fence will keep larger animals out, but you still might have to deal with reptiles and small animals. Some people keep a simple board "ramp" in the pool to help critters escape.

Hiking, Biking, and Horseback Riding

Some of the best country recreation is the simplest—walking, bicycling, and horseback riding. All ages can walk country roads or through the countryside, most can ride a bike, and some enjoy horseback riding. These quiet activities allow you to see and hear nature at its finest.

Remember that because land appears unoccupied doesn't mean you are free to roam on it. Get permission from any landowner before going on their property. Don't climb or go through fences, and close any gates you open. And never walk, bike, or ride through crops.

On-Road Safety

Back roads seem to be safe to walk or ride on because they're less traveled, but that very fact seems to make the motor vehicle drivers less careful of where they are on the road and how fast they're going. If you're walking on back roads, stay on the shoulder where possible and walk *facing* oncoming traffic. Wear bright or light-colored clothing. And remember that you're walking in nature, so leave the headphones behind so you can hear oncoming traffic. If you must walk on back roads at dawn or dusk or after dark, wear reflective clothing or carry a light. Stay as far off the road as possible when you hear traffic, and be especially careful coming up a hill or going around curves.

You might want to carry some pepper spray and a cane or stick to fend off loose dogs. You may also want to carry a cell phone for emergencies. Although we don't like to think about it, a single walker could become the victim of an abduction walking in unpopulated areas, so try to walk with a friend or a big dog.

In most states, bikers and horseback riders are required to follow the same rules motor traffic does. That means riding with the flow of traffic, not against it. That also means only taking up one lane, not spreading out across the road, and obeying yield and stop signs.

> **Rural Rule**
>
> If you bring a dog with you, be sure he's not off getting into mischief as you walk or ride. If he doesn't stay by you and obey voice commands, keep him on a leash.

Bikers and horseback riders should learn the hand signals for turning and use them. (A Google or Yahoo! search for "bicycle hand signals" should yield several sets of instructions.) Keep horses on the road shoulder when possible, especially on paved roads. Motor vehicles are supposed to treat horses on the shoulder as if they're on the road, but don't count on it.

Bikers and horseback riders should wear helmets. They should also wear bright, highly visible clothing. Stick reflective decals on saddles and bridles as well as on bikes. Whether you're on a horse or a bike, you might want to wear a reflective vest.

Horse-drawn vehicles should also follow safety laws for motor vehicles. Most states require that they have a slow-moving emblem on the back.

Horseback riders and bikers are not required to yield to drivers of motor vehicles that come up behind them, but common sense tells you that you'll lose the battle if you attempt to impede or prevent motor vehicles from passing you. As soon as it's possible to do so safely, move to the far right and signal them to pass you. When riding up hills or around curves, or anywhere your view or oncoming traffic's view is obstructed, stay as far to the right as possible and ride single file.

Most states have laws that make it illegal to try to hit or scare a horse on the road. Horn-blowing is also prohibited unless you're signaling imminent danger. It's also illegal to speed pass horses and pass in no passing zones, but don't count on drivers to know any of this. If someone gives you a hard time, try to get a license plate number and inform law enforcement.

> **Sinkhole**
>
> Never try to provoke motorists by pretending not to see them and spreading out across the road to prevent them from passing. Anger causes people to do stupid things.

Ride with a friend, ride when it's light enough for motorists to see you, and try to carry a cell phone for emergencies. If you ride into a town, be aware that you can get tickets for horse or bike traffic offenses and illegal parking. If you see designated parking areas for horses and bikes, use them.

Off-Road Safety

For hikers, bike riders, and horseback riders off road, the problem is more likely to come from something you did rather than from what someone else did to you. Stay off private property unless you have permission. If you're riding or walking public trails, stay on the trails. If you're hiking or biking, be sure you don't get lost. Carry a compass and a map if you have one. Tell someone where you're going, and carry a cell phone for emergencies.

Even experienced hikers or riders can get lost if the weather is bad, if the sun isn't visible, or if they're having a bad day. As soon as you think you're lost, stop and wait for things to clear up or for help to come. If you decide to continue, mark your trail so you'll know if you're going in circles and so others may find you.

> **Country Color**
>
> If you let them choose the route, horses can usually find their way home in a familiar area.

On horses and bikes, don't get going too fast in unfamiliar areas. Hitting a hole or bump or a fence wire can be very painful. Even if you ride frequently in an area the terrain can change. If a woodchuck digs a hole or a tree falls, you need time to react to the situation.

Stay alert because when you stop paying attention to your surroundings, an accident is more likely to happen. When you get too tired, head home. Fooling around and taking chances can get you in a world of trouble far away from help.

Learn what poison ivy, oak, and sumac look like, and learn to avoid them. If you get off your horse, be sure you can re-mount and tie the horse if you leave it. Check the weather before you set out, and don't go out when storms threaten.

Exploring Mountains and Caves

Some people like to climb, and some people like to crawl. Mountain climbing and cave exploration are two things you should never do alone. Although exciting, these activities require some preparation and planning.

If you moved into a country area that has mountains to climb or caves to explore, some of the same basic rules apply as for walkers and riders. Get permission to go on private property, tell someone where you're going, and be sure you have the proper safety equipment.

If, during your exploration of mountains and caves, you come upon *artifacts*, remember that by law, they belong either to the property owner or the government, depending on what they are. You may be the property owner, but in some cases of true archaeological value, the government may claim the finds. If you're on tribal or reservation land, it's very important not to disturb artifacts or bones. If you find artifacts, mark the location and contact local law enforcement, who should know who to contact to investigate the find.

When you go anywhere in the wilderness, don't leave behind graffiti or deliberately damage things. If it's your property, I suppose you can do as you like, but it's a shame to destroy beauty or items of cultural significance.

def•i•ni•tion

An **artifact** is something made by humans, generally in an earlier time and with archaeological interest. Things like arrowheads, old pots, and remains of homes are artifacts.

Skiing and Other Winter Sports

Some people like to be outside in the winter and enjoy living in areas that get lots of snow. If cold weather sports turn you on, there are many country areas you'll probably be happy to live in.

Nearly every area of the United States that gets snow boasts ski slopes. The average homeowner however, won't have the means to groom a slope, even if he has a good hill on his property. You can ski down mountains and hills in the area if you're experienced, but most people will want to go to a groomed slope for good skiing.

Skiing "wild" means there won't be a lift to get you back to the top of the slope, so what took you a few seconds to go down can take a good bit longer to get back up. For some people, that's just fine and they will be happy on local hills.

Cross-country skiing is a fun and much easier way to enjoy the snow than downhill skiing for the average property owner. In cross-country skiing, you glide across the land. It's easy on the joints, but it's still a good workout. This is a sport the whole family can enjoy—you can pull the littlest ones behind you on a sled. Practice close to home until you've mastered the technique.

All the safety tips for hikers earlier in this chapter also apply to cross-country skiing. Have the proper equipment, and wear the right clothes for the weather.

Country Color

Don't forget toboggans and sleds when you think of playing in the snow. A good hill on your property can give your family hours of fun. Establish some rules about how many can slide down at one time, make everyone wear helmets, and try to remove or pad anything sliders could hit. Remember, you have to climb back up the hill, so establish a safe route for that purpose.

Motorized Off-Road Vehicles

One of the things that cause the biggest problems between established country dwellers and new country dwellers is the newcomers' use of off-road motorized vehicles. Some off-road drivers assume all country property and rural roads are fair game to ride on. Not so.

Country people do use quads and snowmobiles, often as farm tools. But sensible country people know that although such vehicles can be useful, they destroy soil and crops and scare animals as well as annoy other people with their noise.

Sinkhole

Snowmobile riders often use frozen lakes and ponds as riding areas. If the lake or pond is public, you may have the right to play there, but be sure to use great caution. The machine and rider are heavier than a skater, and you may end up under water.

If you're moving to the country to be able to ride your snowmobile or all-terrain vehicle (ATV) around home, buy a good, large piece of land to ride on, or buy near established public trails. In many areas, snowmobiles and ATVs are not allowed to travel legally on roads. The shoulder of the road is often used, but this is also usually illegal. Where such vehicles are legal on the road, the driver has the same responsibilities as a car driver and must use the road the same way. He or she must have a driver's license and obey traffic rules.

Drivers of ATVs, motorcycles, and snowmobiles don't have the right to cross private land. Just because a field is covered with snow doesn't mean crossing it won't hurt a crop underneath. And riders are taking big risks that they won't run into snow buried fence wires or debris.

In dry areas, the hot mufflers on ATVs and motorcycles have been known to cause fires. Never remove mufflers or spark suppressors.

> **Country Color**
>
> According to the Consumer Product Safety Commission, children driving ATVs have a 61 percent higher risk of death or serious injury than from participating in 33 sports studied, including football.

It's illegal to chase or harass wildlife or domestic animals with off-road machines. And if you hit a deer with one of these machines, you will likely die with it.

If your kids like to ride these motorized toys, keep them on your property or on public trails. Be sure a child can handle the machine and wear helmets at all times, even on a dirt track out back. Be conscious of disturbing neighbors and animals with too much noise, and always leave the mufflers on the machines.

Recreational Safety

Throughout this chapter I've given safety tips, but safety can never be stressed enough. There are two major components to outdoor recreational safety.

First up, always tell someone where you're going. Even if you're going out to the pond behind the barn to fish, tell someone your plans. If no one is home to tell, leave a note in the house. Then stick to your planned activity. Don't put the fishing pole down and wander off to hike the back 40.

As important is to know your limits. Don't try to do things you cannot safely do, or shouldn't do. There may be limits to your equipment—that rope isn't supposed to carry more than 200 pounds—or limits to your physical strength or ability.

If you're inexperienced with a sport, let an experienced person guide you, or practice in a safe place. If you have medical problems or a disability, don't do things that put you, and possibly others, in jeopardy. Don't let yourself get so tired that you make a mistake or take chances. Keep yourself alert and focused on the activity. It's okay to push the limits a little, but know when to stop.

The Least You Need to Know

◆ The country offers many opportunities for outdoor sports and activities.

◆ Don't use other people's property for recreation without permission.

◆ Always practice safety, tell someone where you're going, and know your limits.

13

Country Safety and Emergency Preparedness

In This Chapter

- ◆ Country emergency planning
- ◆ Your family disaster plan
- ◆ Emergency food, water, and other supplies
- ◆ Safety planning

Accidents and natural disasters can affect everyone. But those who live in rural areas face special hazards and considerations. And if you're a long-distance commuter, you also need to consider emergency preparedness for the road.

Differences in Country Emergency Preparedness

Disasters are possible anywhere. When disasters involve large numbers of people in an urban area, help might arrive faster because emergency personnel are already on duty in those areas, and plans for disasters and people to manage them are often already in place. It's easier to find victims if they're concentrated in one area, and common sense can lead rescuers to areas where they can do the most good with the least effort first.

Depending on your area, in the country, emergency planning may be lacking, and equipment to rescue victims may not be in place. Because people who live in isolated areas may be hard to reach or rescuers may be unaware they need help, country people should prepare to be on their own for at least the first few days of any major emergency.

If you live in the country, you should monitor the weather and news reports automatically. Warning systems, such as tornado sirens, may not be present in your area, so you must know what's going on. You should also check with your local government, county, and township or village to see what emergency plans and warning systems they do have.

Country Color

Since the formation of the Homeland Security Agency, each county and major metropolitan area is supposed to have an emergency plan. The Federal Emergency Management Agency (FEMA) has guidelines for community preparedness. Your local phone book or government website may list an emergency preparedness office, or those duties may be part of another county or township department. Your county plan will list where evacuation shelters and emergency medical care will be set up in disasters and who is responsible for each operation.

Better Safe Than Sorry

"Better safe than sorry" is the theme to live by in the country. When the weather report indicates that an ice storm may be on the way, for example, check your emergency supplies, be sure you have the medications you need, and if you have a well, fill up some containers with water in case you lose power. (A power failure means your well won't work.) If a wildfire is burning nearby or an evacuation might be ordered, have the car packed and the kids and pets accounted for, and be ready to go at a moment's notice. It may not be headed your way now, but the winds could shift at any minute.

With proper planning, country dwellers can survive most emergencies and in some situations may actually be better off than those in urban areas.

Identify Common Hazards

Every area has disasters that may be more common in that area than in other parts of the country. A tornado could hit anywhere in the United States but is more common in the Midwest and South. Floods normally occur close to rivers or lakes, but heavy rain or broken dams may send flood water where it's unexpected.

Wildfires are unlikely to occur in desert areas. Hurricanes probably won't touch Wyoming. Florida rarely gets ice storms, although they have happened. Plan most intently for disasters that happen in your area, but don't entirely discount that once-in-a-lifetime event.

Some disasters, such as house fires, toxic spills, even nuclear attacks or terrorist activity, could happen anywhere. Earthquakes could happen anywhere, too, although they're more common in the West.

Rural Rule

When you've determined what the most likely natural disasters are for your area, check your homeowner's insurance policy to see if you're covered for that disaster damage. Most homeowner policies don't cover flood damage; it has to be added as a separate policy. In hurricane-prone areas, you need a policy that covers flood damage and wind damage. Other areas may require separate coverage for things like mudslides or falling rocks. If you have questions about what your policy covers, talk to your agent.

Pay Attention to Weather Reports

In the country, you'll soon learn to pay more attention to the weather. A weather radio that picks up emergency weather warnings is a valuable tool. If you don't have a weather radio, listen to the radio or TV weather report at least once a day, and more often if the weather looks threatening.

Even things like thunderstorms being predicted should get your country ears up. If you live in one of the mountainous areas where mudslides occur, even rain coming should get your attention. If you're a commuter, also pay attention to the weather near your worksite. Weather can change dramatically in as little as 50 miles.

Establish a Family Disaster Plan

Your family needs an emergency plan. All members of the family should know the plan, and you should practice some emergency procedures occasionally. Each family will have different concerns and special needs, but the basics apply to every family.

Start by deciding where family members will meet outside the home if a house fire, earthquake, or other disaster makes a sudden evacuation from the home necessary. Pick a site that's easy to remember and that's a short distance from the house. At the meeting place you can determine who is missing and the next steps to take.

If family members may be separated during an emergency such as at school or work, establish one number everyone should call to check in on each other. Pick a number outside your area, which might not be affected by the emergency, such as a relative in another state. Also establish a backup number or e-mail address. Everyone should memorize the number, carry it in a purse or wallet, or program it into a cell phone.

Each family member should know where to go for shelter during a disaster at home, such as a basement, storm shelter, inside closet, etc. They should know where emergency equipment such as flashlights, fire extinguishers, and ladders are stored. All family members should know where emergency food and water are kept and where the portable emergency kits are. (I talk more about these in a bit.) More than one person in a family should know how to do things like shut off power or fuel, start a generator, or use the sump pump.

Rural Rule

Hold practice drills with your family so everyone knows what to do when they hear an alarm, smell smoke, see fire, or are told to evacuate immediately. Even one or two practices can give valuable experience and let you know of any glitches in your plan.

If someone in your home is dependent on electrical medical equipment, have a backup power source. If you can't afford a generator, check into battery-powered equipment. Your plan may be to move a dependent person to a hospital or other shelter as soon as possible.

Talk to the family about other types of disasters such earthquakes, ice storms, blizzards, or lightning strikes and what the plans are for each situation. Discuss what to do with pets and livestock. (I talk more about that later in this chapter.)

Evacuation/Survival Kits

You should have emergency supplies in your home, but there might be times when you have to leave your home in a hurry. Everyone should have a personal evacuation kit packed and ready for an emergency. Why an individual kit for each person rather than one kit for the whole family? That one-for-all kit might be too heavy or cumbersome to move in a hurry, and it could get lost or damaged, leaving nothing for anyone. (Note that personal evacuation kits are different from first-aid kits, which I discuss later.)

If you commute long distances, you should always have a personal evacuation kit in the car with essential food, water, and other supplies. If you have pets, you should also prepare evacuation kits for them.

Food and Water

You need a supply of food and water for *sheltering in place* (or staying in your home until the emergency passes) and for evacuation kits. FEMA and the Red Cross recommend that all families have a 3-day supply of emergency food and water on hand for each family member. In the country, especially in more remote areas, you may want to increase that to a 5- to 7-day supply. Many families choose to keep a 2 weeks' supply of food and water on hand, which really isn't that hard to do. If evacuation kits are in the home, that food and water can be counted as part of the home emergency supply.

Let's talk about water first, because it's so important. Every person, including children, will need about 2 quarts of drinking water a day. That's the amount a 2-liter soda pop bottle holds. Nursing mothers and sick people may need more. More water will be needed for cooking and basic washing, so count on another 2 quarts water for every person per day for a total of 1 gallon or 2 (2-liter) soda pop bottles. If you have an emergency hand pump on your well or a generator, you may store less drinking water for sheltering in place, but your evacuation kit must have the proper amount: a $\frac{1}{2}$-gallon or 2-liter soda pop bottles per day (for drinking only). Stored items like carbonated beverages and juices can be counted in a person's water allowance.

It's recommended that you buy your drinking water for storage and keep it in the original, sealed container. Most grocery stores now sell 1- and 5-gallon containers of water as well as small bottles. The 1-gallon or smaller bottles are easier to store and carry.

If you don't want to buy water, you can prepare and store your own. But don't just fill any old container with water and call it a day. There are some specific guidelines in place you should follow when storing drinking water. For information on how to store water safely and clean contaminated water for drinking in emergency situations, go to www.fema.gov/areyouready or call 1-800-480-2520 for a comprehensive emergency preparedness book for families.

The amount of food you store depends on many factors. If you normally keep the freezer and refrigerator full, and your cupboards usually have the essentials, your family can probably survive for several days. It's still wise to always have some foods that require little water or heating on hand for sheltering in place. Always keep items like peanut butter, canned or foil packets of tuna and chicken, foil packets of precooked rice, crackers, canned ready-to-eat pasta, ready-to-eat soup, canned stew and chili, jelly, and canned fruit and vegetables on hand. Canned or bottled juices are also good. Choose things your family likes, use the stored foods before they get too old, and replace them as necessary.

If you're fairly certain you'll have adequate water in an emergency, foods like rice, beans, pasta, flour, sugar, etc. will be good choices to store. Canned shortening or bottled oil and powdered or canned milk may also be needed for cooking. You can also buy powdered eggs.

When shopping for your evacuation kits, select lightweight food that's easy to open and ready to eat. Don't choose items designed to be heated in a microwave as they're usually packaged in containers that can't be used with direct heat such as on a grill or open fire. Things like foil packets of tuna and chicken, peanut butter in individual servings, cheese and crackers, jerky, peanuts or other nuts, energy bars, breakfast bars, trail mix, dried fruit, juice in boxes, hard candy, and pudding and gelatin cups are good choices.

If you have infants in the home, you should always have a 3- to 7-day supply of baby food and things like boxed juice or milk on hand. You may also need ready-to-use formula. You'll also need bottles and nipples. Don't count on the mother nursing the baby during an emergency. If the mother is injured or separated from the baby, he will still need to be fed.

If you don't have a pantry or cupboard for your emergency food and water, you could store it in plastic tubs with lids under a bed, in a closet, in the corner of a room, etc. The area should be dark and cool if possible.

If you have an emergency shelter, that's the ideal place to store food and water. Food must be stored in a dry area, away from animals. If flooding is a possible emergency in your area, store your food and water as high as possible.

Talk to your children about the importance of having emergency food supplies, especially in their own evacuation kit. Check the kits from time to time to be sure no one is sneaking treats. In an emergency, people can make do with short food supplies for a long time, but water is much more important. If you need to skimp, do it with the food.

Rural Rule _____

An old unused, even non-working freezer or refrigerator makes a good place to store food and water for an emergency. It could be put in the basement or garage and would keep the food pest-free.

Other Emergency Supplies

Make photocopies of important documents, birth certificates, Social Security cards, driver's licenses, passports, marriage licenses, insurance policies, doctor or other professional licenses, etc. Your originals, of course, need to be protected in a fireproof safe or box if you aren't carrying them.

Keep copies of the documents in your evacuation kit and copies in a safe place somewhere away from home, such as in a safe-deposit box, your office, or a relative's home. The documents in the evacuation kit should be in a waterproof bag and hidden in the kit.

Always keep a small amount of cash in your evacuation kit, too. Bank cards and ATMs might not work in emergencies.

You should have a 3-day supply of prescription medicines and over-the-counter drugs you use regularly in your evacuation kit. Don't let prescription medicines get too low before refilling them so you always have a week's supply at home.

If you need other medical supplies, keep a 3-day supply in the evacuation kit and a week's worth in the home. If you have an extra pair of prescription glasses or even an old pair, include them in the evacuation kit. Women should keep some personal hygiene supplies in the evacuation kit as well.

If you're a long-distance commuter, keep a pair of comfortable shoes or boots in your car and a change of comfortable clothes in your emergency kit. Commuters in cold areas should always have a warm coat, hat, and gloves in the car. A blanket is also a good idea.

The home survival kit should have matches, candles, flashlights, batteries, and possibly oil lamps and lamp oil. The personal evacuation kit should have waterproof matches or a lighter, flashlight, and batteries. A candle and a small can to melt snow or heat something could also be included.

Along with the food supplies in the home kit, include a manual can opener. Personal kits should have a pocket knife, a can opener if the food stored will need one, and a metal fork and spoon.

You will need something to cook on if power goes out. You can use the top burners of gas and propane stoves, lit with a match. Otherwise, you need a grill or camp stove you can use outside (to avoid carbon monoxide poisoning). Woodstoves and fireplaces can also be used for cooking on.

Heat can be obtained by fireplaces, wood or corn stoves, or kerosene or propane heaters. Be very cautious of carbon monoxide poisoning using unvented heating sources such as portable heaters. Leave windows cracked, and use a battery-operated carbon monoxide detector when using them.

Sinkhole

Don't buy a wood or corn stove or propane heater for emergency heating unless it will run without electricity. Many won't.

Landline cordless phones won't work in a power outage, so keep a corded phone on hand and know how to plug it in. A cell phone battery charger that plugs into a car battery will keep cell phones alive. Commuters should always have a cell phone and battery charger with them.

A hand-cranked or battery-powered radio is great for emergencies. Every home should have one, and maybe consider putting one in your family's personal evacuation kit.

Personal evacuation kits should have several garbage bags and re-closable plastic bags, which can be used in a number of ways. They should also have some plastic tarps or a cheap tent, some rope, and duct tape. Personal kits should also have toilet paper, hand wipes or sanitizer, and a small first-aid kit.

If possible, personal kits should have a blanket or sleeping bag. Pens and paper, whistles or other signaling devices, and pepper spray or protective devices are other considerations.

Home and evacuation kits for infants and toddlers should include disposable diapers, even if you don't use them at home. If you use cloth diapers at home, you might not be able to wash and dry them in an emergency.

Several changes of clothing and possibly training pants should be included in toddler evacuation kits. These can be older things, maybe from a garage sale, but serviceable in an emergency. Remember to check and re-size as children grow.

An extra pacifier, bottles or sippy cups, if needed, should be in toddler and infant evacuation kits.

First-Aid Kits

Every home, car, and personal survival kit should contain a basic first-aid kit. You can buy them preassembled or put them together yourself. A first-aid kit should contain various sizes of Band-Aids, first-aid tape and gauze pads, sterile alcohol wipes, a thermometer, first-aid cream or spray, nonprescription pain reliever, and anti-diarrhea medicine. You may want to add disposable gloves and wet wipes. A first-aid manual is also useful.

Everyone who could be isolated from immediate emergency response should take a good first-aid class. You can often find these at your local hospital, fire department, or local library.

If you're injured, or if you find someone injured, try to remain calm. If you come upon an accident, don't become the second victim. Take a moment to assess the situation and decide on the best way to help. Proceed carefully, get the victim immediate help such as turning off a machine or scaring off an animal, and call for help.

Rural Rule _____

Both parents in a home should take CPR (cardio-pulmonary resuscitation) classes. They are often offered by the Red Cross or hospitals for a small fee. Teens may want to learn first aid and CPR also. Keep a CPR instruction chart with first-aid supplies. In the country or in a disaster with long emergency response times, knowing CPR may save a life.

Pets and Livestock

Since Hurricane Katrina, the government has done an about-face on the subject of evacuating animals in an emergency. In many disaster situations, people refuse to leave their homes if they can't take their pets, or they return to unsafe areas too soon to rescue them. People will always come first, but the government realizes that an orderly and effective evacuation or response to a disaster must include attention to the pets and livestock in a community.

Your Community's Plan

It's now a law that all counties have an emergency evacuation plan for companion animals and livestock. In some areas, people are allowed to take pets to shelters with them; other areas have separate shelters to hold pets and livestock with designated caretakers.

If you have animals, find out before an emergency what the plans are for animals in your county. Locate the designated shelters, and know how to get there. If the shelter won't let owners stay with pets and that's important to you, perhaps you can volunteer to be part of an emergency response team at that shelter.

If you lose your pets during a disaster, you should always check for them at the designated shelters because that's where rescued pets will be brought.

Your Family's Plan

If you have pets or livestock, you should think about what you will do in various emergency situations. Large pets and companion animals such as horses will take the most thought and planning.

All pets and even livestock should have identification that will establish you as the owner. Pets can be microchipped and/or have tags, and livestock can be branded, ear tagged, or tattooed.

Be sure all rabies and other vaccinations needed in your area are kept up-to-date. That will make your animals more welcome at emergency shelters and will protect them as they mingle with many other animals.

Have a safe way to transport animals in an emergency. Dogs, cats, birds, and other small pets should have secure, hard-sided carriers. Large carriers may need to be on wheels. This is the safest way to transport pets. Wire cages, bird cages used in the home, plastic hamster cages, etc. should not be used except as a last resort.

Unless you're sure two animals get along, only one animal should be in a carrier. The carrier should have enough room for the animal to stand, turn around, and lie down. It should have a solid top and ventilated sides. Your name and address should be on the carrier in several places.

Rural Rule

You can often pick up pet carriers at yard sales and flea markets very cheaply. They don't have to look great, but be sure the doors and latches still work well.

Horses and larger pets need a livestock trailer. If you don't have one, perhaps you can arrange with a neighbor or friend to transport your animals in an emergency. You should practice loading your animal into a trailer so you and the animal both know what to do before a disaster strikes.

With large animals, consider finding a friend or relative in an area a good ways away from you who may not be affected by the same disaster and transporting your animals there. It could be a reciprocal arrangement.

Emergency Supplies for Animals

Have a 3-day supply of pet food on hand for evacuations, and be sure emergency pet food is stored at home. If your pet needs medication, be sure you also have several days' supply of the medication. If you must leave your pet, tape the food and medication with directions on top of its carrier.

Don't forget the water. Pets don't get sick as easily from mildly contaminated water, so water may be easier to provide for them. The amount of water needed varies. Count on a 2-liter bottle for small pets and up to 5 gallons per day for large animals, depending on size and the weather.

Include a small litter box in a cat carrier. Dogs and other animals may be kept dry by providing several layers of newspaper on the bottom of the carrier covered by a perforated rubber or plastic mat. Some carriers also have wire grids over the floor. Put newspaper or absorbent material underneath the grid.

You'll need food and water dishes, preferably ones that clip on the carrier door. All dogs should have a collar and leash so they can be safely exercised. Horses and larger animals should have a halter and lead with them.

> **Country Color**
>
> You may have to transport what food and water you can for large animals and hope for the best. If the animal needs special food like senior food for horses, do all you can to provide an emergency supply.

First-Aid Kits for Animals

If you have pets or large animals, you should have a first-aid kit for them. Many of the same items in a human first-aid kit can be used in an animal's kit. A special thermometer for pets and special bandaging tape are needed. Also include pain medication and animal-specific anti-diarrhea medication.

Restraints such as a muzzle or a twitch for horses may be needed. A sturdy canvas cloth that can be used as a stretcher for small animals is handy. A cream that can be used on wounds to keep off flies is also good to have.

If You Can't Take Them with You

It may be heartbreaking, but sometimes the best thing to do is leave your animals behind. Leave as much food and water as possible. If the disaster is an impending flood or fire, turn large animals loose because they may be able to find safety on their own. In a wildfire, shut the doors to barns and stables so animals don't run inside and get trapped.

Turn pets loose before a fire if you can't move them. Some will hide in the house, but at least leave doors and gates open so they can try to escape if they want.

If you leave, mark your home on the outside, stating what kind of animals were left and how many. Leave any special instructions about the animals and where you can be reached if you know.

Personal and Home Safety Issues

Even in the country, bad things can happen to good and trusting people. It can be an accident with no one close to help you or an intruder who steals from or somehow harms you. When you talk about emergency planning with your family, you should also discuss those emergencies that may affect only your family.

Accidents

In the country, people are often working with powerful tools in isolated places. Accidents can happen with no close neighbors to see or hear that a problem has occurred. Even activities that seem harmless can suddenly turn deadly.

When working with tools such as chainsaws, wood splitters, post hole augers, band saws, etc., try to do it when someone else is home and within calling distance. Read the tool's directions, stay alert, and always use safety equipment. Wear proper-fitting clothing around power tools because loose clothing may catch in tools and draw you into the blade. The work area should be free of things that you could trip or stumble on, including cords and gas cans.

Sinkhole

Children should not use power tools until they're old enough and strong enough to do so safely.

When you're working out of sight of the house and any neighbors, try to keep a cell phone on you. If a family member has been gone a long time doing a chore, go check on them.

Large animals can also prove dangerous, even unintentionally. A kick to the head from a horse that's feeling frisky can be painful or deadly. Male animals that have not been castrated are especially unpredictable. Don't relax your guard around large animals, and always practice safe handling, with the proper equipment.

Children should not play around or handle large animals without adult supervision. If animals deliberately try to harm humans, get rid of them.

Home Robberies

Every once in a while, a crime spree breaks out in rural areas where thieves target homes secluded from the road. They watch them, seeing that no one is home for large parts of the day. If you hear of this type of crime occurring in the area, ask a neighbor or friend to drop by your house at odd times.

Lock your house; this will slow them a little. Don't leave valuables in view of windows, especially guns, which are a prime target.

A locked gate at the end of a drive may be a deterrent as they will not have an easy way to load loot, and someone may notice the car by the road. Alarm systems that ring outside the home may not alert neighbors who are far away. If law enforcement is fairly close, a monitored alarm system that notifies them may be helpful.

Country Color

Should you have a gun for protection? Country homes are often isolated from help, and a gun might come in handy someday. If you live in an area with large predators, there's no doubt that a household should have one, and the adults should know how to use it. Keep guns locked up, unloaded, and out of sight of casual visitors. Don't bring the gun out against human intruders unless you fully intend to, and know how to, use it. Otherwise, the gun may be used on you.

Many, many country people leave their doors unlocked, even when they're gone all day. It's a bad practice though, even if you're working somewhere around the place. Chances are, nothing will happen, and maybe you have nothing to steal anyway, but if someone does come in, you'll feel very violated.

The Least You Need to Know

♦ In the country, emergency aid may take longer to reach you.

♦ Your county is required to have an emergency plan for humans as well as animals.

♦ Every home should have an emergency plan and emergency supplies.

Part 4

How Things Work in the Country

For people who always called maintenance when something went wrong, the workings of a country home may seem overwhelming. Even if you owned a home in the suburbs, you might find country home maintenance a little challenging. Knowing how things work takes the mystery out of it and helps you decide if something is wrong.

In Part 4 I cover your country home's well, septic system, and heating system—all very important to your health and well-being. I cover new tools and equipment you may need, and I give you a primer on fence building. Then I discuss sheds, barns, and other buildings you may find or want on your property.

Chapter 14

Wells and Water

In This Chapter

- ◆ Groundwater and how to protect it
- ◆ How wells are created
- ◆ Keeping your well working … well
- ◆ Dealing with water problems

Most Americans couldn't imagine living without safe, clean, good-tasting water. You turn on a tap and immediately there it is. If you live in a city, your water is generally collected from surface water, treated at huge plants, and piped into your home. Small towns may have a municipal well where groundwater is pumped to a tank, tested, treated, and piped into homes. But about 20 percent of Americans, mostly those who live in the country, must rely on home wells.

When you have a home well, you are responsible for ensuring that the water is safe and clean and continues to flow through your pipes when you need it. Wells are fairly simple systems, but because water is so vital to your health, it's important to know how your well works and how to protect your drinking water.

The Importance of Groundwater

Groundwater is the water that's drawn up into your well. It's water just under the surface or deep inside the earth. Most groundwater is a saturated area, where air has been excluded from between the soil or rock particles by water. These saturated areas often occur in layers, with bedrock or heavy clay under them. The top of this saturated area is called the *water table*. (You'll read more about the water table later.) Depending on what type of soil, gravel, or rocks surface water has to pass through, it can take a matter of minutes or hundreds of years for surface water to become groundwater.

Since the beginning of time, groundwater has been contaminated through various processes. Toxic minerals dissolve in water, gases and liquids from the earth's core come into contact with groundwater, animals and plants produce wastes that seep into groundwater, etc. Some of the chemicals man has learned to produce cannot be removed from water by natural processes and, therefore, reach the groundwater intact. Even a few drops of some chemicals can make thousands of gallons of water undrinkable.

A well is a direct link to groundwater, so anything that gets into a well can rapidly reach and pollute the groundwater. This can happen when a well is damaged, as when someone hits the *wellhead* with a car. It can happen during floods when the wellhead is covered with water. When someone dumps used engine oil down an old well, the groundwater is immediately contaminated.

def•i•ni•tion

A **wellhead** is a pipe sticking out of the ground that connects directly to the well. In modern homes, this is outside; in older homes, it may be under the house. Technically, it is the well. The pump is down there in the pipe, in modern wells at least. The part above the ground is where you can access the pump and well. It functions as a vent, too.

Contamination can also occur when things applied to or spilled on the ground seep down to the water table. Fertilizers, animal waste, drugs, pesticides, and chemicals can move through the soil and reach the groundwater. The spill can happen years before the substance reaches the groundwater and pollutes it.

The deeper the layers of soil, clay, gravel, and sand between the surface and the water table, the more likely particles that could pollute groundwater will be trapped or neutralized. Clay has the smallest spaces between its particles and is able to trap and filter potential pollutants better than other materials.

Groundwater can also be polluted by natural occurrences we have no control over, such as leaching of arsenic or radon gas. Anything that makes your water undrinkable will severely impact your quality of life and may make your home unlivable.

Understanding Wells

Man has been digging wells to access groundwater for thousands of years. Groundwater is often available where surface water is not present, and it is better protected from contamination. Homeowners today rarely use surface water for personal use because the cleaning and filtering necessary is a monumental task. Most country homeowners have a well for their home water system.

Types of Wells

In earlier times, all wells were *dug wells*—that is, they were dug by hand. These wells had to have a large opening and could only reach water in the first 20 to 30 feet of ground. Dug wells are easily polluted and dangerous. They are seldom seen on modern home sites and may be illegal in many areas. Old dug wells should be closed as soon as possible. (I discuss closing old wells later in the chapter.)

Driven wells are still seen in some areas and are the easiest wells for do-it-yourselfers to accomplish. A driven well uses a series of pipe pieces that are pounded into the ground. As each piece nears ground level, another piece of pipe is screwed into it. Driven wells cannot go through rock and still can't reach very deep into the ground, but they may be the only option if well drilling machinery can't get into an area.

Drilled wells use a variety of methods and machinery to drill into the soil. Well drilling rigs use percussion, hydraulics, and other forms of force to drill a well shaft. This type of well shaft can go deep into the ground to access water and can even go through some layers of rock. Most modern country wells are drilled.

When a well shaft reaches a pocket of groundwater that's under pressure, the water may flow out of the well under its own pressure. These are called *artesian wells*. Very few artesian wells have enough pressure to pump water through a modern home so they're also augmented with a pump. But in a few instances, water pressure from an artesian well can be more than a home water system can handle.

Springs are areas where the water table is so high, water flows from the ground surface naturally. Most springs just seep water out, although some may run more vigorously. Although they make excellent ponds and wetlands, they're usually not a good home water source. Spring water has no health advantages over any other type of water and can be easily polluted.

How a Well Works

When you turn on a faucet in your house, either your pressure tank or your well pump turns on. A pressure tank stores water and adds pressurized air to the tank to boost water pressure. This keeps the pump from turning on and off as often and lengthens its life.

The size and type of pump used in your well depends on how deep your well is and how much water it needs to supply. When the well is 100 feet or deeper, a submersible pump that fits inside the well casing is generally used. Shallow wells may use a pump that sits on top of the well casing.

When the pump is turned on, it sucks water through a screen on the bottom of the well through the well casing and into the house, where it goes into a holding or pressure tank and then maybe through a water filtration or treatment system and out the tap.

Country Color

For emergency situations, hand pumps can be installed on wells that aren't too deep. They are best installed by a professional so the electric pump isn't damaged.

Because electricity is needed to run your water pump, when the power goes out, you won't have running water unless you have a backup power source such as a generator. Learn to anticipate and plan for power shortages, such as when a storm threatens, by storing water. When the power comes back on, your system should resume operating as usual and need no special treatment.

Locating Your Well

Everyone in the household should know where the well is, how to access it, and just as importantly, how to protect it. I once heard of a woman who cut off the well pipe at ground level because it looked bad. That's a good way to pollute a well. Kids are sometimes tempted to put things down the hole or play on the wellhead. They should also be shown where to shut off the power source to the well pump and the valve that allows water into the house in case of a leak or if someone needs to work on the plumbing.

When locating your well, first look for the wellhead. It will be a pipe sticking up out of the ground. It can be plastic or metal and will be from 3 to 6 inches in diameter. In old homes, it may be under the house in a basement or crawl space or outside in a small building called a *well house*. In modern homes, the wellhead will be outside, usually close to the house.

At the top of the well pipe you will either find the pump or a *well cap*. In modern deep wells, the pump is usually down in the well, submersed in the water. A well cap keeps water and debris out of the well. A screened area under the cap ventilates the well pipe.

If the wellhead is outside the home, a water line (pipe) leads from the well to the house. It will be below the frost line for your area. You should know where it is so you don't dig into it or build over it. Go inside the house and find where the water line enters the house. It will generally be connected to a tank. Follow a direct line from where the line enters the house to the wellhead. Your water pipe is below this line most of the time.

Inside the house near the well, or somewhere close to where the water enters the home, is usually a pressure tank or a holding tank, or sometimes both. These tanks store water so that when you turn on a faucet, the pump doesn't have to come on every time.

Drilling New Wells

If at all possible, have the well put in before you build. There may be limited areas on your property where water can be obtained, and you don't want to obstruct them. A local builder should have a feel for how hard it is to find water in the area and how flexible the site plans should be.

The closer the well to the house, the better, as distance reduces water pressure, but you want your well as far from the septic tank and field as possible. The minimum by law is generally 50 feet from septic fields or tanks or manure storage areas. You also want your well to be uphill from any flow of contaminated water, above or below-ground. The water movement belowground generally flows in the same direction it flows aboveground. Building soil up around the area where your well will go may stop surface contaminants from running into your well, but it doesn't change what's happening belowground.

The wellhead will stick above the ground about a foot. It should never be in a low area where surface water will collect and cover the top of the pipe. This would result in direct contamination of your well. If possible, keep the wellhead away from driveways and garage areas. It's more likely to be damaged by vehicles or contaminated from spills in these areas.

Well Drilling Basics

Because clean, safe water is so vital to your household, hiring a professional well driller is the best way to obtain safe drinking water. Kits are sold to drill or drive your own well, but these rarely work if the water is deeper than 100 feet underground. These may be fine to dig a second well for watering the garden or livestock, but for the home water system, a professional well driller is recommended.

Rural Rule

To find a well contractor/driller in your area who's certified by the National Groundwater Association, call 1-800-551-7379 or go to www.wellowner.org/lookup/contractorlookup.asp.

How Deep Should It Be?

The deeper the well or the more tries to find water, the more expensive the project. Because good water is so important, this is not an area to try to save money. Your goal should be the best well possible.

Good water can come at any depth, but wells that are 100 feet deep or more and that have layers of clay or rock above them are less likely to become polluted from surface contamination. Each municipality has laws that state the minimum depth for a well depending on local conditions.

The Drilling Process

A well driller hopes to find several layers of clay and no deep layers of rock between the surface of the ground and where he finds your drinking water. The end of the well or the *well point* should extend deep into the water level so a drop in the water table will be less likely to result in a dry well.

When he hits water at an acceptable depth, the well driller will check to see how many gallons of water a minute the well will produce. Five gallons per minute or more is best for modern households. He will also check the water for purity and quality. Some quality issues such as water hardness can be addressed by adding filtration and conditioning systems. Other issues, such as bacterial contamination, mean that a new well will have to be drilled.

When water safety and quality is assured, the well driller will add screens to the bottom of the shaft to filter out sand and other particles, the well *casing*, the pump, and the water line to the house. The water line to the house is connected to the casing in a trench that goes down below the frost line. A power line to the pump will be hooked up, too. The casing will continue to about a foot above the ground surface.

The well driller will seal the area of the ground surface around the wellhead and around the water pipe that leads into the home so contaminants from the surface cannot slide down the outside of the casing directly to the groundwater. This is very important, and that seal should always be protected.

def•i•ni•tion

Casing is a metal or plastic pipe that holds and directs groundwater from the aquifer to the home.

The well will probably be flushed with a disinfectant to remove contamination from the equipment and drilling process. You may be asked to let the water run for a while to clear out any particles.

The Well Log

A *well log* is a record the well driller keeps as he drills your well. It tells you the date the well was drilled, the types of soil and rock the shaft went through, the depth of the well, the water quality and purity, the rate of water flow, and many other things.

Most municipalities now require the log be filed in a central place in the county. If your well was drilled in the last 30 years or so, a copy of your well log should be on file in your county. When you have a new well drilled, you should receive a copy of the well log.

Well Maintenance

Your well is the most important system in your household. If you don't believe me, try going without water for a few days. A contaminated well drops your property value in a heartbeat and could make your home unlivable and impossible to sell. And when you protect your well, you protect the drinking water of other people who use groundwater for wells.

Protecting the Wellhead

Although the wellhead is not the most attractive part of the landscape, there are things you should *not* do to it.

- Never raise the soil level around the wellhead. It sticks above the ground so surface water won't run into it.

- Don't tie animals to the wellhead. If they pull hard enough, they can break the casing seal.

- Don't let children play on or around the wellhead.

- Don't use the wellhead for target practice or as third base.

- Never remove the wellhead cap unless someone is working on the well.

- If the wellhead is in an area that isn't mowed, keep a clear area around it so it isn't damaged accidentally.

- Don't plant a garden around the wellhead.

- Don't let trees grow close to the wellhead. They may obstruct access to the well over time or damage the casing with their root systems.

- Don't use weed killers around the wellhead.

Sinkhole

If someone should hit the wellhead with a car or other vehicle, call a professional plumber to examine it for damage. Any cracks in the casing or in the seal around the casing can allow pollutants to run directly into your well.

It's okay to cover the wellhead with a fake rock or wishing well as long as it can be easily moved to service the well. These things should not hold water. In fact, placing large rocks or sturdy posts around the wellhead may keep people from running into it with a car or mower.

Checking the Screen

Under the cap on the wellhead is an area covered by a fine screen that ventilates the well. Wells need ventilation points because natural gas, methane, or other gases sometimes enter the well with water. These gasses need a place to escape so pressure doesn't build up and cause an explosion. That's why wells are no longer put *under* homes.

You should check the screen occasionally to be sure it's still intact. (You might have to use a mirror to see under the cap.) The screen keeps insects and small animals out of the well, so have it replaced if it's damaged or missing.

Rural Rule _____

Consider having a plumber familiar with wells inspect your whole water system for problems every couple years. If you suspect something isn't working right, if there's been damage to a well component, or if the water doesn't look or taste right, call a plumber right away.

When Your Well Stops Working

If you turn on the tap and only a trickle runs out or nothing happens at all, don't panic. First check to see if there is power to the pump. Did a circuit trip or fuse blow?

If it isn't a power problem, you need to explore other reasons for the water shutoff. Sometimes the well pump burns out or quits working. As frustrating as that might seem, it's actually a good thing compared to a dry well. A pump can be replaced fairly easily and cheaply compared to drilling a whole new well.

Dry Wells

If a well has gone dry, there have probably been warning signs. Water may only flow after the well hasn't been used for a while or the flow has been greatly lessened. Neighbors may have had wells run dry. The water may seem discolored or full of particles.

A dry well might mean there's no water, there's insufficient water in the aquifer under your well, or the water level has fallen below your well point. It can also mean that your well screen is plugged with rust or debris. In any case, it's time to call a professional.

Poor Water Pressure

If water is flowing but the pressure is low, it could be a problem with the pressure tank or the pump. This is expensive enough, but it's not as bad as drilling a new well. Have those things checked first.

Low water pressure can also be a sign that the well is going dry. Some wells experience low pressure after periods of drought or at certain times of the year. People learn to adjust to the low pressure or drill a deeper well.

Water Quality Issues

As with each vineyard's wine, each well has its own unique flavor. Flavor comes from dissolved minerals in the water. Iron, sulfur, lime, sodium, and other minerals give you your own "brand" of water. You may grow to love your brand of water over time, or you may never like the taste.

Water can smell, taste, and look bad but still be perfectly safe to drink—and still may be better for you than city water. Water that has particles floating in it or is very cloudy, however, should be tested. Sometimes this water will be fine; other times particles and cloudiness are a sign of contamination.

Hard water isn't as much as a problem as contaminated or bad-tasting water, but you can deal with that and other water quality issues, too.

Testing Your Water

Well water should be tested when you move into a home with an existing well. Most mortgage companies require well water be tested before funding the mortgage. Even after you move in, continue to have the water tested at least every other year. Even the best-tasting, clearest water can be contaminated over time. If the smell, look, or taste of your water changes; if the well has been damaged; or if your family has unexplained illnesses for a while, have your well water tested immediately.

Contact your county health department or your county Extension office to find out where to have your water tested. Many counties and agencies provide well water testing for no fee or a low cost. Many private labs also test water. Whoever tests your water will explain how they want you to collect the water sample.

Chemical and Bacterial Contamination

The Environmental Protection Agency has set legal standards for the safety of public water systems, but those laws do not cover private wells. Your state may have laws about well water safety, but in most cases, it's up to the homeowner to monitor the safety of home drinking water.

There are hundreds of water contaminants. Different problems appear in different areas depending on natural geological differences, the type of industry, mining or farming nearby, and many other factors.

The following table lists some common contaminants and their health effects.

Common Drinking Water Contaminants

Contaminant	Health Concern	Source
Nitrate, nitrite	blue baby syndrome in infants under 6 months, respiratory failure	natural deposits, septic tank/field, fertilizers
Coliform bacteria	nothing specific	indicates fecal contamination
Arsenic	skin, circulatory cancer	natural deposits, pesticides, industrial waste
Lead	mental retardation, kidney failure	old plumbing, natural deposits
Benzene	anemia, cancer	gasoline storage, landfill seepage, industrial waste
Dioxin	reproductive cancer	incinerators, industrial waste
Atrazine	cardio-respiratory problems	crop herbicides

If a test reveals that your water is contaminated, stop drinking the water, bathing with it, and cooking with it. If the test was done through the health department, it will probably give you instructions on what you can do. The Extension office and private labs may also offer advice, but in this case, you should also contact the county health department for its recommendation. Depending on what was found in your well, other state and federal agencies may get involved.

Some well water contaminants can be removed by treating the well, or by installing filters. A new well can sometimes be drilled to solve the problem. Sometimes your water will be considered safe for everything but drinking and cooking, and you can use bottled water for these things.

In the worst-case scenario, you'll never be able to use well water on that property again and the water test will reveal problems that make it safer to move.

Country Color

If you need help understanding your well test results, need more information on safe water, or need to know where to find help with a contaminated well, you can call the Safe Water Hotline at 1-800-426-4791 or visit www.epa.gov/safewater/drinklink.html.

Hard Water

Hard water—water that is very alkaline and full of dissolved minerals—is a very common and annoying problem for many country homeowners. Hard water is safe to drink unless it's otherwise contaminated, but it leaves rust and scale on sinks and tubs, yellows and stains laundry, and clogs showerheads and other fixtures. You can learn to deal with hard water, or you can install a water softener.

A water softener is a tank that acidifies water through the use of salt and other chemicals or uses other methods to remove minerals. The tanks require periodic maintenance and addition of chemicals. The water will more closely resemble the water you were used to in the city. Usually only the water used indoors will go through the softener.

Other Water Treatment Systems

If your water tastes and smells bad, you can install filtering systems to remove minerals and salts from your water. Some systems soften and filter water; some systems only remove minerals. Some very advanced and expensive systems can also treat your water for some bacterial problems. These filters may be used to filter the water in the whole house or just the water going to one location, such as the kitchen sink.

Some chemicals polluting water can never be safely removed, so follow the advice of your health department when treating water, and don't ever rely solely on the salesman's advice.

Closing Abandoned Wells

When you move to country land that's been developed for many years, there may be one or several abandoned wells on the property. You should search for and immediately close any old wells you find on the property. Because they're so dangerous, money is often available on the state or local level to help seal these wells.

Pipes sticking out of the ground near old buildings or where buildings once stood may identify old wells. The pipes can be inside buildings or in the basement of a home. An old windmill or hand pump usually indicates an old well is underneath or nearby. Even more dangerous are depressions in the soil or rings of stone or cement that may signify an old dug well. They may have been covered with boards that are slowly rotting away.

Sinkhole _____

Why are old wells so dangerous? Because people use them to dispose of waste, or waste seeps into them and that contaminates the groundwater we use to drink immediately. Even if it's miles from your well, if gasoline, pesticides, oil, or even bacteria enter the groundwater, even in small quantities, it can pollute your water. If the same waste was spilled on the ground, it might be filtered out before it reached the groundwater or would at least take a long time to reach it. Not to mention that large wells can trap pets and children.

If you identify an old well, call the health department, the Extension office, a groundwater protection agency, or the Department of Natural Resources District office to find out if help is available to close it. These agencies can also advise you on the legal and safe way to seal the well.

A Note on Cisterns

In some areas of the United States, groundwater may be nonexistent or water may be too contaminated to use. In these cases, a home water system may rely on a *cistern*. Cisterns collect rainwater off roofs or hold trucked-in water. Cisterns may be located under the house, above the house for a gravity feed, or just outside the house.

In most cases, cisterns require pumps to move water and filters to screen out debris from water intake. They have to be chlorinated, and the tank requires periodic cleaning and disinfecting. Homeowners who rely on cisterns quickly learn to conserve water.

If you're going to have water trucked in to fill a cistern, be sure a large tanker truck can get close enough to your house in all kinds of weather to fill it.

def•i•ni•tion _____

A **cistern** is simply a water tank, usually steel or some form of plastic.

The Least You Need to Know

- Groundwater is the source of water for home wells and should be protected.

- It's up to the homeowner to monitor and maintain the safety and mechanical condition of home wells.

- A contaminated well can affect your health and the value of your home.

- Bad taste and smell don't equal contaminated water, and good taste doesn't mean water is safe to drink.

15

Your Septic System

In This Chapter

- How septic systems work
- Locating the parts of your septic system
- Maintaining your septic system

In the city, you seldom have to worry about the waste system. In the country, homes usually aren't connected to municipal sewer systems and must process their own waste. If you have a septic system, you need to understand how it works and how to maintain it.

Understanding Septic Systems

When you flush the toilet or take a shower, you generally don't worry about where the wastewater goes. As long as it disappears into the sewer pipe, you don't worry about it. Any solid matter that can pass through the pipes also goes along for the trip.

It's fine to leave it at that, but knowing a little about how your septic system works and the different parts involved is important, too.

Gray Water and Black Water

By volume, most of what goes into the sewer pipe is water. It's classified as either *gray water* or *black water.* Gray water is minimally contaminated water from sinks and showers, and *black water* comes from the toilet.

In some areas, gray water is diverted from septic systems and used for irrigation. Diverting gray water is a good way to conserve water because this water accounts for most of the water disposed of in homes—about 40 gallons per person per day. Gray water diversion systems can be installed in new homes or added later by handy homeowners. Some gray water systems use filters to remove solid particles and grease before using it to irrigate. Homeowners can devise simple sand filters for this water.

Gray water may contain some harmful bacteria and viruses and should not be used for drinking, washing, hosing down areas where children play, or on patios. Gray water should not be used on food crops, although it can be used to water fruit trees at the base. Lawns where children and pets play should not be irrigated with gray water.

Flowerbeds, lawns that are seldom used for recreation, and shrubbery and trees are good places to use gray water.

> **Country Color**
>
> In many areas, irrigation systems that use gray water are required to have purple-colored emitters and outlets to let people know the water is not to be used for drinking or food crops.

Some chemicals in gray water could harm plants, so if you divert gray water, use liquid laundry detergents rather than powdered ones to help avoid salt buildup. Detergents used in dishwashers are very alkaline and can harm plants, so water from dishwashers should go into the septic system and not on plants.

Gray water use is legal in most places and spares the septic system to some extent. Some areas require that gray water be discharged underground and not at the surface. Black water, however, must always go into the septic system.

Into the Tank It Goes

The first place the waste travels is to the tank. Tanks used to be made of cement or metal, and some still are, but many of today's tanks are made of special plastics. The tank has a lid with a port so the tank can be emptied or pumped out when needed. The size of the tank(s) needed is determined by the building code in your area and is based on the number of bedrooms and bathrooms in the home.

Solid and liquid waste are separated in the septic tank. As waste sits in the tank, the heavier solids fall to the bottom. A layer of water forms over the solids; in it, small particles of waste are suspended. On top is a layer of scum, composed of floating waste, fats and oils, and helpful bacteria. The outflow pipe is near the top of the tank. Liquid waste goes into that pipe and flows either to a second tank or to the leach field, depending on the system.

> **Country Color**
>
> If you're also operating a business that produces a lot of waste, such as a beauty salon, the tank needs to be bigger.

In systems that use a second tank, that tank is generally fitted with a pump to control the amount of wastewater being sent to the leach field at any one time.

The Septic Field

In traditional septic systems, the septic or *leach field* is fed by gravity, so the tank needs to be located slightly above the field. In other systems, a pump pumps liquid waste to the leach field. This allows the leach field to be built on land above the tank if necessary.

In the leach field, the liquid waste flows through a series of perforated pipes sitting on a bed of sand and gravel. The liquid waste seeps through the holes in the pipes and down into the soil. The field is buried under topsoil, generally below frost level.

def•i•ni•tion

> A **leach field** is a series of perforated pipes that allow liquefied waste to percolate down into a layer of sand and gravel and eventually into the soil.

Leach fields are put together in a variety of ways. Some have a T shape with smaller branches running off the T arms; others have multiple branches. The septic builder determines what type of pipe system is needed on your property.

What Happens to Waste?

Much of the waste that enters the septic system is liquid and almost immediately runs into the septic leach field, where it percolates through the soil and eventually reaches the groundwater. As wastewater moves through the soil, some contaminants are caught by soil particles and remain in the soil layer. Ideally, by the time the rest of the water reaches the groundwater level, it is cleaned of contaminants.

Solid waste consists of fecal matter, paper, and other things. As it sits in the bottom of the septic tank, bacteria breaks down some of it into liquid and it's discharged into the septic field. Other waste is slowly consumed by bacteria.

As it's broken down, the mass of waste becomes smaller, but remember, waste is continually being added. Eventually, the tank fills with solid waste. How fast this happens depends on how much waste is added and how large the tank is.

When the tank is filled with solid waste up to the outflow pipe, solid waste may move into the leach field pipes and eventually to the leach field. This clogs your system and stops it from functioning. Most septic tanks need to have solid waste pumped out every 3 years. You can hire someone to do this. A truck will come with a vacuum and suck out the waste from a port in the tank lid and haul it away.

Locating Your Septic System

You should know where your septic system parts are located because they sometimes need service, and they always need to be protected from damage. But it's not always easy to know where the septic tank and field are by just looking at your yard.

If you go under your house in the basement or crawl space, you'll see large, heavy waste pipes connected to the toilet, tub, and sinks. They all generally connect to one pipe that runs out of the house. In aboveground crawl spaces, the pipe may run down into the ground. The direction the pipe travels is the direction where the tanks and field are located.

Now go outside to the side of your house the pipes travel to. Septic tanks are usually located 25 to 50 feet from the house. There may be a slight depression in the sod over the top of the tank. The grass may also be a different color. In dry weather, the grass should be brown, not green, because green indicates a leak. In cold weather, the snow may be melted over the tank.

Country Color

Your house might have one septic tank, or some newer systems may have two or three tanks. Usually they're located near one an other but in some special situations, one might be close to the leach field.

If you think you see a depression or low spot where the tank may be, use a metal rod to probe and feel for the top of the tank. It should be buried a few inches to a foot below the soil. If you think you've located it, you could dig down a bit to confirm it. You don't need to dig it out and open it unless there's something wrong.

The septic leach field could go off in any direction from the tank. It could be close or some distance away. One or two main pipes lead to a series of perforated pipes linked together. The field area can take up varying amounts of space, depending on the soil type and the system installed.

The area above the leach field should be grass covered and fairly level. Ideally, no buildings, driveways, large trees, or other things are built or planted over the field. It's probably a good distance from your well, too. It's usually at least 25 feet by law. In some engineered septic systems, the leach field is installed in a mound of soil above-ground. (More on this later in this chapter.)

Because liquid is supposed to seep into the soil from the leach field, the grass may look a little greener there, but there should be no odor or liquid on top of the ground if the system is functioning correctly.

Of course, the easiest way to know where the septic tank and field are is to ask the previous homeowner or the builder to show you.

Septic System Maintenance

Homeowners with septic tanks function as their own sewage treatment station. Most of the time nothing needs your attention. But country homeowners should always remember to protect their health and wallets by properly maintaining their septic system.

One thing you don't need is all the fancy "bio treatments" that are presented to septic owners as miracle cures to break down waste faster and keep you from having to pump the tank as often. There is no unbiased evidence that shows that any of these enzymes and bacteria additives actually work.

The waste that goes into the tank has enough bacteria to break it down. Unless the bacteria are killed by heavy additions of bleach or other chemicals, the tank will function just fine on its own.

> **Country Color**
>
> In the old days, people used to throw a dead chicken, road kill, or hamburger in a new septic system to get it "started." Research has shown this is not necessary.

Septic Do's and Don'ts

Having mentioned bleach, let's talk about some other do's and don'ts of septic maintenance. By thinking about what you do on a day-to-day basis, you can help keep your septic system running smoothly.

Remember that any cleaning and laundry chemicals you use in your sinks, showers, toilets, etc. may eventually end up in your septic system. Many years ago, cleaning products contained some chemicals that weren't very good for septic systems. But as we've worked to clean up the environment, a lot of those chemicals have been banned.

Most cleaning and laundry products used in the normal manner won't harm your septic system. Small amounts of bleach used in cleaning and laundry won't harm the system either. If you're concerned about a certain product, check the label. It should indicate if it should not be used in septic systems.

Pay attention to cleaners and deodorizers that hang in toilets and work when flushing and also drain cleaners. Be sure these products are safe for septic systems before using them.

Do not dispose of old chemicals and unwanted cleaning products by dumping them down the toilet. This may cause a strain on the system by killing off the good bacteria that processes waste. Don't put medications, particularly antibiotics, into drains or the toilet, either. These could kill the bacteria, too.

Almost every type of toilet paper sold today dissolves quickly in water and is safe to use in septic systems. Colored paper is fine also. Just as in city sewer systems, don't dispose of things like diapers and sanitary pads into the septic system.

Rural Rule

You can find garbage disposals that grind food waste into smaller particles and that work much better with septic systems than conventional garbage disposals.

Grease and oils clog septic systems. Homes that have garbage disposers get more grease and more solids in the septic system and need to have the tank pumped more frequently. Try to avoid getting grease and oils into drains. Wipe out greasy pans, and put used oil in a sealed container and dispose of it in your regular trash instead of pouring it down a drain.

Cleanout Schedule

How often you need to have your tank pumped out depends on several factors. The type of system, size of the tank, and the amount of waste put into the system all play a part in how fast it fills. Most experts recommend that the tank be pumped at least every 3 years.

The previous owners of your home may have had a schedule for cleaning out the tank based on experience. If your usage of the septic system is about the same, you may want to follow their lead. Your septic engineer may also give you an estimate of when you need to pump the tank based on his experience.

Signs of Septic Failure

Remember that pipes in the homes of septic tank users can get plugged just as those in the city, so don't assume your septic system is failing because a drain won't run. Now, if *all* the drains won't run very well, it could mean either a plug in the main line or septic failure. If it hasn't been very long since the tank was pumped—say, less than a year—it's probably a plugged line. Try calling a plumber first. He'll let you know if it's the septic tank.

If you don't know when the tank was pumped or it's been a long time, you might need to pump the tank. Other than slow-running or nonrunning drains, signs of septic failure may include water standing on top of the field or tank area and sewer smell in those areas.

Should you open the tank and see if it needs pumping? Maybe, but you need to know what you're looking for and you need to be able to dig up and open the tank. At least the first time the tank is checked, have an experienced person do it while you watch.

Don't delay in having the system checked. Pumping out a septic tank is not expensive compared to replacing the leach field when it's been plugged with solids.

> **Sinkhole** _____
>
> If your septic tank and field are submerged by flood water, they won't work. Never have the tank pumped in this situation, because it will float up out of the ground. You'll just have to wait for the water to recede and use an alternative waste system.

Protecting the Tank and Field Aboveground

Just as important as watching what goes *into* your septic system is watching what goes *over* it. I've mentioned before that you shouldn't build or plant anything over the tank or septic field. The tank must always be accessible to be pumped.

Building over the field will cause it to work improperly because the soil above the field needs oxygen to make all the layers of bacteria in it and down beneath the leach field work properly. Compacted soil may not allow water to move through it freely. Avoid anything that compacts the ground over the tank or fields. That includes heavy machinery, driveways, parking areas, even livestock pens. Don't locate children's play areas directly over the system, either. An occasional car driving over the tank or field area may not do any harm, and lawnmowers are generally okay, too. But avoid routing traffic over any of the system components.

Pay attention to what you plant over and close to the septic leach field. Some plants might get into or otherwise affect septic tanks. The best cover for septic fields and tanks is simply lawn or a low groundcover. This is one area where lawn is actually a sound ecological choice.

Herbaceous perennials (plants that die back each winter) and annuals (plants that live for just one year) are fine to plant over septic fields and tanks. Don't plant vegetable gardens over septic fields and tanks. If there's a sewage leak, the food could be contaminated. Don't plant large trees and shrubs over the leach field or tank or even near them. Their roots can invade and clog the pipes. Keep trees at least 20 feet from the septic system, and plant small shrubs at least 10 feet away.

Sinkhole

Remember that what you plant over septic fields and tanks may need to be disturbed if the tank needs pumping.

Mulch, either organic or stone, is fine over the septic system if it isn't too deep. Don't use landscape fabric or plastic under the mulch in these areas.

Don't construct raised beds over the tank or leach field, as these add weight and change the oxygen flow in the soil.

If you're setting fence posts, trenching a water line or electric line, putting in posts for a swing set, etc., remember where the leach field is and avoid it.

If you accidentally damage the septic tank or part of the field, call a septic engineer to evaluate the damage right away. Waiting may cause even more damage and much higher repair bills.

Engineered and Alternative Septic Systems

In some areas, the water table is close to the surface or there's bedrock under a small layer of soil, so waste liquid just won't percolate away. In other areas, there isn't enough land to support a septic field, especially if homes are close together.

If you can't hook up to municipal sewage systems in these cases, you need to have a septic engineer design a system to remove waste. Engineered systems can simply be a mound of soil on top of ground or a box of special sand set in the ground that leach pipes run through. Some of these systems are very expensive, so when possible, it's best to build your country home in an area where conventional septic systems can be used.

You can create waste systems a number of other ways, but most are much more expensive and require a lot more maintenance than traditional systems. But they do allow you to build on some sites where other systems won't work.

What? An Outhouse?!

There might be times when an outhouse is necessary, such as during the construction or remodeling of a home. And some people truly believe the world is a better place without inside plumbing. And some people like to have an outhouse near animal areas or by a pond for quick use.

If the situation is temporary, you can construct a wooden outhouse over a hole in the ground just like the good old days, or you can rent a porta-potty.

Dig a deep hole—the deeper the better—but at least 6 feet deep. You'll also want to construct a tight-fitting lid over the hole to help keep down any odors. You'll need to add a ventilation pipe from the pit to somewhere outside the outhouse to remove methane and other gases that will build up.

You can build up the traditional wood box with a hole and a toilet seat or even use an actual toilet without the tank over the hole. The house frame should rest well outside the rim of the hole. It should have a sturdy floor with only a small opening for waste to pass through. Doors should be tightly fitting and kept closed to discourage critter visits. An electric or battery-powered light is a real help, especially at night or if your outhouse doesn't have a window.

Rural Rule _____

Add lime, sawdust, or kitty litter to the hole to keep the waste drier, because the drier it is, the less it will smell. It will look better, too.

When the hole is nearly full, or you no longer need the outhouse facilities, cover the hole with at least 3 feet of soil. If you opted for a rented porta-potty, you can have it pumped and disinfected from time to time.

If you're thinking of a permanent outhouse, check with your local government to see if it's legal. Only the most remote areas, or areas with large Amish populations, still allow this method of disposing waste.

Many books and magazines offer plans to help you live closer to nature in all ways. Study them to see how to build a functional, long-lasting outhouse. You may want to consider instead an indoor composting toilet or incinerating toilet.

The Least You Need to Know

◆ Septic systems dispose of waste and clean dirty water by filtering it through the ground.

◆ Septic systems need regular maintenance.

◆ Septic fields should be protected. Don't build over them or plant trees on them.

◆ In some areas, an outhouse or alternative toilet may be an option to dispose of waste.

Chapter 16

Country Home Heating

In This Chapter

- Country home heating options
- Cutting and buying firewood
- Safety considerations for home heating

Natural gas is seldom available in rural areas. Electric heat may be an option, but let's explore other methods of heating your country home.

If you're building a new home or remodeling an old one, give careful consideration to your heating system. In many areas of the country, heating costs eat up a large chunk of the budget. If you spend a little more to get a good, energy-efficient system when building or remodeling, you'll save money in the long run.

If you're stuck with the heating system you have, keep reading to learn how it works and what safety considerations you should be aware of.

Heating with Propane

Propane is one of the most popular fuels when natural gas isn't available. Propane is a byproduct made when producing natural gas and refining gasoline.

Unlike fuel oil, propane can also be used to run the hot water heater, dryer, stove, oven, and any other appliance that can run on natural gas. Special adapters can be put on most natural gas appliances to burn propane.

Propane Basics

Propane is a cold liquid when it's put under pressure. It's delivered to your home as a liquid in a tanker truck. When it's released from the tank, either into the air or into an appliance to be burned, it turns into a gas. In its natural state, propane is colorless and odorless. An odor is added to it so you know if a leak has occurred. Propane burns cleaner and warmer than fuel oil and leaves no odor in the home.

Ninety percent of the propane used in the United States is produced in the United States, but still, the cost varies depending on the season as well as the demand for and prices of crude oil and gas on the market. For the homeowner, heating with propane is slightly more expensive than heating with fuel oil. However, propane furnaces tend to last longer than fuel oil furnaces and don't need to be cleaned and serviced each year, as oil-burning furnaces do.

> **Rural Rule**
>
> To save money on propane, purchase it in the warmer months, either by filling the tank or by paying for a set amount before your heating season begins and locking in a price. Most providers also have payment plans where you spread the cost out over the entire year.

Propane does have some disadvantages: the tanks carry the risk of exploding; propane leaks outside are hard to detect before the fuel is lost; and if you let your tank get empty, you'll probably need to have a professional perform a leak test before you can fill it again.

If you use propane for heat, get used to checking the gauge on the tank frequently and call your provider for a refill before the level gets below 20 percent. Most providers have an automatic fill program and come fill your tank when needed.

Propane Tanks

At your home, propane is stored in a tank. Sometimes the tank is located underground, but it might sit aboveground. Tanks come in various sizes, but the average home has a 250- or 500-gallon tank. The tanks are sometimes affectionately called "pigs" because of their shape.

Country Color

Propane tanks can be the property of the propane provider, or you can purchase them. If they're the provider's tanks, you can only fill them by using that provider's propane company. If you buy a tank, you can shop around for the best price on propane. Many homeowners opt for renting the tanks, finding little difference in local prices, and liking the fact that the propane company generally fixes or replaces its tank without charge if needed.

Most tanks are painted silver or white to reflect heat. On top of the tank is a cap that protects the pressure relief valve and vent, a fill port, and a fuel gauge. Keep the cap on the valves unless they're being used to protect them from the weather and any other damage. The tank must be placed at least 20 feet away from buildings and can't be placed under power lines. A line is run underground to the house to bring the propane to the appliances. The regulator valve is generally somewhere near where the line enters the house. Know where the line from the tank runs underground so you don't build over it or cut into it when digging. Tanks must be located where the tanker truck can get close enough to refill them. Keep an unobstructed, clean area around the tank.

Don't allow children to climb on or play with the propane tank. If they cause a leak, all your expensive fuel can be lost in a short amount of time and you'll have to pay to have an empty tank checked and put back into service. Keep large animals away from the tank, too.

Never burn anything around the tank. Some propane vapor escapes from time to time and could explode. If you ever notice the smell of propane inside or out, contact your service provider at once. Do not light anything if you smell propane because a spark could cause an explosion. You can buy propane detectors for inside the house that work similar to smoke or carbon monoxide detectors.

Country Color

Most modern propane furnaces use electronic ignition systems and won't function in a power outage. You can generally use the burners on your stove if you light them with a match, but the oven and most other propane appliances also use electronic igniters.

Heating with Fuel Oil

Fuel oil is very similar to kerosene. There are different grades of fuel oil, though, and you should check your furnace manufacturer's recommendation to see what type you should purchase. Fuel oil is generally cheaper than propane to heat a home. Fuel oil has less smell than it did 30 years ago, but it still has some odor when it burns.

Fuel oil burns, but it's not explosive, so fuel tanks can be located in the home in many areas, usually in the basement. The tank generally sits outside the house though, usually quite close to the house. A pipe near the bottom feeds the furnace by gravity. In very cold climates, fuel oil may thicken and run into the house very slowly.

Usually fuel oil is delivered by a tanker truck and pumped into your tank, but you can transport it in small quantities to fill the tank when needed.

Some fuel tanks contain gauges to determine the fuel level, but some require that you put a long stick into the fill hole on top and pull it out to see the level—similar to your car's oil dipstick.

Fuel oil leaves a lot of soot and other deposits behind when it burns, and you should have your furnace burners cleaned every year by a professional before the heating season starts. The chimney or *flue* pipes should also be inspected yearly.

def•i•ni•tion

A **flue** is a pipe or shaft that carries smoke and exhaust gases away from a furnace or fireplace. It can be metal, ceramic, clay, brick, or plastic, depending on the appliance.

When propane leaks, it turns into a gas and dissipates into the air. When fuel oil leaks, it goes into the ground and is considered toxic waste. A big spill can turn into an expensive toxic spill cleanup, so be very careful when handling fuel oil.

Also pay attention to how your supplier fills the tank. A friend who uses fuel oil for heating had a supplier park his tanker in the driveway and as he filled her tank, the hose began to leak at the truck. At least several gallons of fuel spilled. The driveway was gravel, so the fuel seeped into the ground. The supplier was required by law to remove all the gravel and several inches of soil beneath the spill and replace it.

Your fuel oil tank should be as far from your well as possible because pollution of the groundwater may occur if fuel oil spills. If spilled on your skin, wash off fuel oil at once. Children should not play on fuel oil tanks, and nothing should be put into the fill hole (except the measuring stick, if necessary). Always keep a tight cap on the fill port so water doesn't get inside.

Geothermal Heating

Geothermal heating is an excellent, "green" way to heat your home. If you're building or remodeling a country home, it's well worth the initial higher cost to install a geothermal system because you'll soon recoup the extra cost with lower heating and cooling bills.

Geothermal systems take advantage of the fact that below the frost level, the soil remains a constant temperature all year round. A series of tubes filled with a circulating fluid are buried in the ground, below the frost level. The layout requires a bit of land, so geothermal isn't easy to use in urban areas, but it's great for the country. Closed loop is the most common type of geothermal system, but open systems circulate water from beneath a deep pond or lake, or a well, pulling it in and then discharging it back into the pond or well. These systems do not pollute the water.

Some electricity is needed to circulate the fluid and to heat the incoming fluid in the winter, but it's modest compared to the cost of heating a home with electricity. The system also works well with solar power panels. The average consumer can expect savings of 30 to 50 percent more than other types of home heating.

Geothermal systems cause no pollution, cannot give you carbon monoxide poisoning, and don't require chimneys or flue pipes. They won't overheat and can't start a fire or explode. They can also cool the home. And they require little maintenance.

The area where the system is buried outside should not be dug into or paved over, but lawns or vegetable and other gardens can be planted over them. Large trees should not be planted near where the system is buried.

> **Country Color**
>
> The energy savings due to the current use of geothermal systems in the United States alone is the equivalent of removing the emissions of 1,295,000 cars or saving 21.5 million barrels of crude oil a year.

Heating with Wood

Heating with wood is probably the oldest method of heating living space. If a country homeowner has his or her own supply of wood or can get some inexpensively, it can be very economical. But there are some serious downsides to heating with wood you should consider.

Although wood is a renewable resource and requires the use of no fossil fuel, it releases a lot of carbon monoxide and other pollution into the air. If burned inside the home, the particulates released from wood burning in even the best wood-burning systems may affect your health.

Burning wood in the home requires a great deal of attention to safety. Chimneys and flue pipes must be kept clean and in good repair. Wood-burning furnaces or stoves are dangerous to leave burning when you're not at home and require that someone replenish the wood at frequent intervals. Children, pets, and flammable materials should be kept away from wood-burning stoves, furnaces, and fireplaces. Ashes need to be removed at frequent intervals and must be disposed of safely.

One of the biggest problems with burning wood inside the home is the smoke and particulates that get into the air. People with asthma, allergies, and lung conditions may suffer more with a wood-burning appliance in the home. The air is also dry, and low humidity contributes to sinus problems.

Burning wood inside means you have to bring wood inside, too. That can be messy and can bring in pests, mold, and dust along with the wood.

> **Sinkhole**
>
> Always keep working smoke and carbon monoxide detectors in your home if you burn wood inside. These safety devices are important in all homes, but the risk of a fire is higher if you burn wood inside.

Wood-Burning Fireplaces

Wood-burning fireplaces are very romantic on a cold winter night, but they're not terribly efficient for heating a home. The area around the fireplace is warm, but the rest of the home is often cold. The best way to use a fireplace is for emergency or supplemental heat. There should be good glass doors on the fireplace to prevent drafts when not in use, and a blower system to circulate air when in use.

Have chimneys inspected every year to remove creosote buildup. Do not burn paper and other trash in the fireplace. Use only seasoned, dry wood for a fire. Compressed sawdust "logs" and other items should only be used for an occasional "recreational" fire for appearance and ambiance, not heating.

Indoor Wood Burners

Indoor wood burners range from small stoves to large furnaces. You can cook on some of the wood stoves, but it takes some getting used to. One of the best indoor wood burners is a unit you add on to a conventional furnace. You can use wood when you're home and have wood, but the regular furnace will run when wood isn't burning. It sits in the basement or other furnace room area and is out of the general living space.

All indoor wood-burning appliances should be installed by an experienced person who understands the building codes and safety issues involved.

Rural Rule

Keep a pot or tea kettle full of water on top of a wood-burning stove in the living area. The steam produced will add humidity to the air. A few marbles on the bottom will rattle and let you know when the pot is nearly empty.

Outdoor Wood Burners

Outdoor furnaces can heat your home and often additional structures like a greenhouse or work shed at the same time. They can supply your hot water, too. They work by circulating heated water, like a boiler and radiator system.

Outdoor wood burners can take large amounts of fuel and may only need to be loaded once a day. Most outdoor burners use wood, but some are made to burn corn, cherry pits, or other available fuel. They're safer than indoor wood-burning appliances in that the risk of fire and carbon monoxide poisoning are greatly reduced.

Outdoor wood burners keep the smoke and particulates out of your home, but they still go into the air. Before you install an outdoor furnace, check your local ordinances. In some areas, their use is banned because they pollute the air and affect neighbors downwind.

Outdoor furnaces are usually placed somewhere away from buildings, trees, or electric wires. They get hot, so kids and pets must be kept away when they're in use. Always keep grass, leaves, and flammable material away from the furnace as well.

Your Wood Supply

If you heat with wood, you need a supply of wood to burn. In some areas, wood is free or very inexpensive. In other areas, the cost of purchasing wood may be almost as much as purchasing propane or other fuel.

You need to have a way to transport the wood or pay to have it delivered. You also need a roofed area to store the wood until you use it. Even if you don't cut the wood yourself, there's labor involved in stacking the wood for storage and bringing it into the home or to the furnace.

Wet wood doesn't burn well, so you should store your firewood in a covered area after it's dried or at least cover the pile with a tarp.

Country Color

All wood burns, and some wood is better for heating than other types, but don't worry about the type of wood. It's how well wood is seasoned and dried that makes it good firewood. Some wood has an enjoyable aroma when burning, such as hickory and apple.

Locate the storage area fairly close to the house so you don't have to carry it as far. Have a spot inside where you can store a day or two's worth of wood so it can warm to room temperature. It will start and burn better that way.

Cutting Your Own Wood

Cutting your own wood is the most frugal way to heat with wood. If you have a lot of standing wood to harvest on your land or permission to harvest wood on other lands, you have an advantage over those who have to buy wood.

I don't have enough room in this chapter to tell you how to select and cut down trees. But to even think of cutting your own wood, you need the proper equipment: a chainsaw, a wood saw, axes, and mauls at the very least. You should also have safety equipment such as a helmet, safety goggles, ropes, and heavy leather or canvas gloves with long sleeves. Trees need to be cut down, cut into manageable log pieces, and split. Because wood needs to dry or season for a good amount of time, it's best to cut wood in the winter and early spring for burning the following winter.

Logs should be cut into lengths to fit your wood burner and then split into smaller pieces lengthwise. Pieces about 6 inches wide are a good size. You can split wood when it's freshly cut or wait until it's dry, but split wood dries better than whole log pieces. Splitting can be done by hand or you can buy or rent a hydraulic wood splitter that runs off a tractor or electric or gasoline-powered splitters.

Stack wood for drying in a single row, about 4 feet high, in the open sun and wind. Don't worry about covering the pile. After it's dry, move the wood to a dry, covered place for storage.

> **Country Color**
>
> Wood is properly dry when the moisture content is 15 to 20 percent. Moisture meters can tell you when the wood is dry.

Buying Wood

You can save a lot of work by buying wood, but there are some disadvantages other than the cost. If you're inexperienced in wood burning, you'll have to take the seller's word that the wood is properly seasoned, and you'll have a hard time comparing prices because of the way wood is commonly measured.

Wood is sold by the *cord*, or more commonly, by the *face cord*. The cost of a cord or face cord of wood can vary tremendously depending on wood species, the seasoning and drying time, and whether it's split or not.

A **cord** is a legal measurement and denotes a stack of wood 4 feet high, 4 feet wide, and 8 feet long. A **face cord** (or a *stove cord* or *rick,* as it's sometimes called) is not a legal measurement and can be different in different areas. It's generally a stack 4 feet high and 8 feet long but varies in depth.

Corn and Alternative Fuel Burners

Some very energy-efficient stoves on the market burn products such as whole dried corn, wood pellets, and even cherry pits. Burners that are versatile and can use whatever alternative fuel is available have the most advantages.

These stoves burn hotter and cleaner than wood burners. Many burn a long time on a single load, and some have a gravity-fed hopper that can keep them burning for days. Most corn stoves burn so hot there's little smoke and very few gases or particulates released into the air, so they are easy on the environment. Inside, they emit a slight, pleasant odor similar to popcorn.

When they were first on the market, corn stoves were advertised as being a much cheaper fuel source than propane and fuel oil. That was before the cost of corn skyrocketed because of increased ethanol production. Still, corn is probably cheaper than conventional fuels and is a renewable resource.

You can get "cleaned" corn that has less dust for inside burning in bags or huge truckloads of corn for outside burners. You can also buy bagged cherry pits in some areas or bags of wood pellets.

Rural Rule

Corn fuel may be very attractive to many animal pests, so store it in animal-proof containers such as metal trash cans.

Home Heating Safety

No matter what type of heating system you have, it should be installed by a professional. New heating systems should not be installed using old chimneys or vents until they are inspected and found to be safe and appropriate for the new use. After installation, having a professional perform periodic checkups of the system, including vents and chimneys, is wise, too.

It goes without saying that all homes should be aware of fire safety in the home. If you see or smell smoke in the home, your heating source, including a wood burner, probably isn't working correctly or you are misusing it. The system should be checked by a professional. There should always be working smoke alarms in the home. If the home uses a combustible fuel such as propane, fuel oil, gas, wood, coal, or alternative fuels inside as a heating or cooking source, carbon monoxide alarms should be installed. A fire extinguisher should be in place on each floor of the home as well.

If you have a wood stove or other heating or cooking appliance that has a hot outer surface, it should be "fenced" so children and pets can't touch it.

Breathing Hazards and Sensitivities

Wood-burning heaters emit smoke and other particles that can be harmful to some people's health. If someone in your family seems to suffer from asthma or allergy symptoms when a fire is burning, you may need to install another heating source.

Wood or alternative fuel like corn, when stored in the home, may also bring in mold and dust or other allergens that some people are sensitive to.

What Not to Burn Inside

Never start a fire in a fireplace or wood stove with gasoline, kerosene, charcoal lighter, etc. Learn how to use kindling and properly start a fire.

You can start a fire with paper, but do not burn wrapping paper and other trash in fireplaces or other inside burners. They increase the particulates in the air, increase deposits in chimneys, and may release harmful gases as they burn. Pieces that are still burning can float up chimneys and land on the roof, starting a fire.

Burn only dry, seasoned wood in wood burners, and be sure the pieces are correctly sized for your appliance. If you're using an alternative fuel burner, read the manufacturer's directions about what can be burned and how to store it.

Safe Ash Disposal

Whenever an inch or so of ashes and small, unburned pieces accumulate in the bottom of your stove or fireplace, they should be removed. Special tools like brushes, pokers or rakes, and shovels can help you remove ashes.

If you can, wait until the ashes are cold and rake and sweep them into a metal container. Take the container outside immediately. Never assume that the ashes and coals are completely cold. Don't set your ash bucket on a wood porch or deck floor. Many fires have resulted from this.

You can spread ashes very thinly over lawn or garden areas for a little fertilization. But too much will cause plants to suffer from an imbalance of minerals and improper soil pH.

The Least You Need to Know

- ◆ You have several options when it comes to heating your country home.

- ◆ Heating with wood is economical but may have health and safety issues. Breathing wood smoke and particulates may be a health hazard.

- ◆ Spending more now to install a high-efficiency heating system may save you money in the long run.

- ◆ All homes should practice fire safety, but homes that burn wood should take special precautions. Be sure to install smoke and carbon dioxide alarms in your home.

Equipment and Tools You May Need

In This Chapter

♦ Vehicles good in the country

♦ Lawnmowers versus tractors

♦ Machines for summer, fall, and winter

♦ When the power goes out

When you moved from the city, you probably brought some common household tools with you. But country life may require some new equipment and tools, some of which you've never used before.

In this chapter, I introduce you to some equipment you might need in your new life in the country.

Pickup or Four-Wheel Drive?

Nothing symbolizes country living better than a pickup truck. Do you need a truck or a four-wheel-drive vehicle when you move to the country? If you intend to have any livestock, if you're going to heat with wood, or if you're doing a lot of home remodeling or landscaping, you'll soon find a truck invaluable.

If you're going to be driving off road, into the field to install fence posts, or into the woods to hunt, a vehicle with four-wheel drive, whether a truck or another utility vehicle, is a wise choice. It's also helpful when your road becomes a quagmire, a muddy mess, or covered with snow. (Just remember that even four-wheel-drive vehicles can get stuck.)

If you'll be pulling a horse or boat trailer, you'll need a truck. You'll also need a hitch on your truck, and consider adding a *winch* so you can pull yourself out of any bad spots you might get into.

If you don't want to drive it all the time, a truck can be your backup transportation when you don't need it for hauling things.

def•i•ni•tion

A **winch** is a pulling device. You attach one end to a bumper, pass a rope or chain around a strong stationary item like a post or tree, and feed it back to a cylinder turned by the power source (your engine or a hand crank), which pulls the vehicle out.

All-Terrain Vehicles

All-terrain vehicles (ATVs) are primarily used for recreation (see Chapter 12 for more on recreation in the country), but country landowners can get some practical use out of an ATV as well. These vehicles can get you around your property in a hurry to check fences or bring feed to animals. If you're a hunter and need a smaller vehicle to go into the woods and fields to place bait piles or bring out game for cleaning, an ATV will work well for you.

Some of the larger, more powerful ATVs can pull good-size loads or plow snow, with the proper attachments. Other attachments are being made for ATVs now such as pull-behind mowers, tillers, dozer blades, etc., but unless you'll be using your ATV extensively where a truck can't go, you'd probably be better off with a garden or farm tractor and truck.

Trailers

Trailers run the gamut from small, light trailers you pull behind a mower to large live-stock trailers you pull behind a truck. If you have more than a few acres and are doing any gardening, landscaping, or remodeling, a small trailer, at the very least, will be a big help. A trailer that's versatile, with sides that remove or fold and a tilt feature to unload things like loads of mulch will likely get lots of use.

If you're going to keep horses or other livestock, you need to think about a horse or livestock trailer. A small horse trailer can be pulled by a car. Horse trailers come in all sizes and styles, from a simple one-horse trailer to elaborate units with dressing rooms and sleeping areas.

If you have boats or recreational vehicles such as snowmobiles, you need to decide if you need a trailer to transport them.

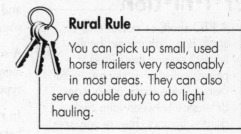

Rural Rule _____

You can pick up small, used horse trailers very reasonably in most areas. They can also serve double duty to do light hauling.

Riding Mowers and Tractors

If you're going to mow $\frac{1}{2}$ acre or more of lawn, you'll probably want a riding mower, lawn tractor, garden tractor, or farm tractor. You still need a small push mower or "weed whacker" to get close cuts next to buildings and garden beds.

Or you could buy a flock of sheep!

What's the Difference?

The lines are becoming more and more blurred between riding mowers and tractors, and the terms used by dealers and the general public are often interchanged, but here's an attempt to define the mowers and tractors out there.

Riding mowers should be the term for machines that only do mowing and have the mower mounted in front of the engine and seat. *Lawn tractors* are designed mostly for mowing, but the mowing deck is in the middle of the machine, under the driver's seat. They are generally smaller with less horsepower than garden tractors.

Garden tractors also have a mowing deck under the middle of the machine, but they're also designed to pull or push various implements. They generally have a higher horsepower, are heavier, and are larger than lawn tractors. Garden tractors generally have numerous corresponding implements such as plows, brush cutters, and snow blades. Usually you have to purchase implements that go with that particular model, but some things may fit many models.

Farm tractors come in large and small versions. Farm tractors generally run on diesel fuel. They pull or push implements that you purchase separately. They generally have one or more ways to power other implements, including a *PTO shaft* and a hydraulic

def•i•ni•tion

A **PTO shaft**, or *power take off shaft*, is a shaft rotated by the tractor's engine that's used to power pulled or stationary implements. These shafts are a main difference between farm and garden tractors. They're very useful but also very dangerous and should never be used without a shield.

or electric power source. Things like post hole augers and wood splitters can be hooked up to these power sources.

A sort of farm tractor–lawn tractor hybrid is called a *compact utility tractor* and has features of both tractor types.

In recent years, all forms of tractors and mowers have been gussied up, and high-price models feature things like cup holders and radios. They've been made safer, too, with many safety features now required by law.

What Size Do You Need?

Many people feel the need for power in anything they purchase. It's senseless, however, to pay for more machine than you really need. Not only are those large, powerful machines more expensive to purchase, but operating and repair costs are higher, too.

If you have a $1/_2$ to 1 acre of lawn to mow, you probably only need a riding mower or small lawn tractor. If you have 1 to 3 acres to mow, need to occasionally pull a small trailer, and need a small snow plow for the drive, choose a garden tractor.

If you need to pull a brush cutter, plow a large garden, scrape out manure from the barn, or do other heavy work, choose a large, powerful garden tractor or small farm tractor. You may want to consider a two-cylinder model, which, although more expensive, runs cooler and is more powerful.

Sinkhole

When you get mower decks wider than 42 inches, you might have trouble getting the deck through many doorways or in the bed of a pickup to take it for repairs.

If you're mowing less than an acre, a mower deck 36 to 42 inches wide on a tractor with a minimum 14-horsepower engine should do the trick. For 1 to 3 acres of mowing, choose a 42- to 46-inch mower deck and an 18-horsepower or greater engine. If you're mowing more than 3 acres or you need to plow snow or haul heavy loads, try a 46- to 54-inch mower deck with a 20-horsepower or greater engine.

All mowers and tractors should have these safety features: cutting blades that disengage when you get off the seat, discharge chute protectors, and a system that prevents the mower from starting unless the blades are disengaged.

When choosing mowers or tractors, there are many things to consider besides color, the deck size, and horsepower. How does it "fit" you? Are you comfortable driving it and operating the controls? How easy is it to take off the deck to sharpen blades or change a belt? What type of warranty does it have? Does it allow you to use accessory implements you want like trailers and tillers?

Read your operator's manual and pay attention to basic maintenance such as checking and filling the oil. The most common cause of engine failure in mowers is the owner failing to keep oil in the machine. This voids your warranty and requires a new engine, which is very expensive.

Replace or sharpen your mower blades every spring. Sharp blades make a clean cut, which makes the lawn look better. If your model has an air filter, clean it often and replace it when it is too dirty or worn.

Plan on having a place to store mowers or tractors out of the weather. They last much longer that way. When putting them away for the winter, empty the gas tank or add a fuel stabilizer.

> **Rural Rule**
>
> If you need large areas of brush or heavy weeds cut just for the initial installation of a lawn, or if you don't mind keeping part of your property a little wilder most of the year, you can hire someone to cut the property once or a couple times a year instead of buying a heavy-duty mower to keep it nicely trimmed.

Snow Plows and Snow Throwers

If you live in an area with winter weather, you need to consider how you'll clean your driveway and walkways after a snowstorm. If you have a short drive and few walks, a snow thrower you walk behind may be all you need. If you have six stout sons, you only need six shovels!

If you have a long driveway, you'll either have to hire someone to plow it or purchase a plow blade for your truck, tractor, or ATV to do the job yourself. Garden tractor and ATV plows are not meant for clearing $1/2$-mile driveways. If you have a very long driveway, you need a farm-type tractor or truck with a plow.

Sinkhole

New snowplow owners are often eager to use their machines and decide to plow the main road, too. Although this might be okay in an emergency situation, most road commissions frown on citizens helping in this way. There are certain ways that public roads need to be plowed, and the road commission has the liability for how the road conditions are maintained. You may even get a ticket for trying to be helpful.

Rototillers, Leaf Blowers, and Chipper-Shredders

If you're a gardener, you might want a rototiller, but you can garden without one. In fact, some people do more damage to their soil with a rototiller than help it. But if you have a large garden in mind, they can be helpful if you don't have a tilling attachment for your lawn tractor.

You probably don't need a leaf blower. You can rake leaves into a pile faster than blowing them into one. Besides, leaves are valuable soil amendments and nature's way of returning nutrients to the soil.

Chipper-shredders are very handy if you have trees on your property. Shredding yard waste makes it break down much faster, and you can make yourself valuable woodchip mulch. When shopping, buy the largest-horsepower motor you can afford—you won't regret it.

Chainsaws and Wood Splitters

If you have mature trees on your property, at some point, you'll need a chainsaw. If you're going to cut your own firewood, a chainsaw is a must. A small gasoline-powered chainsaw will help most homeowners trim trees or clean up moderate storm damage. If you live with a lot of large trees and storm damage is common, you may want to purchase a heavy-duty chainsaw.

Sinkhole

Electric chainsaws generally aren't practical for country homeowners. After a storm, power is often lost, and on larger pieces of property, electricity may not be present where you need to work.

Chainsaws are not toys, and safety precautions should always be used around them. They generally have a two-cycle engine for which you must mix the oil and gas. You also need to lubricate the chain with bar oil as you work. Choose a chainsaw you can handle and control, and keep the blades sharp.

Wood splitters are handy if you use wood for heating. Powered models run off a tractor, or you can find models you run with gasoline or electricity. You can also split your wood the old-fashioned way with an ax or maul.

Take great care with powered wood splitters so you don't hurt yourself or anyone else. Children should not operate or even be around them.

Generators

In the country, after a serious power outage, you might have to wait a long time for power to be restored. If you can afford it, a generator can give you much peace of mind—and electricity to operate essential household appliances. People who depend on electric medical equipment are most in need of a generator or other emergency backup.

Generators generally operate on gasoline, diesel, natural gas, or propane. You need to keep at least a small amount of this fuel on hand, or the generator will be useless when you need it.

There are two types of generator systems, *standby*, or permanently installed; and *portable*. A standby system turns on either automatically when power goes out, or you flip a switch to start it. An electrician needs to install them, in part because they have a transfer switch that prevents power from being back-fed into electric lines. Standby systems are hooked up to a fuel source. Because gasoline and diesel have limited storage life, you need propane or natural gas for these systems.

A portable generator needs to be filled with fuel and started when the power goes out. You'll need heavy-duty outdoor-approved extension cords to plug your appliances into the generator.

> **Country Color**
>
> In many places, standby generators must be inspected and issued a certificate. Keep this certificate in a safe place because if you sell the home, you'll need to produce it.

What Size Do You Need?

The more power a generator can provide, the more expensive it is. If you're on a limited budget, choose a small generator that will operate just the basics such as medical equipment and the furnace igniter and blower.

In some emergencies, fuel is able to be replenished, but it won't be in others, so also consider fuel storage in your generator planning.

To see what size generator you need (or want), first determine what you'll want to run during a power outage and write down the watts each item needs to run. You can usually find the wattage on the cord or a tag on the item or in the owner's manual. On large appliances, you should also note the running and startup wattage. Many appliances take three times as much power to start as to run.

Add the wattages for the things you feel are vital, and also add the starting wattage load for the highest-rated item. Then add an additional 20 percent to the figure. This generally gives you a safe wattage total for your needs. It's better to have a slightly larger generator than you need rather than a smaller one. If you overload the generator, your appliances could be ruined or a fire could start.

> **Country Color**
>
> Compact fluorescent lightbulbs give you the same amount of light and use less wattage than regular lightbulbs. They also save on your electric bills when you aren't using a generator.

Remember, you don't have to start or run everything at the same time. You can plug in and unplug appliances to run what you need when you need it, but be careful doing this so you don't ruin any of your appliances.

The highest users of electricity are electric dyers, electric hot water heaters, and air conditioners. You may not want to run them during a power outage. Medical equipment, the furnace or a fan, and your water pump are probably the most important things to keep going. Keeping a refrigerator or freezer running may also be a priority. You may want to keep only one TV or computer operational on the generator, limit the lighting and cooking with electricity, and only run water when the furnace or fan isn't running.

Generator Safety

One of the most important things you can do to operate a generator safely is to have a professional electrician install a standby one or to install a switch for a portable generator that keeps power from flowing into utility lines.

Generators must be installed outside of the living areas or any place where fumes could enter the home. They produce carbon monoxide, which is colorless and odorless but can still kill you. Generators need to be close to the house, but don't place them under windows or near doors.

Generators are generally noisy when they run, so think about your neighbors when you install your generator. They should be positioned so air can circulate around them. And they're a popular item for thieves to steal, so make them as unobtrusive or hidden as possible.

Generators must be kept dry, and they must be grounded. Follow the manufacturer's guidelines for grounding portable generators. Do not stand in water or have wet hands when touching a generator.

Generators get hot, so be sure to keep children and pets away. When you must refill the fuel, turn off the generator and let it cool so you don't start a flash fire. The extension cords going to appliances may also get hot. If they do, unplug them and let them cool or buy higher-rated cords. Keep a fire extinguisher near the generator.

> **Sinkhole**
>
> Never just plug a portable generator into a home circuit and rig it to power your home. Not only is it illegal, but if electricity flows into a power line, it can be amplified and sent miles down the line and may kill a worker trying to repair lines.

If you're not familiar with generators, ask the electrician or someone who is experienced to show you how to run the generator before an emergency arises. At least two people in a household should know how to run the generator. Keep the instruction manual near the generator.

Handy Hand Tools

If this is your first house or first house with a yard, you may wonder what sort of basic hand tools you need for lawn and yard work. Start with a shovel, a leaf rake and a garden or bow rake, and a push broom. If you live in an area that gets snow, add a snow shovel to that list. You also probably need a hose and hose nozzle.

Other tools you might need depend on your situation. Gardeners will want pruning shears, loppers, a hoe, hedge shears, weed trimmers (hand, electric, battery, or gas models), an ax, a spreader, sprinklers, etc.

Homeowners should have a sturdy ladder that reaches to any window on the house for fire safety. You will need trash cans, and a wheelbarrow or garden cart is also always nice to have, as it can go where pulled trailers or trucks can't.

> **Rural Rule**
>
> If you tend to misplace tools, paint the handles a bright color so you can better see them if you don't remember where you set them down.

Buy the best tools you can afford, and take good care of them. Good tools last a long time and are less likely to break and injure you. Keep tools stored out of the weather and the blades sharp.

The Least You Need to Know

◆ You may need a truck or four-wheel-drive vehicle to manage country roads and country chores.

◆ Your mower needs to be sized for your needs.

◆ A snow plow or snow thrower may be necessary in the country.

◆ A generator can provide power in emergencies but must be installed and used correctly.

Chapter 18

Barns, Sheds, and Other Outbuildings

In This Chapter

- ◆ Making your outbuilding wish list
- ◆ Saving or demolishing old outbuildings
- ◆ A primer on new buildings
- ◆ Other kinds of country outbuildings

One of the first things new "4-P" country dwellers want besides the *pickup*, *pond*, and *pony* is the *pole barn*. You have many options for barns and other outbuildings; the pole barn is probably the most popular. Prefabricated steel buildings can be delivered to your site. Wood and pole barn kits are available if you want to build them yourself. You can even find small buildings made of plastic and resin.

There are other outbuildings you might want, or if you bought a pre-owned home, you may have many buildings on the property you're considering using and need to know about.

In this chapter, I briefly discuss the types of outbuildings you might encounter in the country and offer some tips on how to maintain the buildings you already have.

What You Need Versus What You Want

If you've just built a home on a bare piece of land, you might need a shed or other building to store your lawn tractor and other equipment. You may covet a 50×75-foot gleaming blue-steel pole barn, but maybe all you really need is a good-size shed.

Some people (myself included) find outbuildings, especially barns, as important as the house. Sometimes a perfectly functional building exists on an older homestead that can be adapted for your use. A restored older building lends character to the homesite and may actually become an asset.

It's always nice to have a place to park the car out of the weather. If your home doesn't have a garage, you might want a building that can hold a car or two. If you want animals, they may not need much shelter, but you'll be far more comfortable caring for them with one. If you're going to burn wood, you'll need a wood shed. If you have lots of equipment, lawn tractor, trailer, snow thrower, ATV, etc., a shed will keep them dry and can be locked to deter theft. If you have a hobby such as woodworking, a workroom may be part of your needs list.

Sometimes one building can serve many functions. You could store lawn tractors and snow throwers in a garage next to a car or have a shop on one end of the garage. But sometimes multiuse isn't practical or safe. Animals shouldn't be housed in machinery storage areas, for instance. Hay or other flammable items shouldn't be stored in an area where welding or other open flames will be present.

> **Sinkhole**
>
> If you have a lot of storage space, you might be tempted to store a lot of stuff. But really, how many buildings full of stuff do you need?

If a big pole barn is what you want, but you only need a shed, be careful about overbuilding. I've known many people who went into serious debt erecting huge buildings they now get little use out of. Too often I see new country people put up things like indoor riding arenas or 30-stall horse barns and then lose everything because they can't afford the payments. Bigger is not always better. You can always add on later.

Can That Barn Be Saved?

In Chapter 5, I discussed what to look for with existing barns and outbuildings when you're considering buying older property. In this chapter, let's discuss what to do if you have a building on your property that deserves rescuing.

Older buildings have charm and often have wonderful workmanship that can become a distinctive part of your homesite. Old barns and sheds can become useable again, many times for less effort and money than building a new structure. Some features might need to be modified for a modern use, but that can often be done. Old barns and carriage sheds can even be turned into homes. I've known people who bought property simply because of a magnificent barn.

Barns that are leaning, have crumbling foundations, or are missing siding and doors can be repaired. The value of a properly restored and cared-for timber-frame building is often many times that of a new pole barn of the same size.

In some areas, barns may have historical significance and funds may be available to help preserve them. This is more frequent in the East and upper Midwest. Or someone may be willing to take the barn down and move it. Octagon, hexagon, and round barns are particularly valued because they're so rare. Every effort should be made to restore them. Even a small shed or old chicken house can be restored and used. Could you move that chicken house next to the garden and use it to store tools? Can the old milk house make a clever artist's studio?

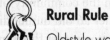

Rural Rule

Old-style wood barns are quickly being replaced by pole barns and steel buildings, and as a result, a part of our heritage is slipping away. Whenever possible, try to preserve old barns. Go to www.barnagain.org to see what others have done with restored barns and get tips on what you can do.

If you're thinking of getting rid of an old barn, especially one that isn't in very bad shape, ask a local historical society if there would be any interest in it.

Restoration Tips

When restoring older outbuildings for use, don't just slap up metal siding. Metal roofs are usually fine, but metal siding over old wood holds in moisture, which may cause it to rot. It's better to replace rotted boards and give the structure a good paint job.

Red and white are the most common colors used to paint barns. Yellow comes in a distant third, and green and brown are also often used. When repainting old barns, avoid paint colors like lavender or pink.

Country Color

Barns were traditionally painted red because red paint was cheaper. It was made with iron oxide, which helped prevent mold and rot. The inside of barns were often whitewashed to use up excess milk and lighten the inside.

If you're lucky enough to have a barn with an old advertising sign on the roof, you may want to try to restore it. Also try to restore hex and good luck signs painted on barns, usually above a door. These are unique and valuable additions to the landscape.

Safe Demolition

When old barns are too damaged by weather and too unsafe to be left standing, they should be taken down. If the roof timbers are rotting and the roof has been open to the weather a long time, the rest of the frame is probably rotting, too. Or your county or local government may ask that you remove an unsafe barn or repair it.

Barn experts in the community often can give you estimates and help you make decisions on whether an old outbuilding is repairable. A straight demolition and cleanup of a big old barn can cost thousands of dollars. Be sure you and the demolition crew have a signed contract and the demolition crew has insurance.

You might think you can demolish the barn yourself, and that's possible, but it can be a massive and dangerous task. First, check to see if you need to have a permit. Then, start with the roof and work down. If you slowly take apart the barn for a wood harvest, be sure the remaining parts of the structure are secured so nothing can injure curious children or animals.

Before demolition, remove all electric, water, gas, or propane lines to the structure. If the demolition is to be sudden, such as with a bulldozer, be prepared for a lot of dust. Old barns were often painted with lead paint and lead may be in the dust, too. Ask the contractor if wetting the building and its surroundings will help keep down dust. You may want to do this if you're demolishing the building yourself and water is available.

Selling the Lumber

In some areas, you can sell old barns and outbuildings, or at least their wood. Highly valued barns contain hand-hewn timbers, unusual woods such as chestnut or walnut, or carved wood, which may make the barn worth several thousand dollars. Other more common barns may only sell for a couple hundred dollars. Cupolas, weather vanes, and carved artwork or signs on the barn can be very valuable antiques as well.

If you only get a few hundred dollars but the buyer has done the demolition and cleanup work in exchange for keeping what he or she wants of the wood, you've still saved money. To make a sale worthwhile for the buyer they will need to be able to

> **Rural Rule**
>
> It may take several months or even longer to sell a barn for the wood. Try contacting artist groups; the wood is often used in crafts, and high-end builders or decorators may use the old barn wood in new homes or remodeling jobs as a decorative accent.

get up close to the barn with a trailer and other equipment and will need lots of time to finish their work. To ensure that the best pieces don't get harvested and then the mess left behind, have a clear contract and pay attention to the process.

Pole Barns

If you have no existing outbuildings and want to have one, you have a wealth of choices, including the popular pole barn.

> **Rural Rule**
>
> Before beginning construction on any type of building, check your local ordinances to see if you need any permits or if there are restrictions on what kind of building you can have. Be sure you stress that the building isn't for human habitation when inquiring about permits. Many country areas don't require permits for agricultural buildings. In some areas, you may need to furnish blueprints for a permit. And before building, be sure you're building it on *your* property and that any required setbacks from property lines are followed.

In a pole barn, the posts for the structure are buried in the ground and a horizontal framing is used (instead of vertical, as in most framed buildings). Lightweight aluminum or steel panels cover the building sides and roof quickly and easily. Pole barns can be built with plywood panels, too. The kit concept, which contains everything precut and numbered and directions tell you just how to assemble the building, popularized the buildings.

Pole barns have evolved from simple rectangular structures rarely more than 30 feet wide to elaborate, 2-story buildings and even huge arenas 50 or more feet wide. Pole barns are easy for one or two people to assemble and generally cost less than conventional framed buildings. They don't need foundations, and the maintenance is also less. The posts or poles of the structure used to always be wood, but some are now steel.

Except for the more elaborate arena-type pole barns, two people with the right tools and a little handyman knowledge can build a pole barn. (I say two people because placing the roof trusses calls for some help.) Your most important consideration in building will be to get your poles straight and your corners square; accurate measuring and leveling is everything. Putting sheet metal panels on with screws instead of nails and anchoring posts in cement are also important.

Having someone lift the roof trusses with a forklift or backhoe and support them in place until they are secured will save you time, frustration, and possibly injury. You may be able to rent the machine needed.

Speaking of roof trusses, go the extra mile and slight extra expense, and use storm or hurricane clips in construction. These help tie the roof trusses to the frame and prevent the roof from blowing off in all but the most powerful storms.

A concrete floor can be poured after the frame is up, or you can leave the floor as soil or add sand for a floor. Concrete is generally used for equipment storage or cars; animal shelters are often left with sand or soil floors.

All types of doors and windows are now available for pole barns. Just be sure the doors you choose are wide enough and tall enough to get your equipment through. Some pole barns are built with translucent panels near the top or even in the roof to let in natural light.

Rural Rule

Websites such as bioengr. ag.utk.edu/extension/ ExtPubs/PlanList97.htm have plans for many types of pole barns, sheds, and other outbuildings. Your county Extension office may also have outbuilding plans.

When building a pole barn for horses or other large animals, line the inside with heavier wood at least halfway up the walls to prevent damage in case the animals kick. Animals should not have access to support posts, because they're often treated with toxic chemicals that might be harmful if the animals chew on them.

Many plans for pole barns are available free from lumberyards, farm stores, and online. If you design one yourself, consult with lumberyards or a farm store to see the dimensions of building materials available and design so you do as little cutting as possible. If you buy a kit or have a building designed with help from a lumberyard, plans are included. Blueprints are different from plans, so if your building code requires blueprints for a permit, buy from a company that can furnish them or have someone draw one for you.

In many areas, crews specialize in putting up pole barns and other small buildings. A lumber or farm supply store should be able to give you numbers to reach these people.

Country Color

Steel buildings shaped like an upside-down C are gaining popularity. These can be anchored right to the ground or put on short side walls. They are delivered to your site and set on the walls with machinery. It is sometimes hard to finish the ends of these, though. Small steel C buildings are sometimes used for livestock shelters and are light enough to be towed to new locations with a tractor.

Sheds

Sheds are small structures generally for storage. You can buy many pre-assembled sheds and have them delivered. Sheds are also easy to build, and small ones may not require any permits. A homeowner can generally handle the construction of a small shed, from a kit or otherwise.

What you plan to use the shed for determines what kind of shed you'll need to buy or build. Let's review some common sheds and their uses.

A run-in shed is three-sided and generally used to shelter animals or large equipment. It is similar to a pole barn except one side is open. The open side should face away from prevailing winds. These may sail off in strong winds, so be sure they're anchored well.

If you heat with wood, you need a wood shed. An area in front of the shed where you can split wood is always nice. Wood sheds can be open on one side or enclosed.

Tool sheds should be near the area you use tools such as the garden. You may want to put a lock on them. A shed near the pond to store fishing equipment or fish food is nice to have.

If you have a boat or snowmobiles, you should consider a shed to shelter them in off seasons. Be sure the doors are wide enough to get them in and out, and be sure a trailer can get close enough to load the equipment.

Sinkhole

If you live in a windy area, always anchor sheds to the ground so they don't fly away. Never store fuel in sheds with expensive equipment, and try to empty gas tanks before long-term storage. Be sure the sheds that house expensive boats and machines are insured, including the contents.

Shops and Work Rooms

Shops in the country are generally special work places (or hiding places!). A shop often has 240-volt electric service for heavy-duty power installed to run power tools, good lighting, and a source of heat. (Homes may have 120 and 240 power systems.) Unless you have electrical knowledge, this is best left to an electrician.

When planning and building your shop or work room, give yourself enough space to work on large projects or with small machines and have plenty of shelves and storage racks to keep things neat. Concrete floors are preferred in shops.

Sinkhole

Have a licensed electrician do any wiring or other electrical work. If not, insurance may not cover any losses caused by electrical problems.

Some country dwellers need special work spaces for pottery kilns, artist studios, or home offices. In most cases, these are treated like agricultural buildings as far as permits go, but check before building. Any building that gets regular client visits, is used as a public store, or processes food, needs special permits and inspections and will probably be considered a business for zoning purposes.

Garages

If your home doesn't have a garage and you're thinking of building one onto your house, check with your local government before doing anything because this may be prohibited or require a special permit. Free-standing garages may or may not require permits in your area.

You need to decide if you want the garage just for parking cars—and how many garages do you know where that happens?—or if you want extra storage space, too. A one-car garage without much storage is 12×12 feet; a 12×24-foot garage parks two cars and allows for some storage space.

Garages are usually built close to the home and in a style that complements the home. Be sure you're not building over septic tanks or fields, the well, or other buried lines. You'll probably also want electricity in your garage.

Most garages have concrete floors. High walls in a garage allow for loft storage space. Windows should be high on the walls so light gets in but your possessions aren't in easy view of potential thieves.

When installing garage doors, electric door openers are nice, but when a power outage occurs, remember that you have to manually lift the door to get your car out, and two smaller doors are easier to lift than one large door. Be sure there's at least a walk-through door to get in and out of the garage in a power failure if you don't think you're strong enough to lift the overhead door.

The Least You Need to Know

- A restored older barn can be more valuable than a new barn.
- The wood from old barns may be valuable if you can find a buyer.
- Homeowners can generally handle the construction of pole barns and sheds.
- You have many options when it comes to barns, sheds, and garages.

Chapter 19

Fences and Gates

In This Chapter

◆ What type of fence do you need?

◆ All about fence posts

◆ Tips for electric fences

◆ The importance of good gates

Good fences make good neighbors … and save you a lot of time and grief. Before you moved to the country, you may have lived in a suburban or city area where fences were frowned on or even prohibited. But you're in the country now, and country people appreciate a good fence.

You may not need to fence all your property, but if you have animals or just dogs, you need to fence some of it. Fences can keep your kids safe and help protect you from liability lawsuits if you have an attractive "nuisance" on your property such as a pond. Some fences also protect your landscaping from loose cows and night raids by deer.

Putting up a good fence is one of the hardest country skills you may need to learn. It looks a lot easier than it is. You need the right kind of fence, the right tools, and some basic knowledge. And practice makes perfect; the first fence you put up may not be the best-looking one, but you'll learn as you go.

Before You Do Anything

You first need to decide what you need your fence for and how much fence you can afford. You also need to honestly assess whether you and your friends or family can tackle the job or if you need help. Putting up more than a few hundred feet of fence is generally a two-person job, but even a smaller fencing project benefits from extra hands.

Check for Rules

Unlike urban areas, most rural areas have few rules about where and how you can fence your property. However, if you're in a new rural subdivision, you might need to check the fence rules.

If you have right of ways for utility lines or easements on your property, you may have some fencing restrictions. You may have to have gates that allow equipment access to utilities, or you may be restricted from fencing across easements.

Know Your Boundaries

Many, many, neighbor disputes begin over a fence being put up on an unclear boundary. Don't assume an old fence line denotes your property's boundaries. Be *sure* you know where your property line is. Before you even start measuring, find and mark the property boundaries. Plan to put the fence up at least a few inches within the boundary lines. Don't give up too many inches on a fence that's close to the line, though, or the neighbors may make the assumption they own more than they do.

If the fence is on a boundary, talk to the neighbor or neighbors who share the boundary and tell them you're putting up a fence. In some cases, neighbors may even pay for half of the fence or help you put it up.

If neighbors have strong feelings against a fence, find out if there are good reasons behind it and if you can do something to ease their concerns. For example, if a neighbor feels horses on his side of the fence may be harmed by the barbed wire you're thinking about putting up, you may want to change to electric fencing.

Types of Fences

Depending on what the fence will be used for—to keep in or keep out—will, in large part, determine what kind of fence you need.

Field fence generally has the largest openings; sometimes the openings are smaller near the bottom and get larger near the top. Field fence keeps in large animals, but not smaller ones. It must be stretched well and attached to wooden posts for it to be effective and last a while.

Woven or welded wire fence has openings of various dimensions and also comes in different wire thicknesses or gauges. Chain link fence is one example, although you don't see it much in country settings except for kennels.

For horses and goats, which tend to walk down fences with larger openings—or stick their heads through it—welded wire fences with openings of 2×3 or 2×5 and that are 5 feet high are often used. This type of fence works well with dogs, also. Shorter fences can be used with children and some dogs.

Country Color
The lower the gauge numbers, the thicker and stronger the wire is. For example, 6-gauge wire is thicker than 12-gauge.

There are very strong welded wire panels called cattle or hog panels, usually found in 16-foot lengths. They are used when heavy animals are confined to small areas and might go through lighter fences. They're usually too expensive for large areas.

A few hog or cattle panels are nice to have around the homesite. Clipped together, they can make a quick pen, a lightweight gate, and a trellis for tomatoes or grapes, etc. They can be bowed, anchored to the ground, and covered with a tarp for a quick shelter or plastic for a greenhouse. There are many other uses.

Barbed wire fence is not used as often as it used to be. Most other types of fence are safer. It's never a wise idea to use it with horses. It's better to use it at the top of a woven wire fence where you need to keep people from climbing over.

Electric fences shock animals that come in contact with it. It also shocks you if you forget and back into it or touch it. Although the shock is slightly painful, it does no permanent harm, even to small children. Electric fences now come in a wide range of styles. There's the simple, old-fashioned, single bare wire and also electrified straps, webs, and woven multicolored strands that look like rope. There are also woven wire electric fences.

Electric fences require many accessories, from the charger to insulators that hold the wires. Even a permanent electric fence setup is fairly easy to do, and movable electric fences are often used to subdivide animal areas or make a temporary enclosure. An electric wire is often used in connection with wire fencing to keep animals from leaning, rubbing, or walking on it or to keep predators out.

Sinkhole

Electric fence may keep farm animals in, but many predators such as dogs learn to go under the fence. In situations where predators are a problem, use woven wire with an electric wire on the outside of the fence near the bottom and an electric wire at the top of the fence.

Wooden fences come in a variety of styles and range from utilitarian to purely decorative. Board fences are commonly used to keep horses confined. Board fences are expensive and require a lot of maintenance. New vinyl or plastic wood "boards" are lower maintenance but have a much higher cost.

Split rail and post and rail fences are good boundary fences if you just want to make a statement and keep snowmobiles out. Picket-type fences may keep some dogs in but are generally for looks. A white picket fence screams to have flowers planted along it, cottage garden style. There are plastic picket fences now, too.

There are now plastic and nylon netting type fencing. Using black netting keeps deer out of large areas in an unobtrusive way. Netting is also used to cover large areas to keep birds out. Netting is not for use with large farm animals or dogs.

If you live in snow country, you may want to put up a snow fence, which keeps snow from drifting over the driveway or paths. Snow fences can be wood slats or plastic netting. They must be installed about 10 feet from the area you want to protect, in the direction the wind comes from, normally north or west. The posts need to be put in before the ground freezes.

In some regions of the country, other types of fences are made from locally available material. Stone walls, metal pipe, and fences made of pulled tree stumps are examples.

How Much Do You Need?

You'd think measuring would be pretty straightforward, but many people have problems with calculating how much fence they need.

Start by marking the corners of the area you intend to fence. Be sure you measure a straight line from corner to corner—this is harder than you think. Without surveying tools, you just have to sight down the line. If the area is a simple square or rectangle, measure two sides, one short and one long in the rectangle, and double the amount; or measure one side in a square and multiply by four. If you have an odd shape, measure by using a measuring wheel around the entire perimeter or by marking where a change of direction occurs, placing markers there and measuring from point to point and adding it together.

Woven wire fence is generally sold by 100- or 330-foot rolls. Divide the number of feet you measured by 100 or 330 to get the number of rolls you need to buy. It probably won't be an exact amount. For example, if you need 820 feet of fence, you'll have to buy 9 rolls of 100-foot fence or 3 rolls of 330-foot fence.

Electric wire, electric strapping, and smooth and barbed wire fences are also sold by the roll. The roll can be marked by feet, or more commonly marked in mile increments such as $\frac{1}{4}$ mile. A mile is 5,280 linear feet, so $\frac{1}{4}$ mile is 1,320 feet.

The important thing to remember when measuring for this type of fence is to multiply the number of feet you need to go around the perimeter one time by the

Rural Rule

When planning a fencing project, find out what size roll the fence you want to use comes in. Try to adjust your dimensions so you aren't buying a whole roll of fence when you only need 30 feet more. This can save a lot of money.

number of strands of fencing you're going to install. For example, if your fence will consist of three strands of electric fence and you need 1,000 feet to go around the perimeter one time, you need 3,000 feet altogether. If the wire you choose is sold in $\frac{1}{4}$-mile rolls, you need to purchase 3 rolls. Two (2,640 feet) won't be quite enough, and although some places do sell less than a roll, you'll generally pay more for it this way and it's very inconvenient to package and move home.

Most electric, smooth wire, and barbed wire fences require 3 strands of wire if they are for keeping animals enclosed. If you're just marking property or keeping humans out, two strands or even one may be enough. The various electric webbing and strapping variations require different configurations of strands.

Fencing to keep deer out of areas requires at least 5 strands of whatever you use because the deer will crawl under, leap over, or wiggle through gaps in fence. Deer fencing should be at least 8 feet high. You could use a combination of woven wire on the bottom and electric or barbed wire on top.

Split rail and most other types of wooden fencing are usually sold in 8-foot sections. Pay attention to whether the price is for each piece or for a section, which may consist of a post and two or three rails or boards.

Roughly, for woven wire fences of all types, you'll need a post for every 10 feet. For barbed or electric fence, you'll need a post about every 15 feet. For wood fence posts, they are generally 8 feet apart. Count on extra posts if the shape is irregular and for gates. Some fences require two types of posts. Wooden posts are used on the corners and gates, and metal posts are used in between. (Find lots more on fence posts a little later in the chapter.)

Gather Your Tools

No matter what type of fence you're putting in, be sure you have a good pair of gloves, preferably leather. Your hands can really take a beating when installing a fence, even the smaller, decorative fences. Good gloves are a wise investment, so don't skimp on this purchase. Be sure they fit comfortably and are strong and durable. The fingers should fit well lengthwise so you can pick up things easily.

You need something to measure with. A measuring wheel is very handy if you're going to fence large areas. A 100- or 200-foot tape measure is also a good start. Some small stakes and lightweight string are very handy for laying out a straight line.

You need a *post hole digger,* or a *post hole driver,* depending on what type of posts you're installing. A regular shovel can be used for digging and is sometimes needed to start holes. If you're putting in more than 20 to 30 posts, you may want to buy or rent a *post hole auger* instead of trying to dig all those holes by hand.

def•i•ni•tion

A **post hole digger,** also called a *clamshell shovel,* has two curved shovel blades that face each other. You move the handles apart to get the blades apart, jab them into the soil, and move the handles together to pick up soil and remove it from the hole. A **post hole driver** is a heavy piece of pipe with a weighted, closed end and two handles. You put the open end over a metal post and lift it up and let it fall, driving the post into the ground. They are inexpensive and nice to have around. A **post hole auger** is a giant corkscrewlike tool powered either by a gasoline engine or a PTO shaft off a tractor that bores holes into the ground.

You need wire cutters, pliers, and probably a hammer and nails or screwdriver and screws. You may need a fence stretcher depending on what type of fence you're installing. A level and a square will come in handy, too. You may also want something to cut weeds or brush with you.

If you don't have a pickup or trailer, you might want to have some sort of cart. Rolls of fencing and posts can be very heavy if you have to move them any distance.

If you're setting wood posts in very wet areas, you'll want some gravel for the bottom of the post holes. In sandy soil and at corners, you may need cement for posts. It usually takes about one bag of ready mix cement per post. You'll also need water to mix with the cement.

Besides the fencing material and posts, you might need certain "accessories," depending on the type of fence you're putting in. Corner braces, fence ties, and post caps are some examples. Electric fences require some additional accessories described later in this chapter.

Fence Posts

Electric fence can use metal posts pounded into the ground or what is called *step-in posts*. Step-in posts are a rod with a triangle-shape piece of metal welded on the bottom. You place the triangle point down and step on the top, pushing it into the soil. Simple rods can also be hammered into the ground.

Field fence requires wood posts at least at the corners and preferably every 30 feet or so, with metal posts between or every 10 feet if used alone. Field fence has a real tendency to sag after a short time when attached only to metal posts.

Welded and woven wire fences can use metal posts, commonly called *T posts*, exclusively. T posts also have a triangle-shape piece of metal welded on them near the bottom. Wood posts at corners and occasionally along the line help keep fence from sagging.

When you attach fence to metal posts you use little pieces of wire called *fence ties* that generally come with the roll of fence. These are supposed to catch on raised knobs along the post. In reality, a lot of the wires slip down the post after a while and the fence can buckle or sag.

Setting Posts

Set the corner posts of your fence project first. Measure to be sure you're exactly where the two sides meet at a 45-degree angle. If you're digging a hole, make it as small as possible in diameter. If you're pounding in a post, keep the post straight as you move the driver up and down.

Posts should go in to about $^1/_3$ of their height. If you want a 4-foot post aboveground, use a 6-foot post and sink it 2 feet into the ground. Pound in metal T posts until the top of the triangle-shape brace is below soil level.

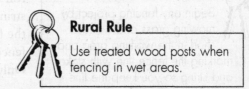

Rural Rule

Use treated wood posts when fencing in wet areas.

If you're putting in a wood post and your soil is very wet, dig the hole about 18 inches deeper and fill it with gravel to where you want the bottom of the post to sit.

In sandy or light soil, where the posts tend to move freely even after being set deeply, add a couple scoops of cement to the hole. For extra strength at corners, cement in both wood and metal posts.

Use braces on corner posts. Braces keep the corner square and absorb some of the tension on the fence. Wood posts generally use wood post braces. Braces run in the direction the fence will take, generally on the inside of the fence. Special clips are made for metal posts that allow you to use two other metal posts as braces.

Removing Posts

There are times when a fence post needs to be moved or removed. Most of the time, posts can be quite a trick to remove.

Posts that were cemented in may need to be dug out or pulled out with a heavy truck. Sometimes in wet weather and the right soil, metal or wood posts can be wiggled a little then pulled straight up and out.

Metal T posts can be removed with a device called a post puller, which you can sometimes rent from hardware or farm stores. If you don't have a post puller, move the T post back and forth to enlarge the opening around the top of the triangle-shape bottom brace, and pull upward. If that doesn't work, you'll need to dig down along one side until you've loosened it.

Installing Wire or Wood Fencing

When you've chosen your wire fence and posts, gather all your supplies and take them to the area to be fenced. Set the corner posts first and then use stake and string to lay out the line between corners. First, mark where each post is to be placed and put in the posts. Then roll wire fence out along the ground, just inside your string line. You may need something heavy to keep the fence from rolling back up. Lay out wooden fence boards or sections along the fence route, too. Only lay out what you can finish in a day.

Stretch field fence and chain link fence before attaching it to the posts. You can rent a fence stretcher at

Rural Rule

Begin any fencing project by mowing grass and weeds short in the working area and marking the fence line with stakes and string so you keep the line straight.

most places that sell fencing. This type of fence cannot be stretched enough by hand to keep it looking nice after it's installed. You stretch a section, attach it to the posts, and move down the line. You want it nice and taut and set a couple inches above the ground. On chain link fence, the pointed ends go down. On field fence, the largest openings and the largest wire are on the top.

If you're working with most other welded wire fencing, it can be set up, pulled tightly by hand, and attached to the posts.

Wood fencing varies as to how it needs to be attached. Work with a level on wood fences so your top line remains straight.

Installing Electric Fence

Electric fence is somewhat easier to install but requires more parts and hand labor. Wires need to be stretched tautly so they don't sag. In some instances, you may want to have only the top and bottom wire hot, or charged. Some people also put a single hot wire at the top of welded wire fence. In this case, the hot wire must not touch the top of the fence.

You must have an unbroken expanse of wire from the fence charger to the end of the line, which can be back at the charger or somewhere else along the line. Each strand of wire must be attached to the previous; usually a wire is just continually looped or a "jump" can be made by attaching a piece of wire from one level to the next.

Rural Rule _____

Keep the area under the bottom wire of an electric fence clear of tall weeds so it doesn't short out the fence.

Where there's a gate, the wire needs to be buried underground inside a protective tube or stretched high overhead. You can also use insulated handles with a metal hook to hook and unhook a wire strand. These are better for seldom-used gates.

Insulators and Other Accessories

The charged wire cannot touch a metal post and really shouldn't touch wood posts, either. Insulators, plastic pieces attached to the post, hold the wires out away from the post. In most areas they are yellow or white. Insulators come in a variety of sizes and shapes. A salesperson at the farm store can help you pick the type of insulators you need for your job.

You need an insulator for each strand of wire or electric tape on each post. For example, if you have a three strand fence, you need three insulators for each post. Buy extra insulators. They snap off or become lost easily.

A fence tester is an inexpensive little gadget that keeps you from having to touch a fence to see if it's hot. You stick one rod in the ground and touch the other end to the fence. If the fence is working, a little light will flash on the fence tester.

Chargers

A charger keeps the electricity running through the fence. There are a variety of types and sizes. You need one rated for the amount of wire you plan to install. They're generally rated by the mile, such as "powers a ½ mile of fence."

Most chargers send pulses of power along the line rather than a continuous stream. Some chargers send a stronger shock than others, especially if they're made to power through weeds that may touch them. You can use a lower-rated charger if you faithfully keep weeds trimmed below the fence and vines off it.

Electric chargers can work by hooking up to your power source, or they can be solar-powered or battery-powered. They need to be grounded when installed, and they should be protected from the weather and close enough to the house or barn that you can check them easily.

Chargers raise your electric bill, especially if they frequently ground out (see the following "Special Maintenance" section). Solar seems nice, but a backup is generally needed in winter or in cloudy areas.

Special Maintenance

Electric fences seem to need a lot of checking. Anything that touches the fence and touches the ground or something touching the ground will short it out beyond that point. Sometimes these grounds are hard to find, and you can walk the fence three times before you find the problem.

Sinkhole

Electric fences will not contain extremely amorous, frightened, or angry animals. It should not be the sole fence used to contain dangerous animals.

Animals learn to hear the tiny clicks a grounded fence gives off, and some take advantage of the outage. And some animals learn that if they run through the fence the correction is only temporary and leads to a good reward.

Marking and Training

Animals need to be trained to respect electric fence. If you use smooth, plain wire, tie strips of plastic or cloth in a light color every 3 or 4 feet along the top and bottom wires, this helps the animals see the wire.

Encourage your animals to sniff the fence. They'll get a shock and jump back, which is what you want. Most animals learn very quickly to avoid the wire.

To use electric fence to discourage deer, cut small strips of aluminum foil about 4 inches wide. Smear them with peanut butter near evening and lay the strips over the wire. Deer should approach, lick the strip, and get a shock. You want them to know the fence is there and jump over it or avoid it rather than just run through the wire.

Gates

Think about gates carefully before you put up a fence. It's much easier to install them as you're putting up the fence rather than later. Err on the side of too many gates rather than too few. Gates should be easy to open and to secure.

If cars, tractors, and other machinery need to get through the gate, it needs to be 10 to 12 feet wide. Walk gates need to be anywhere from 24 inches to 48 inches wide. A 48-inch-wide gate is wide enough for most lawn tractors to pass through.

Gates should have stout wood or round metal posts installed on both sides of the opening. The opening needs to be a few inches wider than the gate to accommodate the hinges. The gate posts should probably be set in cement.

Gates for large openings are easier to use if they're in two pieces. The weight of a large, wide gate tends to make the unattached end sag and drag on the ground. You can use a small wheel on that end or attach a wire that runs from the top of the gate back to the gate post and turns on a swivel. Gates should be as high as the fence if you have animals.

Country Color
Hang gates so they swing toward you in snow country, so you can clear away snow to open them.

The latches you use depend on what you're trying to keep in or out. You may want to padlock seldom-used gates, especially if they're out of sight of the house.

The Least You Need to Know

- ◆ Before beginning a fencing project, check for rules and restrictions.
- ◆ Measuring and laying out the fence line is important when putting up a good fence.
- ◆ Get the right type post for the fence you're installing.
- ◆ Be sure gates are large enough to get required machinery through.

Part 5

Farm Fresh Food

One of the healthiest things you and your family can do is grow your own fruits and vegetables. This alone is one of the reasons many families move to rural areas. Homegrown food is good nutrition and tastes great—and working in a garden is good exercise for you, too!

But you're not limited to soil and seeds. Want farm fresh eggs? Get yourself some chickens! Crave homemade maple syrup or honey? I've got you covered. In Part 5, I discuss ways you new country dwellers can produce some of your own food.

20

Fruit and Vegetable Garden Basics

In This Chapter

♦ Where to start your garden

♦ Tips for deciding what and how much to plant

♦ Starting from scratch (or seed, or bulb …)

♦ Is organic right for you?

Homegrown food is better tasting, safer, and more nutritious than food grown in foreign countries that's covered with all sorts of pesticides and that's picked green and transported thousands of miles. One of the reasons many people move to the country is to grow some of their own food. The love of growing things, of providing food for the family, is embedded deeply in some of us. We need to smell the soil and feel the earth in our hands. We know that the food we grow with love will be the best food our family can eat.

In this chapter, we explore the important decisions about where to plant your garden, soil building, and site preparation. We also take a brief look at some crops you can grow in your country garden.

Where Does Your Garden Grow?

The location of your garden is important to its success. It should be located in the sun, where it gets at least 6 hours of sun and preferably the whole day. Only a few things will grow well in a shaded location.

Your site should drain well. That means water shouldn't stand there for more than a few minutes after a rain. When you dig down for at least 2 feet into the soil, you shouldn't hit water.

Your garden should be close to the house. Being close to the house gives you access to water. If you can see the garden from the house, you're more likely to keep it neat and weeded. You're also more likely to run out to the garden to get some onions or tomatoes or basil when you're preparing dinner.

Keeping the garden close to the house also discourages animal predators. Deer are more likely to destroy an apple orchard planted way out by the woods than one located close to a house.

> **Sinkhole**
>
> Do not plant food gardens within 25 feet of a road. Toxic exhaust particles and dust can settle on the plants, and roadsides are sometimes sprayed with vegetation killer, which could harm a garden.

A Word About Microclimates

Microclimates are areas in your yard where conditions may be just a little different from surrounding areas. A low spot may collect cold air and get frost earlier and later than other spots only a few feet away. The top of a hill can expose plants to drying wind and stress them. The south slope of a hill, however, may keep them warmer and protected.

An area slightly blocked from the wind is beneficial to many crops. This could be the south side of a tree line or building. However, plants too close to a building that reflects light, such as a white metal shed, may scorch in warm areas.

How Big Should It Be?

A 20×30-foot garden is fine for two people, and one 20×50 feet is probably big enough to feed a whole family. If this is your first garden, start small, but choose your site so you can expand in the future as you gain experience.

The biggest mistake new gardeners make is to bite off more than they can chew. If you start with a huge garden, you're more likely to be overwhelmed with caring for it that first year and just give up and let it go to weeds in subsequent years. It's better to have a few small crops that look nice and don't strain your muscles—or your sanity.

Improving Your Soil

Good loose, fertile soil with lots of organic material is ideal for your garden, but don't worry if you don't have that. Adding organic matter is the key to improving any type of soil, clay, or sand. Organic matter includes compost, shredded leaves, straw, green cover crops that are tilled under, etc. Over time, any soil can be improved with organic material.

But never add sand to clay soil or clay to sandy soil. This just makes cement. Add organic matter instead.

Manure Basics

Manure is good for gardens because it adds some organic matter, especially if animal bedding is mixed in with it. But manure varies tremendously in its fertilizer value, depending on what the animals that produced it were fed and how the manure was stored.

Do not put fresh manure on gardens or orchards. Fresh manure is hot from the decomposition process and will burn plants chemically. Manure is best put on gardens in fall or very early spring and then worked into the soil.

Rabbit, goat, and sheep manure is less likely to burn plants but would still be better spread a month or so before planting. Manure that was stored outside in piles for more than a few months loses much of its nutrients but is still a good soil conditioner.

Without having the nutrient content of manure analyzed, which can be expensive, don't count on manure to replace fertilizer. Compost is not fertilizer either, although it is very good for the soil.

Rural Rule

Manure may be easy to find in the country. Ask horse owners or those with dairy farms if they need to get rid of manure. Sometimes they'll even deliver to you. In some areas, though, you may be charged for manure.

Fertilizer and Lime

Don't add fertilizer or lime until you've had a soil test done on your garden area. (See Chapter 7 for information about soil testing.) Then only add the fertilizer recommended in your soil test results.

Never just add lime to the soil as you start the garden. Wait for soil test results. If you make your soil too alkaline, it's much harder to undo the mistake than adjusting acidic soil, and many plants won't grow well in alkaline soil.

Most vegetable and fruit crops will benefit from some nitrogen because nitrogen is quickly lost from the soil. Some crops are heavier feeders than others, too. Your soil test will tell you if other elements are needed and how much nitrogen to use.

> **Country Color**
>
> Fertilizer doesn't "feed" plants. It provides the minerals they need as they convert sunlight to food for the whole planet. Think of fertilizer like the vitamins we take to supplement our diets.

You can try organic and nonorganic or synthetic fertilizers. Plants can use either one, so the decision is up to you. Whatever type of fertilizer you use should be a slow-release formula for vegetable gardens or fruit trees. Use it as the label directs every year when planting vegetables or in the spring for fruit plants.

What and How Much Should You Grow?

It's best to grow foods that do well in your climate. Some crops don't do well in cold climates—citrus, sweet potatoes, and peanuts, for example. Likewise, some don't do well in warm climates—apples, pears, and some other fruit crops, for example, won't make fruit unless they have a certain number of cold days.

Check the variety of the vegetable crop you intend to grow to see how many days it needs to mature. This information is on seed packages, plant tags, and in catalogs. Find out how long your average growing season is (it's usually calculated from the last frost in spring to the first frost in fall). Ask your Extension office or a gardening neighbor when the last and first frost usually occurs.

To complicate things, you may see some varieties listed in catalogs as "not good in the south" or "needs long days to set fruit." Although some crops may grow all across the United States, not all varieties of the crop grow well in your area. Try to choose varieties listed for your area.

How much you should grow depends on many things. Many vegetable garden or fruit-growing reference books give you the amount of food a certain size row or number of plants will provide. Your Extension office can also tell you how to calculate an average yield from a certain space or plant.

If you don't intend to can or freeze produce for the winter, you can plant less of the crop. Because you need two trees of some fruits for pollination, you will need to plan for more fruit produced than you may be able to eat fresh.

Choose Your Method

Everyone seems to have some new method they want to tell you about when it comes to planting gardens. Let's look at some of your options, starting with vegetable gardens.

You can lay out your vegetable garden in traditional rows with paths between them big enough for a rototiller to fit. This is good when you have lots of space; good, loose soil; and lots of time to tend the garden.

If you have less-than-perfect soil and less space and time, you may want to consider other methods such as *raised beds*. Raised beds have better drainage, give plant roots deeper soil, and clearly mark where crops are planted. The rows between can be narrow and kept mulched.

Raised beds with amended good soil can be planted intensively and yield more crop in the same space than other methods. After they're made, the soil isn't tilled or walked on, which is good for the soil structure. Plus, a garden of raised beds looks nice and often is easier to tend.

Raised or mounded rows can be used for growing strawberries, but most other small fruit such as raspberries are planted in regular rows. Grapes need to be planted near a trellis or a system of posts and wires to support them. Fruit trees are usually planted in rows or scattered in the landscape. Some small dwarf trees can be trained to grow along a trellis or wall.

def•i•ni•tion

With **raised beds**, you actually build a frame aboveground and fill it with soil. This can be soil from the paths, soil you purchase, or a combination. This is a good method when you have very poor soil that needs lots of organic matter and other amendments because the added material is put just where plants will be growing.

Before You Plant

Before you go putting anything in the ground or even tilling a plot of dirt, you have some pre-planting planning to take care of first, starting with the area where your garden will grow.

Start with a Clean Slate

For both vegetables and fruit, a weed- and grass-free planting area is best. If you start the summer or early fall of the year before you intend to plant, you can smother an area to get rid of all other growing things. Mark out your intended garden spot, and lay down heavy layers of mulch or some other light-blocking material. When you remove the mulch the following year, you should have a nice, bare planting area.

> **Country Color**
>
> Old pieces of carpet laid upside down in areas where you want to kill grass and weeds work very well. So place thick layers of newspapers covered with some wood chips for appearance.

If you didn't start the year before, you can remove sod and weeds by hand or hire someone to plow. For large areas of heavy turf, hiring someone to plow the first year is wise. You can do it with a rototiller, but it's a lot of work. After plowing or tilling, rake out all the weed and grass roots.

You can also use chemical vegetation killers a month or so before you plant. This is hard to do the same season you want to plant as most vegetation killers with short-term effects need plants to be actively growing before they work. You then need to wait a certain number of days before you can plant there.

Make a Plan

Get out that trusty notebook and graph paper I talked about in Chapter 7. After you've chosen what you want to grow, lay out your garden on graph paper to see how much space you need and to keep yourself organized.

Vegetable crops and strawberries need to be rotated from year to year, so you should note on your plan where they're growing each year. Tomatoes, peppers, eggplant, and potatoes should ideally have a 3-year rotation between the time when a member of the group is planted there and the same crop or group is planted there again. Rotate other crops from year to year, too. Strawberries should not follow the tomato, pepper, eggplant, and potato group in rotation.

A plan also helps you remember where to plant future purchases of fruit trees and other perennial vegetables or small fruit.

Beware of Overtilling

Soil is a living thing, full of organisms all doing their own beneficial things at various levels within the soil. Every time you turn over those levels, you disturb the community and put many of the beneficial processes on hold for a while. Imagine what happens when someone with a new rototiller goes out and tills his new garden spot every day for 2 weeks! Not only has he disturbed the soil food chain, but he's possibly broken down the soil structure.

All soil needs pockets of oxygen and water for plant roots. Chunky soil provides the most spaces. I'm not talking about fist-size clumps, but tiny, fingernail-size clumps and chunks of organic matter. When you overtill the soil, you destroy that soil structure. It seems like that powder-fine soil you made would be great for plant roots, but it isn't.

If you're making a new vegetable or small fruit bed from a piece of ground with sod or weeds growing on it, it's fine to till it one or two times. You can also use a rototiller to shallowly till the soil between rows to get rid of weeds. But don't overdo the tilling.

Getting Dirty: Planting

Many types of vegetables take a long time to mature so they're started inside early. Peppers, tomatoes, and eggplants are among the early starters. Some crops such as cabbage, broccoli, and brussels sprouts are also started inside in colder areas but planted outside as seeds in warmer ones.

When choosing transplants at the garden center, look for stocky, dark, green plants without flowers or fruit if they're in tiny cell packs. If the plants are tall and yellowish, or are blooming in the cell pack, they are stressed and will never make good garden plants. If plants are individually planted in large pots it's fine for them to have flowers or small fruit.

Onions may be started from seed, from tiny plants, or from sets (or small onion bulbs). Potatoes are started from pieces of cut potatoes called seed potatoes or eyes.

Many other plants should be started from seed in the garden. These include peas, beans, corn, vine crops, carrots, beets, and the various greens. These are sometimes offered as plants, but if the soil conditions are right they'll grow just as fast from seed as from plants because they won't suffer transplant shock.

For many vegetables, you can just plant the seeds in the row outside. Follow the directions on the seed package for how deep and how far apart to plant the seeds. Seeds must be kept moist to germinate, so water them if the season is dry.

Rural Rule

Thin seedlings as they grow to the spacing recommended on the package. It's very hard for some people to do this, but if you don't thin enough, the whole crop will be small and weak.

When you plant is almost as important, if not more so, than what and where you plant. Here's a guide to when to plant what:

- Plant tender vegetable plants such as tomatoes, peppers, eggplant, beans, sweet potatoes, spinach, sweet corn, okra, melons, cucumbers, pumpkins, and squash after the last frost in the spring.

- Semi-hardy crops like cabbage, broccoli, brussels sprouts, cauliflower, potatoes, carrots, and beets can stand some light frost but no freezing weather.

- Plant peas, lettuce, radishes, and chard outside as soon as the soil is unfrozen.

- Strawberries are planted early, but only after hard frost is past.

- Grapes, blueberries, raspberries, and blackberries are planted when dormant, in early spring, or from pots after frost.

- Most fruit trees are planted when dormant and bare rooted in early spring, as soon as the soil can be worked. If potted and growing, wait until after hard frost has passed.

- Citrus should not be planted where frost threatens.

Organic Growing Versus Integrated Pest Control

For vegetable gardens, a completely organic approach is fairly easy to manage. Organic gardening means using no synthetic pesticides and, in some definitions, no synthetic fertilizers. If you've planted the garden in a good spot and have worked your soil into a fairly decent state, you should be able to get healthy crops of vegetables and small fruit like strawberries without a lot of pesticides and fertilizers.

Organic methods with fruit trees aren't quite as successful. If you can live with wormy, scabby fruit, don't spray your fruit trees. A few organic products for fruit trees exist, but there's also a lot more work involved using them to keep the trees somewhat pest-free.

Integrated pest management (IPM) is the practice of monitoring a crop for pest activity and taking the least-harmful method necessary to control a problem. Pesticides are used but only when a certain threshold is reached. If you want to grow good tree fruit like apples and peaches, a moderate spray schedule and monitoring for more aggressive pests is probably the best way to go.

Sinkhole

The directions on a pesticide bottle tell you the only legal ways the product can be used. If you mix higher concentrations or use the product on a plant or pest not mentioned on the label, you are breaking the law.

Growing Perennial Crops

A few vegetable crops can be considered perennials, including rhubarb, asparagus, and Jerusalem artichokes. When you decide you want to grow these crops, pick your site carefully because the plants will be around for a long time.

It's important with these crops to mulch them so the weeds don't overtake them. If weeds get out of hand, the best thing to do is prepare a new weed-free location, dig up the plants, remove any weeds in the roots, and transplant them to the new spot.

Growing Culinary Herbs and Flowers

No vegetable garden is complete without some culinary herbs (herbs used for cooking) and some pretty flowers. Flowers may help deter pests, too.

Some herbs are perennial and should be given their own bed so they can grow undisturbed. Sage, rosemary, oregano, and thyme are among these herbs. Other herbs such as basil and dill are annuals or treated as annuals. You can plant them among the crops and clean them up in the winter with other crop residue.

For planting among vegetables, annual flowers are best. Nasturtiums and calendula have edible flowers and are pretty, too. Other annual flowers that do well in a vegetable garden are tall marigolds, zinnias, cosmos, painted daisies, gladiolas, and dahlias.

Growing Tree Fruit

Fruit trees generally won't bear fruit for several years after you plant them. But while you wait for them to fruit, you must protect them from deer and other animals, prune them, and keep them disease-free. Fruit trees take more space than small fruit, but your yield is also greater.

Most tree fruit comes in three sizes—dwarf, semi-dwarf, and standard. Homeowners should choose semi-dwarf trees even if they have lots of room. Semi-dwarf trees bear sooner and are easier to care for and harvest than larger trees. The very small dwarf trees should only be used for special situations, where you want a potted tree, or to grow trained along a fence or wall. Dwarf trees need special care, and the yield is small for the work involved.

Most fruit trees are *grafted* trees because the fruit flavor and quality varies tremendously from seed-grown trees. The root part of the grafted tree controls the tree height.

One of the most important things to remember about fruit trees is that many cannot make fruit without two trees being present. In most cases, these trees cannot even be of the same variety because they are too close genetically. Apples, pears, sweet cherries, and Japanese plums require that you plant two trees of different varieties within a $^1/_4$ mile of each other. Not all varieties will *pollinate* each other, so you should consult a good reference, catalog, or your county Extension office to see what will pollinate what.

def•i•ni•tion

Grafted trees have a piece of one tree with good fruit inserted into another tree grown for strong, hardy roots and certain growth characteristics to produce the best of both worlds. The two parts grow together and become one tree. **Pollination** is when pollen from the male parts of one flower is carried to the female part of another flower. Pollen contains sperm cells, which, if the female part of the flower is receptive to it, will work their way down to eggs in the ovary. A certain number of eggs must be fertilized and become seeds for a fruit to form.

Peaches, nectarines, apricots, citrus, tart cherries, and European plums can set fruit without two trees being present. However, research suggests that they'll set more and better-tasting fruit if two trees are near each other for cross-pollination.

Some fruit trees, especially apples and pears, are also fussy about what area of the country they're grown in. All apples and pears require a certain number of cold days to set fruit buds. Originally, apples and pears didn't grow well in the south, but a few varieties have been developed that make fruit in warm areas.

Fruit trees are often purchased as dormant, bare root trees. The roots should be kept in moist paper, sawdust, shavings, etc. until you plant the tree, but they should not be left standing in water. Plant them in the spring as soon as you can dig the hole.

Potted fruit trees can be planted at any time, but they must be kept well watered in dry weather. Keep the weeds and grass away from newly planted trees, and protect the trunk with tree wrap or a circle of fence. Tree tubes made of translucent plastic are good to use on fruit trees, too.

Apple trees need the most pruning to shape them, but all fruit trees need some pruning and shaping as they grow. (This technique varies by fruit type and is too detailed to go into here. You can get the information from reference books or your county Extension office.) If you don't prune your trees, you'll soon have a messy, unproductive tree on your hands. If you intend to grow tree fruit, you need to learn and practice pruning.

Tree fruit also requires care to prevent disease and insect problems. Some diseases and insects are cosmetic problems but some will kill the trees. Start with disease resistant varieties of fruit trees. They are on the market and are easier for homeowners to grow.

For best results with fruit trees you will need to follow a preventative spray schedule for disease and insects. There are some products on the market considered organic but they are expensive and must be applied more frequently than conventional pesticides.

If you follow the label directions on pesticides your fruit should be safe to eat and just as nutritious as organic produce. Whether you choose organic or conventional you must follow a schedule. Contact your county Extension office for a fruit tree spray schedule for your area.

Growing Small Fruit

Small fruits such as strawberries, raspberries, grapes, and blueberries are fairly easy and satisfying for home gardeners to grow. A large amount of fruit can be grown in a small space, and small fruits need less pest control than tree fruits.

Strawberries can last for several years in some parts of the United States but are treated as annual plants in the far south and far north.

June-bearing strawberries have all their fruit in one large spring crop, are everbearing, and produce small crops sporadically all season. Short day strawberries are planted in the fall in the far south and bear crops in late winter or early spring.

Raspberries and blackberries come in summer, fall, and everbearing varieties. These bramble crops are perennial and can be grown for many years before needing replacement. They produce fruit without another plant.

Blueberries need to have slightly acidic soil to do well. Homeowners can use acidic fertilizers to successfully grow blueberries. Some blueberry varieties are good for the north, and some do better in the south. Blueberries are attractive in the landscape and can be worked in around the home. You need to have more than one plant for the best fruit set, preferably of different varieties.

Grapes can be a bit trickier than other small fruit. You need to choose a variety hardy in your

---

Country Color

The bramble crops do need the right kind of pruning to remain productive. Some varieties also do better in some areas of the country than others. Consult a reference book or your county Extension office for care needs and help choosing varieties.

Rural Rule

Consider planting a row of vegetables or fruit to donate to the hungry. Write to PAR@ gardenwriters.org or call 1-877-492-2727 to find a program in your community. You could also donate excess produce to a local soup kitchen or shelter.

planting zone and also provide some support for the vines. Grapes also need to be trained and pruned to remain productive. You can eat all grape varieties, but some make better table grapes and some are better for juice or wine. Grapes do not need another plant for fruit to set.

If you can't grow all your fruit and vegetable needs, try to buy them locally. Buying locally and seasonally helps both the local economy and the environment.

The Least You Need to Know

♦ Homegrown veggies and fruits taste better and are more nutritious than store-bought produce.

♦ Improving your soil with organic matter enables you to grow more vegetables and fruits.

♦ Plan before you plant for the best results.

♦ Homegrown fruit requires pest control and proper pruning.

Chapter **21**

Chickens, Eggs, Honey, and More

In This Chapter

- Chickens and eggs
- Homemade maple syrup
- A bit of honey

Nothing says country like a few chickens strutting around the place or a rooster crowing in the morning. And after you taste farm fresh eggs, you'll never want store-bought eggs again. Chickens are easy for country newcomers to raise and are a fun project for children, too.

And to go with those eggs, you might want to add some honey or maple syrup. These aren't as easy, but they're fun projects to consider.

Country Chickens and Farm Fresh Eggs

First things first: before you get excited about producing your own eggs, be sure it's okay to keep chickens on your property. There are some places in the country where chickens aren't allowed. Some places may restrict the number of chickens you can keep or how they're housed.

Before You Shop for Chickens ...

If you've checked around and gotten the green light to get some chickens, it's time to go buy some, right? Not so fast. Before you can bring home your flock of chickens, you need to have some specific things.

Chickens don't need much space, but they do need a warm, dry shelter and a pen so they can get some fresh air. You can let your chickens roam around your place, but you'll want a pen to shut them in at least part of the time. You'll also need a strong wire pen if loose dogs roam the neighborhood or if your own dogs don't like to play nice. Sometimes chickens must be confined for their own safety. If you have close neighbors with gardens, you'll probably want to confine your chickens. Chickens don't respect boundaries and can do some major damage to gardens.

The shelter can be a partitioned-off part of a barn or shed, or you can build the chickens their own little house. You can buy cute little pens with attached houses that look like dog houses. These might be okay for one or two *hens*, but chickens really prefer a shelter where they can get up off the ground to roost at night.

def•i•ni•tion

Hens are female chickens that have started laying eggs.

A 4-foot-square house 6 feet high can comfortably shelter 4 or 5 hens with room for 2 nest boxes and a roost for the night. If you want 10 adult hens, your shelter should be at least 4 feet by 8 feet. The shelter should have a solid floor and a door so you can get inside to collect eggs or catch hens. You may also want a small door for the hens to get out into their pen, so the large door can be closed against the weather. You also may want a vent or window in the shelter for hot days.

Inside, you need a nest box for every two hens. (They share well.) The boxes should be about 1 foot square. They can be simple open boxes on the floor, but hens like covered boxes where it's dark to lay their eggs. You can buy or build nest boxes, but good, reasonably priced substitutes are covered kitty litter boxes. These plastic boxes are easy to clean and you can find them in any pet store.

Nest boxes need something inside to cushion the eggs and give the hens something to fluff up. You can use hay, straw, dry leaves, or wood shavings. Replace the material whenever it looks too dirty.

Inside furnishings should also include a roost, a place where hens go to sleep at night. They like it up off the floor, but heavy laying hens can't fly up very high, so 3 or 4 feet off the ground is good. The roost should be about 1 foot wide per hen and could be a 2×4 turned on end or a pole 2 or 3 inches in diameter.

Your hens also need a food dish and a water container. They need to be heavy enough not to tip easily, easy to clean, and large enough to hold a minimum 1 days' worth of food and water.

Be sure your hens have an outside pen. They love it outside. Make the pen as large as possible. A minimum would be 2 square feet per bird. Don't use flimsy *chicken wire* on the bottom part of your pen. Dogs and other large predators can rip through that. Save the *poultry netting* for the upper part of the pen and the top. Use strong welded wire with small openings on the bottom 3 or 4 feet of the pen.

Have a door on the pen so if you need to get inside you can and so you can let the hens out to roam a little when it's safe. If you let them out later in the day, they'll go back in the pen before it gets dark and you can safely shut them in for the night.

def•i•ni•tion _____

Chicken wire and **poultry netting** are names for lightweight wire fencing with six-sided openings either 1 or 2 inches wide. It's generally inexpensive, but it's not very strong and it rusts quickly.

Choosing Your Chickens

What chicken breed do you want to keep? Some breeds lay more and larger eggs than others. If you want large, high-quality eggs and gentle hens, some breeds stand out. Likewise, some of the strange and flamboyant breeds of chickens aren't good layers. Many of the Banty or dwarf chickens look like their larger cousins but produce tiny eggs.

Some hens produce white eggs; others produce various shades of brown eggs; and still others produce eggs in shades of green, pink, and blue. As a general rule, the hens that produce white eggs are lighter in weight than those that produce brown eggs. They also have white ear lobes. White egg layers include Leghorns, Anacona, and Lakenvelder.

Country Color
Chickens come in many colors, sizes, and feather styles. A good place to look at the different breeds is at a county or state fair. You can also look in reference books, baby chick catalogs, and poultry magazines.

Hens that lay brown eggs are generally heavier bodied and good for meat as well as laying eggs. As far as feather color goes, darker birds usually produce brown eggs, but this rule doesn't always hold true. Good brown egg breeds include Issa Browns, Rhode Island Reds, Plymouth Rocks, Black Australorps, Welsummers, Golden Comets, and Wyandottes.

The few breeds that produce colored eggs are generally intermediate in size. Some lay a lot of eggs, but most aren't very productive. Colored eggs taste just like white or brown eggs. Colored egg layers include Ameraucana and Aruacana.

If you're not concerned with maximum egg production, you can pick any hens that appeal to you. But remember that they'll all eat about the same amount of food and require the same care.

How Many Hens Do You Need?

A good layer will lay 1 egg a day about 6 days a week. If you have 4 hens, you'll probably get 2 dozen eggs a week from good layers. You can pick the number of hens you need by the amount of eggs your family can eat in a week.

Hens stop laying eggs when it gets very cold or hot and when they molt, which happens once a year. As hens get older, they lay less often. Hens need good feed and minerals to lay well, also. In the winter, your 4 hens may only lay 4 eggs a week each.

Don't keep just one hen. Chickens are flock birds and get very lonely if they're kept as a single. A flock of four hens is a good minimum. Don't get too many hens. Eggs don't store as well as some other produce.

Do You Need a Rooster?

You don't need a *rooster* for hens to lay eggs, and a rooster on the place doesn't affect the number of eggs laid or the taste or nutritional value of the eggs.

def•i•ni•tion

A **rooster** or *cock* is a male chicken that's become sexually active, generally when he begins to crow.

That being said, there are reasons to keep a rooster. If you enjoy hearing a rooster crow—and they crow *all* day, even sometimes at night—get a rooster. Roosters can be very beautiful and entertaining to watch as they care for their hens. A rooster will cluck and call his girls to come get the choice tidbits he finds. He'll herd them or lead them back home at night and protect them if he can. Hens seem to enjoy having a man around, too.

Getting Started

Okay, now it's time to get your birds. Whether you start with adult birds or baby chicks is up to you. You can sometimes find adult birds for sale in your area. If you're inexperienced with poultry, you're really taking a gamble that the hens you're buying are (1) hens, (2) not too old, and (3) healthy. Young hens just starting to lay are much more expensive than older birds.

Hens don't have big combs (the red leathery stuff) on top of their heads and their tail feathers are usually shorter. Hens do not crow. Old hens have thick scaly skin on their legs and often have long toenails. Older hens may lay some eggs but will eat a lot for what they give in return. Watch out for sick chickens that are missing lots of feathers, look sleepy and dopey, sneeze, have runny eyes, or have feathers plastered around the tail area from diarrhea.

If that sounds overwhelming for you, maybe you should begin your farm flock with baby chicks. You can get a wide variety of breeds shipped to you in the mail. Farm stores also sell chicks in the spring. Don't go overboard ordering cute baby chicks from a catalog. There's usually a minimum purchase of 25 chicks for shipping, and that will be more than enough for most families. If you buy chicks from a feed store, either by pre-ordering or right from stock on hand, you probably won't have a minimum to worry about but will have fewer breed choices.

Chicks are sold as sexed or unsexed, also called *straight run*. Straight run chicks are cheaper than *pullets* but more expensive than *cockerels* in most breeds. If you're interested in producing eggs and have no desire to eat your chickens, buy pullets. Straight run chicks can be anywhere from 0 percent to 100 percent males, but they're generally 50 percent.

If you buy straight run chicks, you probably won't know which are hens until they're almost grown. You'll then have to get rid of the excess cockerels because two roosters should not be kept together.

Baby chicks generally don't eat or drink for the first 24 hours after they hatch, which is why they can be shipped directly after hatching. However, some shipments take longer than that and chicks can be subjected to many temperature extremes.

def•i•ni•tion

A **straight run** is a group of chicks that have not been sexed. You'll get males and females. Sexing chicks requires an expert, so sexed chicks cost a little more. **Pullets** are baby female chickens or hens. **Cockerels** are baby male chickens or roosters.

Welcome Home, Chicks!

Open the box and inspect your chicks as soon as they arrive. One or two deaths are not unusual, but count the living ones before you complain. Often more chicks are sent than ordered to cover losses. The chicks should be active and noisy if they're healthy.

You need something to hold and protect the chicks, a heat lamp or other source of heat, a room thermometer, a baby chick waterer, a feed pan, chick starter feed, and some kind of litter for the floor of the pen. You can get most of these things at a feed store.

Rural Rule

Metal or plastic water troughs make good homes for baby chicks. You can often find leaky troughs for free or cheap, and these work fine. Old bathtubs, wash tubs, wading pools, and even old freezers can also be used. You need a cover for it, too. Do not use newspaper as litter on the floor, it's slippery and causes leg problems. Use sand, sawdust, ground cobs, or shavings instead, and change the litter if it gets wet or too dirty.

Baby chicks need to be kept warm—about 95°F the first week—and dry. You should have a pen all set up and waiting for their arrival so you can put them into it immediately. The pen should have a heat lamp set up in one corner so the chicks can get under it if they're cold or move away from it if they're warm.

Put your thermometer close to the heat source on the floor of the pen so you can see how warm it is. You need to be able to adjust the cover or the size of the lightbulb to regulate the temperature in the pen. As the weeks go by and your chicks grow, you can lower the temperature a few degrees each week.

Sinkhole

Heat lamps and other heat sources can start fires, so be sure to anchor them so they don't fall into the pen. Be careful not to splash water onto hot bulbs, and keep them away from flammable objects.

Contented chicks are quiet, calm, but busy. If chicks huddle together and chirp loudly and continuously, they are cold or something else is wrong. Chicks that are too hot will spread out and lay flat and may pant. Chicks can die of overheating in temperatures of more than 100°F.

Be sure to keep the water and feed dishes full. Chick waterers usually consist of a red plastic ring that screws on a jar filled with water. It keeps just a narrow ring of water open to the chicks. As you take each chick out of the packing box, dip its beak carefully in the water. This helps get them started drinking.

You may want to scatter feed on a white, heavy-duty paper plate for a few days to start them eating. They are attracted to movement, so sprinkle some on the plate in front of them. After a day or two, use a feed trough.

Chicks need light to eat and drink. If you're using a heat lamp, that will generally be enough light. If you're using a heat source that doesn't produce light, you need a light on for at least 16 hours a day.

Handling Baby Poultry

Baby chicks are not toys, and children can easily kill them with a tight squeeze. If they're handled too often, the chicks won't grow well. Observation is fine; handling is not.

Children can also get sick from handling chicks. Some baby chicks carry the salmonosis virus, and if children or adults handle chicks and don't wash their hands well, they could become ill.

Raising Laying Birds

When baby chicks have all their feathers and are a couple pounds each, you can move them to your adult chicken quarters. A nightlight in the shelter area is very helpful when they're getting used to their new quarters.

Until they're 4 months old, feed young chickens chick starter and then chick grower feed. About the fourth month, start feeding them laying feed or laying mash. You can buy these feeds at the feed store.

Read the bag label. Some feeds are complete and don't require minerals and grit. Some suggest you add grit and minerals to the diet.

Chickens fed greens or allowed to range free a few hours a day will have egg yolks that are much darker than penned hens. You can feed your chickens greens from the time they are a few days old. You can even give table scraps to older chickens.

> **Country Color**
>
> Chick and grower feed come in medicated and un-medicated varieties. Medicated feeds contain antibiotics that are supposed to keep chickens from getting ill and aid growth. The first bag of starter feed should be medicated to combat shipping stress. After that, it's up to you.

Laying Schedule

It takes at least 5 months and sometimes longer before your baby pullets lay their first eggs. The first eggs are very small, but after a week or two, they should be full size.

If your hens are reaching 5 months old late in the summer or fall, adding light to the shelter so they get light 12 hours a day may start them laying faster.

Healthy hens generally lay their entire lives, but after the first year of laying, they lay fewer eggs per week. As they age, they may also stop laying through the winter months. Some people cannot part with old hens, having named them and become friends and that is fine. You can add a few young hens each year to keep your egg production going. Or you can sell your older hens when you've raised a new batch to production size.

Hens may also stop laying if they get broody. Getting broody means they want to raise a family. This usually happens in late summer and happens more often in some breeds than others. The hens won't want to leave the nest box and if possible will sneak off to lay eggs.

Collecting Eggs

Eggs are generally laid before 10 A.M., and you should keep your hens confined until at least 11 A.M. to be sure no eggs are hidden from you.

Collect eggs immediately after they're laid if you can. In most weather, eggs won't be harmed by sitting in the nest until you can collect them later in the day. But in very cold weather, the eggs will freeze. The freezing creates small cracks that can allow bacteria to enter the egg, so discard frozen eggs or cook and feed them to pets.

> **Country Color**
>
> Sometimes eggs are flecked with tiny spots of darker pigment. This isn't anything to worry about. Keep your eggs rotated in storage so you use the oldest ones first.

After collecting the eggs, wash them with cool water until they look clean, dry with a clean paper towel, and refrigerate. Don't wash the eggs with hot water or any soap. Eggs have a protective waxy covering that keeps bacteria out and moisture from evaporating from the egg. Washing with hot water or soap removes that protective layer. If eggs are really dirty, which happens sometimes, you may just want to discard them.

Homemade Maple Syrup

Real maple syrup tastes better than any store-bought corn syrup-and-flavor "syrup." If you live in the right part of the country and have a few maple trees, you can cook up some of this sweet treat yourself. (If you're not sure whether or not you have maple trees, get someone to help you identify them.)

You'll need some basic equipment and a place to cook the syrup for up to 24 hours per batch. This cooking spot needs to be outside because the steam from boiling sap can coat your walls and ceilings inside with a sticky mess.

Please note that the following paragraphs are for a homeowner wanting to produce a little syrup for his or her own use. If you're thinking about producing a lot of syrup, consult with your county Extension office and other experts.

It's All in the Trees

Sugar maples and black maples are the best syrup producers because their sap has the highest sugar content. But all native maples produce some sweet sap, even box elders, an odd member of the maple family. The trees need to be at least 10 inches in diameter before they can be safely tapped. Each tree can produce up to 1 gallon of sap a day, depending on size and other conditions.

Sap starts running in the spring, when the days are warm, sunny, and above freezing and the nights slip back below freezing. In most areas, this begins in February and continues into March. The season ends when maple buds begin to swell. When the buds start swelling, sap still runs but it turns bitter. In some years, the weather is only right for a few days; in other years, you can collect sap for weeks. You can store sap for a day or two, but after that, it needs to be turned into syrup.

Gather Your Supplies

You need a drill, probably battery-powered, with a $^7/_{16}$-inch bit. You need some taps—clean pieces of rigid pipe, metal, or plastic about 4 inches long and $^7/_{16}$ inches in diameter. One end is cut slanted so there's a point on the end, and the other end is left round. You can sometimes buy these from mail-order places or you can easily fashion your own.

You need some clean plastic tubing that fits over the round end of the tap. You also need some clean jugs or other containers to run the tubing into to collect the sap. If trees are close together, you can run several pieces of tubing into one larger collection container. Use food-grade containers to collect sap, such as milk jugs cleaned out with boiling water, plastic buckets from bakeries and restaurants, etc. The container should be covered to keep out bugs and debris.

To cook the sap, you need a large, flat pan with sides at least 6 inches high. Cheap foil pans won't work. A big metal turkey roaster might work. The more surface area you can provide, the better. You need metal spoons with long handles for stirring and a metal funnel. You also need a candy thermometer. You need some containers for storing the finished syrup, preferably sterilized pint glass jars or similar containers.

Wear old clothing or have an apron on and have some pot holders or oven mitts nearby to handle hot items.

As mentioned earlier, you need something to cook on for an extended period of time, and it should be outside. Many homeowners use gas grills. Be sure you have lots of propane when you start!

Making Syrup

On a sunny day when temperatures are going to be above freezing, drill holes into the maple trees you're going to use. Drill them at a comfortable working height for you and just drill far enough to get past the bark into the cambium layer underneath. This is the layer where the tree's "veins" run. Drill only one hole per tree unless the tree is very large in diameter, more than 36 inches. Then you could make one on each side.

Insert one of your taps, pointed end first, and lightly tap it to seat it. Attach a piece of tubing to the other end, and run it to the collection container. If you've done things correctly, the sap will soon flow down the tube into the container. If not, try again. Maybe back up the tap a bit because the sap won't flow if you went too far into the heart wood. Let the sap run. You can leave it for more than a day, but most people collect the sap at night so animals don't get it.

Only collect sap for a day or two before cooking it, and keep it cool in storage. It should look clear or slightly yellow. A tree can give you 1 gallon sap in a day under good conditions.

It takes about 43 gallons sap to make 1 gallon maple syrup. To make 1 quart maple syrup, collect about 11 gallons sap. That would take 6 trees 2 days under ideal conditions.

When you're ready to begin cooking, pour the sap into the pan and turn on the heat. Leave several inches of space at the top of the pan. If all your sap doesn't fit, you can add it gradually as water boils off the sap in the pan.

Sinkhole

Making maple syrup is fascinating for children, but the syrup can cause some very bad burns if spilled on skin. Be sure children are carefully supervised during the process and the cooking surface is stable.

Bring the sap to a full boil and try to keep it at that stage. It needs to cook a long time, up to 12 hours, and you need to be nearby. If it starts to foam up, stir it and reduce the heat a bit. It will thicken, darken, and reduce in volume as water evaporates.

When the syrup first boils, insert the candy thermometer and note the temperature. (Don't let the thermometer touch the bottom of the pan, though.) When the temperature reaches 7.5° higher than the temperature it boiled at, it should be done. If it goes higher, add a bit of fresh sap until it reaches the correct temperature.

Pour the hot syrup through a mesh screen strainer into a sterilized jar. Then pour it through the funnel into your sterilized jars for storage.

The Buzz on Beekeeping

Our native bees are disappearing at an alarming rate, and we need bees to pollinate most of our fruit and many vegetable crops. Many country homeowners keep a hive of bees as a hobby or to produce honey.

Rural Rule _____

The following few paragraphs barely buzz the surface of beekeeping but might give you an idea if this is something you want to research further. Or check with your county Extension office, a nature center, or someone who sells honey to see if there's a beekeeping club nearby you can join. Beekeeping magazines can be helpful, too. Do some learning and observing before beginning your own hive.

If you decide to keep a hive of bees for the honey, you'll also be helping many gardeners and farmers nearby. Your bees will fly out and forage for pollen and nectar to make honey and will, in the process, pollinate many crops. Bees are making the honey to feed themselves and their young, but they usually make enough to share without any harm to the hive. One hive can easily supply a small family with honey.

Before getting a beehive, consider if anyone in the family is allergic to beestings. Honeybees are generally pretty docile if handled carefully, but stings can occur. If you have close neighbors, you may want to ask if anyone there is allergic to beestings.

And once again, you might want to check those ordinances, although bee hives are rarely prohibited. Keep the hives away from property lines and road sides.

The Basics of Beekeeping

Beekeeping equipment costs you a little money, but often you can pick up secondhand equipment. Bee hives are actually several pieces or components that fit together. The best way to start is to buy a beginner's or starter's package.

You also need equipment to handle the bees such as a protective suit with a hat and face netting. You need equipment to smoke the bees when you work on the hive. You need an extractor to separate the honey from the comb. A hive tool is essential. It's a flat instrument with a scraping side and a prying side. You use it to pry apart the parts of the hive to collect honey and to scrape bees and wax off the parts you remove.

Of course, you need bees. You generally purchase them by mail and receive a queen bee and a thousand or so worker bees. Sometimes a local beekeeper can supply you with a starter package.

Place your hive in a sheltered place, away from human traffic, with the opening facing east if possible. Set up the hive on a stand of some sort so it's off the ground and above most of the grass and weeds.

Country Color
The flowers bees visit affect the flavor of honey. Gourmet honeys include orange blossom, tupelo, and yellow star thistle.

The bees do most of the work, foraging all day until sundown. The honey they make goes into cells in trays inside the hive called *supers*. These have a framework of wire coated with wax just like the natural wax honeycomb bees make in the wild. When the cell is full, the bees cap it with wax.

Collecting Honey

To collect honey, you don your protective gear, smoke the bees to calm them, and check the hive from time to time. If the trays or supers are full of honey, add another one. If all the trays are full or if you want to harvest the honey, remove one or more trays. Always leave some trays in the hive. These feed the bees and produce more bees, which are also sealed in some of the honeycomb.

The wax caps on the cells have to be removed before the honey can be extracted. This is done with hot knives. The trays are spun to remove the honey from the comb. A commercial extractor can be expensive, but sometimes a bee keepers' club will share an extractor. The honey is filtered and put into sterilized glass jars and sealed for storage.

The Least You Need to Know

- A few hens are easy to keep, and nothing beats the taste of farm fresh eggs.

- If you have the right trees and the right weather, you can make homemade maple syrup.

- Keeping bees provides you with honey and a hobby.

- Providing some of your own food is a good project for the whole family and will create many fond memories.

Part 6

Country Pets and Other Critters

Some people move to the country so they can have more or larger pets. Some people want to have more dogs, cats, horses, chickens, or other animals the typical city ordinances don't allow. But before you stock the barn, read Part 6. Here, I present some things you should consider before attaining more animals.

In this part, I also discuss wildlife—including those critters you want to invite to your homestead and those that invite themselves.

Chapter 22

Country Dogs, Cats, and Bunnies

In This Chapter

◆ Country dogs

◆ Country cats

◆ Country bunnies

Dogs, cats, and bunnies are all common pets for country homeowners. You may have had the same pets in the city or maybe you'll be able to have them for the first time now that you live outside the city.

There are some aspects of living in the country that make pet ownership different than when living in the city. In this chapter, I discuss responsible pet ownership in the country.

Your Dog in the Country

Some people move to the country so they can have the dog they've always wanted. But most people moving to the country are bringing the dog along as part of the family. There's no denying that many Americans think of their dogs as children, or at least as part of the family. And yet dogs are so often mis-understood by the people who are supposed to protect and guide them.

If we think of our dogs as children, we should also know that dogs need supervision just as children do. They also need someone to make educated decisions for them.

Preparing a City Dog for the Country

Just as it's wise to prepare your kids for a country move, some preparation for your dog is also wise. There are many things you can do to make the transition smoother and safer for your dog.

First let's discuss the actual move. Many pets get lost during the chaos of moving. Not all of them find their way back home, following your scent across hundreds of miles like in the movies. Shortly before you move, update your dog's identification with your new address and phone number. If your dog doesn't wear an ID tag or isn't *microchipped*, get him some identification.

def•i•ni•tion

Using a needle, a veterinarian can insert a tiny plastic **microchip** with your identification information on it under your dog's skin. Most animal shelters and many vets have scanners they pass over the dog to detect the chip and access the information. (This works for cats, too.)

Microchip identification systems generally rely on an agency that maintains owner information. The vet or animal shelter calls this agency when a chip is found, and contact information for the owner is given to the finder of the pet. To be sure your dog's info is current, call that company and update your contact information before you move.

Also, before you move, contact your vet and tell him or her where you're moving and ask if any additional vaccinations are needed for your dog. If booster vaccines or a rabies shot is needed, get it done. If the dog requires prescription medication, get it refilled.

You can ask your current vet for a recommendation for a new vet in your area, if you're moving too far from the current vet to use his or her services. Or you can ask some of your new neighbors or people at the local animal control center who they consider a good vet for pets in the area.

Make a plan for the day of the actual move. If possible, leave your dog at the old home until the very last moving trip. Plan where the dog will be put when you get to the new home, so he'll be safe and out of the way of movers. Be sure the dog can't run out of gates or doors as people come in and out.

If you're building a home or if you're remodeling and can take the dog for visits before the actual move, do so. That will make him feel a little more at home in your new house after the move.

Beware of Too Much Freedom

If you have a well-behaved dog that responds to commands, you have hundreds of acres out in the middle of nowhere, and you're with him, your dog can enjoy a romp on your property. But otherwise, don't let your dog roam freely without supervision. It's not safe—or legal—in most places for your dog to roam on others' property. You may have 2 acres of land and it might seem like a lot of space to you, but a dog can cross that area in minutes and be off on the neighbor's property or in the road before you know it. Even if you're outside mowing or playing with the kids and your dog is loose, keep tabs on him so he doesn't make a little trip when you aren't watching.

You may think your dog is harmless, and he may well be. But a little bit of "harmless" fun can become very expensive or even deadly. A strange dog chasing sheep, chickens, or other animals can cause them to panic. They may run into fences, crush each other, escape and run into the road, or become overheated from running and die. And it doesn't take long for the damage to occur. A half-hour of chasing sheep, half a mile away, and the dog is back home before you ever realize he's gone.

Meanwhile, the sheep owner is treating animals with broken legs, cuts, and abortions; burying the ones that died; and repairing fences and buildings. He or she is angry and has lost a lot of money, which you, if the dog is located, will be paying back.

Once a dog begins chasing and killing livestock, it's extremely hard to prevent him from wanting to do it again. Dogs are more prone to do this when they're in packs, but your single dog may join up with another neighbor's dog. The nicest, friendliest dogs can become monsters when they're away from home and running with friends.

Sinkhole _____

Unfortunately, there's often an unspoken rule in the country called SSS—shoot, shovel, and shut up. If a dog is seen chasing or hurting livestock, it's shot, buried, and that's the end of that.

Dogs out roaming the countryside and encountering livestock can also be killed by the animals. Cows and horses with young are very protective and may kill dogs that get too close. In areas with coyotes, wolves, bears, or other large animals, dogs may be killed. If a dog is chasing game animals such as deer, a hunter may shoot it, or if it's hunting season, a dog moving through brush may be mistaken for game and shot.

Dogs running loose get caught in traps, eat poison bait, get hit by cars, or get caught in farm machinery. Very small dogs have even been picked up by eagles and owls. Dogs fall through thin ice and into swift rivers. They get sprayed by skunks and bitten by raccoons.

Even dogs that stay fairly close to home when loose can cause problems. Dogs that chase cars can cause someone to lose control of the car. Dogs that chase horseback riders can cause a rider to be thrown and killed.

Sinkhole

Invisible fence that's buried in the ground may keep your dog home, but it won't prevent other animals from coming into your yard and attacking him.

If you're not supervising your dog, he belongs behind a fence, for his safety and the safety of other animals and people. Lucky for you, in the country you can fence a large, safe area for your dog to play in.

Dogs may seem happy when they're roaming free, but people who love their dogs don't let them roam free without supervision.

Dog Laws

Most areas, even rural ones, have laws about dogs running free and trespassing. Most areas also require licensing and rabies vaccinations. Some areas limit the amount of dogs that can be owned or require kennel licenses if more than a certain number are owned. Check your ordinances if you own more than one dog.

If your dog kills or injures livestock, you are required to pay the owner of the livestock for damages. In some cases, the livestock owner is awarded double or triple what the damage amounts to, if negligence is proved. Dogs may also be confiscated and destroyed.

On the other hand, most places have laws that state a dog cannot be killed unless it is threatening someone's life. That means the farmer who shoots the dog chasing chickens is doing something illegal, and so is a hunter who shoots a dog chasing deer. A game warden, animal control officer, or police officer usually can shoot dogs in these circumstances. You, however, cannot shoot someone else's dog that trespasses. Poisoning is also prohibited.

Don't count on these laws protecting your dog. Only you can do that by keeping him from running freely through the countryside.

Special Health Concerns

If you and your dog are moving to a new climate, take care to see that your dog adjusts to the differences. Dogs moved from cool areas to hot ones are at risk of heat stroke. Be sure he doesn't overdo the new romps in the country in hot weather and that he always has shade and water. Never leave your dog in your car while you shop, even with the windows cracked.

If your dog isn't used to cold, limit his outside time. If he's to be housed outside, be sure he has a warm, dry shelter with plenty of bedding. Increase an outside dog's food supply in cold weather and offer him water at least twice a day or have a heated water bowl.

Vaccinations

In some areas, dogs may be exposed to animals that carry certain viruses or parasites. Your new vet should be able to advise you on this. Sometimes a problem will occur in one area that requires either a vaccine or a test to see if an animal is infected.

Leptospirosis is a disease dogs can get from wild animals. People can also catch this disease. In the city, vets are no longer recommending Leptospirosis vaccines, but dogs in the country who may encounter wild animals may need them.

A country dog should always have a rabies vac-cination and commonly prescribed vaccines for distemper, parvo, adneovirus, parainfluenza, and corno virus. There is a vaccine for Lyme disease, carried by ticks, and for Giardia, a parasite found in polluted water. Your vet may recommend them.

> **Country Color**
>
> Much research is currently being conducted to see how often dogs need booster vaccines, including the rabies vaccine. Your vet can advise you on the latest information.

Pest Control

Country dogs often get ticks, so use a spray or collar to repel ticks. Usually this repels fleas also. Fleas are not as much of a problem as they used to be, and if your dog gets fleas, see your vet for some highly effective flea control products.

Flies and mosquitoes can really bother dogs that spend a lot of time outside, especially short-coated dogs. Black flies and deer flies can bite your dog's ears until they're bloody. Ointments are available you can rub on the ears to repel flies. Some fly and mosquito repellent sprays are safe for dogs, also.

Because dogs will eat nearly anything, country dogs are often exposed to internal parasites. Have your dog checked for worms at least twice a year, especially if he's known to eat dead things or animal poop.

Skunk Encounters

Skunks do not like dogs and are quick to show it. Most dogs won't ever bother a skunk again after they've been sprayed once, but some never seem to learn. If skunks are known to prowl your yard at night, be very careful when you let your dog outside. Dogs will also crawl under porches and sheds and encounter skunks in the daytime. Some seem to go out of their way to hunt them, maybe as a grudge.

A dog that's sprayed by a skunk will howl and cry. The skunk's spray hurts his eyes and is extremely unpleasant, to say the least. The dog may come running to you for comfort or run into the house. Try to keep him out of the house. As much as you sympathize, you might have a hard time getting near the dog to comfort him.

Sinkhole

Tomato juice has long been used for removing the smell of skunk, but it's not terribly effective.

Wash your dog with a mixture of 3 percent hydrogen peroxide (a whole bottle), ¼ cup baking soda, and a few drops dish soap or dog shampoo. Mix in a container with a little water, and lather up your dog. Rinse and repeat. Don't get the peroxide mix in the dog's eyes. If his eyes are irritated from the skunk spray, give him a few drops of plain saline eye drops. Use old towels or paper towels to dry the dog, not new or good towels because they'll pick up some of the smell. The smell won't totally go away for many days, but it will be more bearable.

Snakes and Other Reptiles and Amphibians

Dogs often encounter snakes, other reptiles, and amphibians in their explorations. In most areas of the country, poisonous reptiles are rare. The far south and the southwest have the most poisonous reptiles.

If your dog is bitten by a snake and the bite begins to swell, and/or the dog begins to act ill, get him to a vet as soon as possible. Teach your dog from an early age to leave snakes and other reptiles alone.

Dogs can eat frogs with gusto, but a toad will have them spitting and gagging. Generally after they've had this experience they'll leave all frogs and toads alone.

Porcupine Encounters

If porcupines are common in your area, your dog could have a nasty encounter with them. Porcupines rarely come up around homes and try to avoid human and dog contact. However, some dogs still find them.

Contrary to popular belief, a porcupine doesn't shoot his quills. Your dog has to come in contact with the porcupine to get stuck. The quills are very painful, and the dog will probably snap and bite at you if you try to help.

The quills have a barb similar to an arrow and cannot simply be pulled out. The best thing to do is to get the dog to a vet, who will tranquilize him to work out the quills.

Encounters with Other Wild Animals

Dogs in the country may tangle with animals that they later wished they'd left alone. Unless you have a hunting breed and know what you're doing, don't encourage your dog to kill wildlife. I have seen dogs that were seriously maimed and killed because they messed with the wrong animal.

Raccoons can take on a good-size dog and do some major damage. Opossums don't always play dead, and they have more teeth than any other mammal. Badgers are also terrific at defending themselves. A pack of coyotes, very common in many areas now, can kill a domestic dog in minutes. A mountain lion or cougar will even jump into fenced areas to carry dogs off for dinner. And of course a dog will be easily overpowered by a bear.

With the exception of cougars, most of these animals don't seek out dogs; the dogs attack them. Dogs can find some of these animals, like raccoons, right around the home, so it's up to you to stop the encounters from happening.

> **Sinkhole**
>
> It's tempting to send your dog under the porch to kill the woodchuck; but even if he is successful, you may end up with major vet bills.

Eating the Wrong Things

Lots of things around a country home can harm a dog if he eats it. Even some landscaping plants can be dangerous. I knew of a small dog that was tied to a yew tree every day. One day in frustration he chewed on the trunk and roots of the tree and died. Yews are extremely toxic. Other plants that can harm dogs include daffodil and narcissus bulbs, mushrooms, datura, lilies of the valley, azaleas, onions and alliums, tomato and potato plants, English ivy, oleander, foxglove, and mountain laurel. Cocoa shell mulch can also harm dogs. The good news is most dogs don't eat plants unless they're young or very bored or hungry.

Farm and garden chemicals can also harm a dog. Sometimes they will walk through spilled chemicals or find old buried stuff and either absorb it through their skin or lick it off their paws. Rat poison can be eaten at your place or a neighbor's if the dog roams.

Medicines for livestock should be kept out of your dog's reach. Restrain your dog from chewing on old painted wood, which may contain lead, and drinking from water in puddles that may be full of pesticides from crops.

Keep dogs from eating dead animals. Dogs don't get food poisoning as easily as humans do, but they can come home and vomit on your carpet. Some of what they eat, especially spoiled meat, can harm them if certain organisms are growing in it.

Other Problems Country Dogs Can Get Into

Many dogs love to roll in anything nasty, and they have more opportunities in the country. Manure is a favorite of many, as are dead animals. Baths and closer supervision are the only cures for these habits. If the smell is really bad, try the skunk spray remedy given earlier.

Take extra care of your dog's coat, especially if it's long. Burrs are uncomfortable and can cause sores. A dog with a dense undercoat that gets wet from swimming and doesn't dry well in humid weather may get maggots on his skin. The maggots release toxins as they feed and can kill the dog.

Rural Rule

To help separate mats from burrs, rub peanut butter or cooking oil on them.

You may want to keep your dog's coat trimmed short for comfort and easy grooming.

Your Cat in the Country

Unless you're going to let your inside city cat run loose in the country, the city-to-country transition for an indoor cat is simply from one house to the next. But for that reason, it's even more important to be careful not to lose the cat during the move.

Most cats don't like either change or strangers. They also have a tendency to crawl inside things and get accidentally shut inside where they shouldn't be. So put your cat in a safe place while you're packing and moving, and have a place at the new home where she can be safely locked up until things calm down.

Be sure your cat is wearing a collar with your new ID on it and be sure she has had all her current recommended vaccinations, including rabies.

Inside or Outside?

A cat can live happily and safely inside its whole life, but many people want their cat to experience the great outdoors. Many cats are eager to try this, too. Let your cat get adjusted to the inside of your new home for a few weeks before you let her go outside. This is true even if your cat was an inside-outside cat at your old home.

Cats new to the outdoors may panic, climb a tree, or go down a hole and be hard to rescue. If she's never been outside, it might be wise to put a harness and leash on her and sit outside with her the first few times.

Cat owners are increasingly building kennels for cats outside a window or cat door. These allow the cat some outdoor sunlight and fresh air but still keep her safe. Of course, cat kennels must have roofs because cats are such good jumpers.

Barn and Feral Cats

It's hard to imagine a barn without a cat roaming around it, and if your new home has barns, you probably have barn cats around somewhere, too. I call them barn cats if they allow you to touch them and expect to be fed and feral or wild cats if they want nothing to do with you.

If you want cats to keep away mice (they don't do a good job on rats), you need to feed them. Cats don't kill just when they're hungry but they need to be healthy to hunt well. A good dry cat food and some water is all they need.

Barn cat turnover can be high, but you may end up with new cats in the barn from time to time. Cats seem to know how to find a good place to live, and some people think any place with a barn is a good place to drop off a cat.

 Rural Rule

If you can, spay and neuter your barn cats. They'll stay closer to home, and you won't be overrun with kittens.

Most cats don't bother adult chickens but may kill chicks and even adult rabbits. Cats also kill many birds, including songbirds and game-bird chicks. This doesn't endear them to many people, and cats that stray are often shot.

Special Health Concerns

Barn cats and indoor-outdoor cats need to be wormed frequently because they can pick up tapeworms and other parasites from things they kill and eat. Unneutered male cats often develop huge abscesses from fights.

Cats often climb into machinery, so be very careful when starting machines in an area with cats. A cat once had kittens under the mowing deck of our mower, which had been parked outside overnight. Luckily, my husband didn't engage the blades until he had rolled over the kittens, which survived unharmed.

Cats also climb into feed bins and storage areas and get locked in. Look carefully before you shut the doors on these things. Cats also get stepped on by horses, tripped over, and eaten by pigs.

Coyotes and great horned owls enjoy a meal of cat from time to time. Some other predators may also kill cats or kittens. There's not much you can do to protect barn and feral cats, but if it becomes a problem in your area, you might want to keep your indoor-outdoor cat inside at night.

Vaccinations

Cat diseases often sweep through an area—nature's way of reducing the cat population I guess. Some are preventable through vaccines, and some are not. All cats should have a rabies vaccination.

Cats are often affected by rabies and can be very aggressive when they have it. If an unvaccinated feral or barn cat becomes unusually friendly, aggressive, or acts weirdly, avoid it at all costs. If you get bitten, see your doctor right away. The cat may need to be sacrificed and tested for rabies.

Flea and Tick Control

For some reason, cats don't seem to suffer much from ticks, possibly because they remove them while grooming. But they do get fleas. It will be almost impossible to control fleas on feral cats and even barn cats. Fleas can be the source of tapeworms and disease.

Your indoor-outdoor cat may need to be treated frequently for fleas. Ask your vet for the most effective treatments. Your house cat can get fleas, too, if you bring them in on you from the barn. As soon as you see even one flea, begin treating your cat.

Bunnies as Pets

Rabbits have become popular pets, but in some cities they're considered livestock and not allowed. In the country, bunnies are seldom banned, although you will want to check your local ordinances.

Bunnies are cute, quiet, easy to care for, and don't require expensive equipment. They have personalities, can become very tame, and come in a wide range of sizes and colors.

> **Country Color**
>
> Rabbits make an excellent beginning to keeping livestock as a 4-H project, and many adults also show rabbits. Pet rabbits can even be housetrained.

Rabbit Housing

In the country, bunnies are generally kept outside, although they can be kept as house pets. The most important thing to keep in mind with the housing is that it must protect the rabbit from weather and predators.

You can find many wire cages on the market, and most are lightweight and easy to keep clean. They can be hung inside a shed or barn or protected by suspending them off the ground outside and roofing them. Although rabbits like to be around other rabbits, each will need its own cage to prevent fights. Some cages have pans underneath to collect droppings and urine. In other cases, this falls on the ground. Rabbits can stand a lot of cold, but they must be kept dry. Heat is a killer for bunnies, so don't put cages in the sun.

If the cage is outside, the rabbit needs a nest box to get into. Inside the rabbit may only need a board or plastic platform to rest on. *Does* that have young need a nest box for *kindling*. Because they tend to spray urine, *buck* rabbits need a shield around the bottom of the cage on three sides about 4 inches high.

Buy the largest cage you can afford. A dwarf bunny needs a cage at least 3 foot by 18 inches. A giant rabbit such as a French Lop needs a cage at least 5 foot by 3 foot. Bigger is always better for these rabbits.

def•i•ni•tion

A **doe** is a female rabbit. A **buck** is a male rabbit. **Kindling** is when a rabbit gives birth.

Feeding Bunnies

Many complete and balanced pellet feeds are on the market for rabbits. Rabbits also appreciate a little hay and occasional treats of carrot or apple. You can feed them once or twice a day or use a self-feeder that enables them to eat when they want.

Rabbits should always have clean water. They can learn to drink from a water bottle, which keeps it clean. In winter, because bottles will freeze, remove them and give your rabbits warm water twice a day.

Rabbits are notorious for spilling their feed or scratching it out of the dish. Anchor their dishes to the cage wall to help combat this.

Protecting Bunnies from Predators

It's tempting to let your bunny out on the grass to nibble it and get some exercise. But watch it carefully. Bunnies are high on the preferred food list for many animals, including hawks, which can swoop out of the air and fly away with your bunny before you know what's going on.

Keep rabbit cages off the ground and securely anchored. If weasels or minks are present in your area, the holes in the cage wire should not be more than 1×2 inches. Some large animals can pull cage doors open, so if large predators are in the area, keep your rabbit cages inside a secure building.

The Least You Need to Know

- ◆ Do not allow your dog to roam freely. It's for his own safety.
- ◆ Cats and dogs need rabies vaccinations in the country.
- ◆ Cats in the country often need less supervision than dogs do, but they do still need your care.
- ◆ Rabbits make good pets and can be a good introduction to raising livestock.

Chapter 23

Horses and Ponies

In This Chapter

- ◆ What owning a horse involves
- ◆ Horse and pony requirements
- ◆ Horse and rider safety

You've moved to the country and have all this open space on your land. Your dog loves it. He runs and runs and runs—under your supervision, of course. Maybe you've even practiced critter ownership with a few chickens and a bunny or two. Now you feel like you're ready for the big one: a horse or a pony.

In this chapter, I go over the basics of what an animal this size needs and what to expect with horse or pony ownership.

Are You *Really* Ready for a Horse or a Pony?

Before you get too excited about getting a horse or a pony, check to see if you're even allowed to have one in your zoning. Horses and ponies are often allowed where other large livestock are not, as the smell is less and people are more tolerant of horses and ponies. Be sure you check how many horses and ponies are allowed on your property size, as the numbers are sometimes restricted, also.

If your child is begging you for a pony or horse, how do you feel about chipping in with the work? If you don't want to deal with the day-to-day feeding and caring for a horse, do not get children younger than 10 a horse or pony. They need daily help and supervision. Even older children need supervision and occasional help. Teenagers who are busy with school and jobs may neglect a once-loved friend. And if your child gets into showing or barrel racing, you will become very, very involved.

If an older child is responsible and has been reading and talking about horses and ponies their whole life, they are probably going to be good horse or pony owners. But if the child just wants a horse because a friend got one, or you sense the interest is a passing one, hold off on the purchase.

And then there's a little matter of money. If you look for them, you can find many free and low-cost horses and ponies. But horses and ponies can cost *a lot* of money if they're well bred and well trained. No matter what they cost to acquire, horses will cost you money—sometimes lots of money—to care for.

Horses and ponies require hoof trimming or shoeing every 6 weeks or so, whether they're ridden or not. They require vaccinations and worming on a regular schedule. And they eat a lot. *A lot.*

Some people may be moving to the country because they are presently keeping a horse at a boarding stable and want to save money and time keeping it at home. Even these owners may be a little surprised when full care of the animal reverts to them.

def•i•ni•tion

A **farrier** is someone who works on horse and pony feet, trimming and shoeing them.

When you keep one horse or pony or a few, the economies of large purchases of bedding and feed are lost. *Farriers* also charge more when they come to work on one or two horses. And because horses get lonely when they're kept alone, it's always better to keep two or some kind of companion animal such as a goat.

Decisions to Make

Why do you want a horse or pony? Not everyone who buys a horse wants to ride him. Some people want pasture pets, horses they can love and play with and who will keep the grass mowed. If that sounds like what you have in mind, consider getting a miniature horse or a small pony.

Some people want a good horse for riding the back roads. Others may want a horse they can enter into shows or competitions. Some may want a cart or buggy horse. Some people are interested in racing horses or horses for breeding.

You need to decide what level of experience you have with horses—and be honest with yourself here. The worst thing new, inexperienced horse owners can do is buy a young, unbroken horse or pony or one that has bad habits and needs firm control.

You need to decide how much you can afford to spend on a horse or pony. You also need to decide if you can afford the basic maintenance of the animal. And some animals cost more to keep. Older horses may require special food, and younger horses may require money to train them.

Horses can eat pasture grass if you have good pasture and enough of it. But almost every horse needs some supplemental feed and hay at some time of the year. And as mentioned before, you'll have medical and farrier expenses. It's a rare horse owner who has never had an emergency vet bill, and those bills can be large.

Plus, there's equipment and *tack* to buy to handle and care for the horse. You can get some of this second-hand, but you'll still have expenses there.

As mentioned earlier, free and nearly free horses and ponies will always exist. But in this case you *do* need to look a gift horse in the mouth. Inexpensive horses may be unwanted horses, or they may have medical problems, bad behavior, or both. If you buy an emancipated, wormy horse who limps, you may end up spending hundreds of dollars on vet and feed bills just to end up with a sleek, shiny horse that tries to kill you every time you get near it.

def•i•ni•tion

Tack generally refers to the items put on a horse, such as halters, lead ropes, saddles, bridles, etc., and things you use to groom the horse with, such as brushes and hoof picks.

But don't discount rescuing a sad case. Some of the best horses I ever owned were rescue animals, but some of the worst were, too. If you're considering rescuing a horse, buying at an auction, etc. and you don't have much experience with horses, bring someone with you who does and whose head will keep your heart from making a bad decision.

What You Need to Keep a Horse

You don't need a whole lot to keep a horse, but as with any animal, some essentials are, well, essential. Let's look at some of what you need before you bring home a horse.

Shelter

Some people will argue that you don't need more than a stall in a barn to house a horse, but a stall is less important than a good secure area for the horse to exercise in outside. A horse doesn't really need elaborate shelter. If you asked a horse, he would tell you that he would like a place to get out of the weather and wind, but from which he could come and go from at will.

A small shed and a large pasture are ideal for most horses. The shed should have a door or gate that can be shut to keep the horse or horses inside in emergencies.

Rural Rule

Most horses that have the freedom to come and go from a shelter eliminate their waste outside the shelter, saving you a lot of cleanup.

But those conditions aren't always ideal to groom and work with a horse, and so horse owners build elaborate barns and stalls for their animals. If theft or large predators are a problem in your area, a barn that can be locked up may be the best solution.

All kinds of plans exist for designing and building horse barns and stalls. The important things are that stalls be roomy and comfortable and safe for both owner and animal.

Fencing

When fencing horse and pony areas, safety is the number-one consideration. Never use barbed wire fence with horses. If they get tangled in it, they struggle, and serious injury can result. Other types of wire fencing are generally fine.

Well-behaved horses are often fenced with a single strand of electric wire, but this is risky. All electric wire fences should be marked with white or light flags so horses see them.

Some smart horses and particularly ponies learn to crawl or roll under strands of wire!

If welded wire fencing is used, the openings should not be large enough that the horse or pony can get his head through them, which can cause injury. Cover metal fence posts tops with plastic guards so your horse can't injure or impale himself.

Board fences are often used for horses or metal rails. These types of fencing look nice, but they're often quite expensive. These kinds of fences aren't necessary for keeping in horses, and if you can fence a larger area with another type of fence, it's the better route to take.

Other Horse-y Equipment

You need food and water dishes for your horse or pony. You need water in both inside and outside enclosures if the animal is locked up part of the time. You can choose dishes that are on the ground or those that hang. Consider rubber dishes around horses. They last a lot longer.

Larger water containers aren't necessarily better, unless several horses are in a single pasture. If you fill a large tank, the tendency is to let it go a long time before empty-ing and refilling it. Tanks should be emptied, scrubbed free of algae, and refilled with clean water frequently—at least twice a week. This eliminates mosquitoes breeding in the water and other problems.

You need tools to clean a horse stall. Get a flat shovel, manure fork, and some sort of wheelbar-row or cart.

And of course, you need bedding for the stall. Wood chips, sawdust, or straw are commonly used.

> **Country Color**
>
> Children quickly outgrow ponies. If there is no other child to inherit him, a gentle horse is a better choice for a child.

Tack

Look at any horse catalog or tack shop, and you'll find hundreds of horse accessories. If you're using a horse or pony for a particular purpose, you need tack to support that purpose. For example, a riding horse requires a saddle, saddle blanket, girth strap, bridle, and bit.

At the very minimum, you need a well-fitting halter, lead rope, brush, comb, and hoof pick for any horse or pony. From there, the sky's the limit.

Feeding a Horse or Pony

For a large animal, your horse has a very delicate digestive system. More horses are probably overfed than underfed when they are kept as pleasure animals, and that can cause problems in a big way. The health of the digestive system can affect the horse's feet, believe it or not, and without healthy feet, the horse is in trouble.

Too much food, a sudden change in diet, or too rich food causes blood to pool in horse's feet, which swell and become painful and hot. This is called *foundering*. If not treated, the condition can cause changes in the leg bones and hooves that might cause permanent lameness and sometimes death.

The wrong food or too rich food can also cause bloating, which, if not treated, can kill a horse in a matter of hours. Horses also choke on food from time to time. Don't allow people to feed your horse anything without permission, and limit treats.

Rich, lush pasture seems like it would be wonderful for your horse, but if he's not used to it, an hour of lush grass could cause foundering or bloating. Horses outside all the time adjust gradually to seasonal grass changes and are usually fine.

Ask the previous owner of a horse if he has been on pasture and what type of grain and other supplements he has been receiving. Try to adjust a horse to new feed gradually, and keep a close eye on him for problems.

Unless he's being ridden or driven frequently (or she's in the last part of pregnancy or nursing), your horse or pony really doesn't need more than good pasture or good hay and water. Almost all owners, however, feed some grain or other supplement. Don't overdo the grain or pellet feed. A tiny bit is all most horses need. Older horses with worn teeth are an exception. They lose weight even on pasture because they can't chew well. Modern soft, pelleted feeds for old horses do a marvelous job to keep them healthy, but watch that they don't get too fat.

> **Country Color**
>
> Horses can live to be 30 years old or older. A horse is considered aged when he's older than 20 years.

Horse Health Care and Other Needs

Horses need regular worming. You can learn to do it yourself or pay a vet to do it. The area you are in and the way the horse is kept dictate how often and with what the horse or pony needs to be wormed.

Your horse needs a rabies vaccine and a tetanus vaccine. Ask your vet how often booster vaccines are needed. If you get a horse and have no proof of these two vaccines, get the vaccines just in case. Other vaccines, such as the West Nile vaccine, may be recommended for your area. Ask your vet.

Certain tests such as a Coggins test may be needed to move your horse from your home to a show or to an event, or to sell it. Before you buy a horse, ask a local vet who works with horses about your state rules and regulations and be sure your horse has the required vaccines and tests.

Taking care of a horse or pony's feet is one of the most important things you can do. If you don't ride the animal or only ride occasionally on soft surfaces, he may not need shoes, but he does need regular hoof trimming. Hoof trimming is not something the average owner should do. A wrong trim can lame or permanently harm the horse. The process requires special tools and the strength and knowledge to use them. If the feet are neglected and become overgrown, the horse may become lame and the correction will cost much more than a regular trim.

Rural Rule

Most country vets treat horses, but some vets specialize in horses. If a horse vet is nearby, it's worthwhile to use his or her services. Ask horse owners in the area who they recommend.

Special shoes are sometimes put on horses to correct feet and leg problems. A farrier needs to come to your home every 6 to 8 weeks to check and adjust the shoes if necessary.

Grooming your horse or pony is important for his health and helps you find injuries or sore spots. A horse should be brushed and his hooves inspected before every ride and at least two or three times a week. Comb burrs and mats out of his tail and mane, and give him a good brushing to remove dirt and loose hair.

Have another horse owner teach you how to inspect and clean a horse's hooves. You need to remove stones and hard clumps of soil before riding and a few times a week.

If your horse or pony spends a lot of time in a pasture, don't trim his mane and tail more than you need to keep him looking neat. His mane and tail give him protection from insects and shade his eyes.

Buying a Horse or Pony

The way most new horse and pony owners get into trouble is by buying an animal they like the looks of or feel sorry for. If you want your first equine-owning experience to be good, you need to do your homework and pay attention to what your head says, not what your heart says. Get and study some good horse care books. If your kid has been studying them, it's time to borrow the books and do your own research. Try to find some horse-owning friends or neighbors to answer some of your questions and volunteer to shop for a horse with you.

A horse auction may be a good way for you to examine horses and see why some are valued more than others. Listen to the comments as people examine the horses. Just be aware that everyone talking isn't an expert, and leave your money home. A horse auction or sale probably isn't the best way for a beginner to buy a horse, though. A private sale is generally less stressful and will let you find out more about the horse. Be aware that some people buy and sell horses for a living, and some of them are scam artists.

def•i•ni•tion

A **gelding** is a neutered male horse or pony. A **mare** is an adult female horse or pony. A **colt** is a young male horse or pony. A **filly** is a young female horse or pony. A **stallion** is an adult male horse or pony that's not neutered.

If this is your first horse or pony, get an older animal, one who's about 10 years old or older and well trained. Get a *gelding* or *mare. Fillies, colts,* and *stallions* are best left to experienced horse people.

Get an Expert's Opinion

Most horses are going to cost enough that you don't want to make a mistake you can't undo. If you can't find an experienced horse-owning friend or neighbor to go with you to look at horses, consider hiring an expert. Some veterinarians and some horse trainers will examine a horse for you for a fee. If you're paying a lot of money for the horse—and horses can cost thousands of dollars—don't skip this step.

A few good horse sellers will allow you a trial period to handle and use the horse and return it if you aren't happy. If this is offered, get it in writing.

Get the Paperwork

Always get a bill of sale and receipt when purchasing a horse or pony, no matter where you buy it. Horse theft still happens and is still a major legal problem. If your horse or pony is registered, you should get those papers also.

In many places, proof of certain vaccinations or tests are required to move a horse. Find out what's required in your state and county before buying a horse or pony, and be sure you get the paperwork that proves the vaccination or test has been given.

Getting Your Horse Home

If you don't own a horse trailer, you can sometimes hire someone to move the horse or pony for you. They need to have copies of your bill of sale and health papers with them in case any problems develop.

If you're pulling a trailer with a horse for the first time, take it slow and easy. If the horse panics and becomes violent, be careful about opening the trailer and going inside with the horse. He could escape or hurt you. Try to calm him from outside the trailer. Some horses may need to be tranquilized to proceed safely.

Safety and Horses

Always expect the unexpected around horses, and pay attention to what you're doing. Even the gentlest, best-trained horse can come unhinged by something as simple as a plastic bag blowing by. Horses are large animals, and the simplest unintentional blow can pack a wallop.

Learn how to move around a horse safely. Always talk to the horse when you're coming up behind him in his blind spot. Don't put yourself in a position to get pinned in a stall or caught between two unfriendly horses—or even two friendly horses.

Learn to anticipate problems and deal with them proactively. If it's near the Fourth of July and your horse becomes frantic with loud noise, keep him in a safe stall with loud music playing nearby if your neighbors are going to set off fireworks.

A child may be able to handle a gentle horse or pony most of the time, but adults should always supervise children around horses. All riders should wear helmets. Tack should be inspected frequently and repaired or replaced when damaged or worn.

When you turn an animal into a pasture or stall, walk him in and turn him around so he faces the gate or door. Then remove the lead and back out of the door or gate. This keeps you from getting kicked.

Horses seem to be as bad as 10-year-old boys about getting into accidents. Be sure to remove anything that can cut or poke them from pastures and stalls. Check the pasture for holes from woodchucks and other animals, and fill them at once. If icy conditions exist, keep your horse inside.

Introduce your horse to new things, including other animals, and new situations carefully, calmly, and gradually. In hunting season, keep your horse close to the house or barn and not out in the woods or tall grass. You may want to put a orange blanket on them.

Sinkhole

Never try to separate fighting horses without help. Most horse fights resolve quickly, but always stay out of the way and call for help if necessary. And don't keep a horse or pony you can't handle or that deliberately tries to hurt you. Know when to admit you made a mistake. There are too many nice, well-mannered horses out there to keep a killer.

The Least You Need to Know

- ◆ Horses cost money, no matter what you paid for them.

- ◆ Beginners should get expert advice when purchasing a horse.

- ◆ A horse's diet should be carefully controlled.

- ◆ Always expect the unexpected and pay attention to what you're doing when working with horses.

Chapter 24

Dealing With Unwanted Critters

In This Chapter

♦ Co-existing with nature

♦ Controlling pests

♦ A little about animal habits

When some people move to a rural area, they may be shocked and frightened by what animals want to share their space and not know what to do when wildlife become pests. One of the best ways to deal with a pest is to learn as much as you can about your enemy. It's also best to start sooner rather than later to control pests and be alert for signs of pests moving in.

First Things First: Check Game Laws

Before you do anything with unwanted animals on your property, check your state's game laws. Even though certain animals may be on your land, the state actually owns them and it's illegal for you to kill or trap them outside of hunting seasons with the proper license. But the state game control also realizes that in some cases, game animals become nuisances or dangerous and need to be dealt with.

Get a copy of your state game laws, and learn what animals are protected. Then, if you're having a problem with a game animal, call your local Department of Natural Resources (DNR) to see what your options are. In many cases, you'll be issued a permit to deal with the problem.

Some licensed pest control companies have permits to deal with problem animals and know what's allowed under the law.

Can't We All Just Get Along?

If you move to the country, expect to run into wildlife. And if that wildlife isn't harming you or your property, learn to live with them, no matter how scared you are.

Take snakes, for example. Most of the snakes you'll see around your property are beneficial, not harmful. If you leave them alone, they'll leave you alone. Just because a snake likes to sun itself on your cement steps does not make it a problem. Sure, it might startle you, but it'll probably take off quickly when you scream. There's no reason to kill it. Besides, many snakes are endangered, which means it's illegal to kill them.

Don't kill animals just because you don't like to see them or are afraid of them. A little damage to fruit or a hole dug in the lawn should not make you crazy. It's better to spend some time observing and appreciating the animal than obsessing over how to kill it.

Nature has this rule about territory. If the territory can support an animal, it probably will. When you remove one animal, another will soon move in. Sometimes it's better to get used to what you have than get a new invader with worse habits.

Sinkhole

I've seen some people who go too far co-existing with wildlife and put themselves or their families in danger. Don't allow bats, rats or mice, or any other wild animals to live in your home. Wild animals can carry disease and damage your home. In the barn or shed is fine, if you are happy with it there, but don't have these animals in your home.

Why Live Traps Aren't That Kind

Although many people think live traps are the more humane way to trap animals, they're generally not a good solution to a pest problem. It's kinder to kill a skunk, for example, than to let it die from thirst in a trap because you're afraid you'll get sprayed.

It's hard to control what you catch in a live trap, too. You may have been trying to catch a groundhog and get a skunk instead. When you do catch the right target and are willing to transport it to a new environment, there's another problem. Animals establish territories. Animals in the area where you release an animal are going to try to kill or run off the newcomer. If you see a lot of raccoons in an area, it is *not* a good place to release one you caught. The transported animal is not familiar with where the water and food supplies are and is at a disadvantage from the moment you let it go. Many try to return home, and unless you have transported it quite a ways away, may be home before you are.

> **Rural Rule** _____
>
> If you're setting a live trap where a skunk may be captured, cover the trap sides with dark plastic or an old blanket. If a skunk is caught, you can handle the trap, with it inside, safely. And if a skunk can't get its tail up, it won't spray.

Some fish and game agencies prohibit moving animals from one place to another because the trapped animal may introduce disease to a new area. In my area, for example, any trapped raccoon must be destroyed or released where trapped.

Handling a trap with a large angry animal in it can be dangerous and can expose you to disease. Live traps must be checked every day and the animal removed or destroyed. If you can't do this, no matter what's in the trap, don't set one.

Rabies and Other Diseases

Rabies is serious business—it's almost always fatal to humans. Although all warm-blooded animals can get rabies, animals like rats, other rodents, and rabbits rarely get it in the wild. Wild cats, raccoons, foxes, and bats, on the other hand, are a concern for rabies transmission.

Rabies is transmitted from a bite or by getting salvia from an infected animal in a skin break. Not all animals with rabies attack; they can just seem confused, overly friendly, or ill. Avoid any wild animal that acts too tame, approaches you aggressively, or seems ill. Nocturnal animals that are wandering aimlessly in the daytime are suspect, too.

Teach your children that they should not try to help sick animals or catch wild animals that seem tame. Instruct them to tell an adult instead.

Animals also carry other diseases and parasites that can infect humans. Plague, histoplasmosis, leptospirosis, salmonellosis, guardia, roundworm, and hookworm are a few.

When Bambi Isn't So Cute

Deer top the list of pest animals, causing the most damage, including dramatically altering natural plant habitats, causing many native plants across the country to be endangered. Deer also cause many human deaths each year.

Deer need "edge" conditions and predator protection to thrive, and human civilization has given them just what they need. We clear dense brush and forest and plant crops and landscaping deer love, while allowing just enough wild space to hide. We chase off the wolves and prevent hunting on our 10-acre parcels. But there are far too many deer in many parts of the country, and they are destroying many native plants and changing the environment for many other species that can't compete with their destructiveness.

Don't Feed the Deer!

Don't feed the deer you see on your country property. Deer don't need supplemental feeding, and bringing them up close to your house so you can see them from your window is a bad idea. They'll get used to human noise and activity and become bold—even eating your tulips in broad daylight! Deer don't understand that your apple tree and the privet hedge aren't the same as the three bushels of corn you spread on the lawn for them. The damage will only get worse the more you feed them.

> **Sinkhole**
>
> Think twice about feeding deer. You might be held responsible for someone hitting a deer with their car if it was crossing the road to get to your feeding station.

Many counties and states may have regulations on how much and when you can feed deer, even on your own land. Animals that congregate to feed pass diseases such as TB to each other, which can become human health problems, too. Deer also carry disease-laden ticks to your property.

Keeping Deer Out of the Garden

Even if you never intentionally feed deer, they may use your yard and garden as a buffet. A good dog or two within a fenced yard will help. Deer-proof fences should be at least 8 feet high. They can be woven wire or electric wires.

Black plastic netting can either protect special plants or a larger area from deer. If installed correctly, it's almost invisible so it needs to be marked with a lighter material at first so deer know it's there. If they run through it by accident, they soon learn that they can continue to do that.

All the little anti-deer tricks you might have heard about—human hair in bags, bars of soap, predator urine, etc.—work only for a short time, if deer aren't numerous in your area or there are easier places to eat. After a while, you need to change the type of product so they don't get used to it. Some of the newer chemical deer-repellant sprays are fairly effective, but they're not very good for edible crops. Fencing is your best choice. A motion detector that turns on a sprinkler can be quite an effective deer repellant because it makes noise and also hits deer with water.

In many areas, homeowners are issued permits by the DNR to shoot nuisance deer. In some cases, you can give the deer to others who want the meat.

Deer-Proof Your Landscape

Deer don't like some plants, although they may occasionally munch on them if they can't find anything else. These include daffodils, alliums, bleeding heart, chrysanthemums, coreopsis, lily of the valley, iris, foxglove, salvia, sage, lavender, liatris, lupines, yarrow, Russian sage, lilacs, spruce, junipers, larkspur, barberry, astilbe, honey locust, sassafras, holly, tomatoes, potatoes, peppers, agave, aloe, ferns, and English ivy. Deer will eat some plants, like yews, that are poisonous to livestock.

There is some regional variance in what deer will eat, and in times of food scarcity, all bets are off.

They Only Come Out at Night ...

Some animals forage at night, and these critters can do considerable damage while we sleep. When you hear strange noises at night and find a mess the next day, one of these pests may be to blame.

Do your best to discourage all these nocturnal pests from taking up residence in your barns or even your home. They bring a risk of disease. But if animals are in their proper environment and not causing any or much harm, leave them alone.

Skunks

Skunks are found throughout the country. Skunks eat grubs, worms, insects, fruits and berries, and mice and rats. They sometimes kill chickens and steal and eat eggs. Skunks are attracted to garbage cans and pet food that's left out. Skunks don't climb, so a fence will generally keep them out of gardens and the yard where your dog can run safely. They do burrow and sometimes make their home under porches and sheds.

Skunks aren't too afraid of people and might move away slowly if confronted. Don't try to hurry them along, or you will be sorry. They don't like dogs and are quick to spray when a dog approaches.

Rural Rule

If your dog has been sprayed (or if you have!), see Chapter 22 for a recipe to get rid of skunk odor.

Skunks are solitary except when breeding and caring for their young. Sometimes, however, they'll sleep in groups in the winter for warmth. Skunks don't truly hibernate and may appear outside in winter during mild spells. Skunks breed in early spring and have 4 to 10 babies about 9 weeks later. The young stay with the female until the fall. If a skunk has young under your porch or shed, try to be patient because they move their young every couple weeks. The best way to keep them from using your property as a den is to be sure all holes are sealed up under porches, sheds, and crawl spaces.

Skunks often damage lawns by digging small, cone-shape holes looking for grubs. If you keep the grub population down in your yard, you probably won't have this problem.

You can use canned dog or cat food as bait to trap a skunk.

Raccoons

Raccoons are cute as can be but one of the nastiest animals when cornered and most destructive to property. Do not feed or encourage raccoons. They often carry rabies and a type of roundworm that can kill or seriously harm humans. Raccoons are persistent, very clever, and difficult to discourage when they feel at home at your place.

Fed raccoons can become aggressive to humans. A friend was always feeding some young raccoons scraps from his lunch bucket when he returned home at night from work. One day he didn't have any scraps, and the raccoons literally tore the lunch bucket out of his hands and ripped it open, growling and snarling at him.

If raccoons are in your area, lock up your trash cans in an enclosed place, pick up pet food at night, and bring in bird feeders. Close up all openings under porches and sheds, cover chimneys with wire guards, and fix any holes in barns and garages—high and low.

Raccoons mate in early spring and give birth in early summer to four to six young. Baby raccoons begin following Mom out of the den when they're about a month old and will remain with her until the following spring, just before she has new babies.

Raccoons are territorial, but hundreds can congregate at a good food source, although there will be a lot of fighting. In the north, raccoons spend a good deal of the winter holed up and sleeping, although they are not true hibernators.

Sinkhole

Be careful using automatic garage door closers when you can't see inside the garage. My sister closed the garage door from inside the house and trapped a raccoon inside that had been getting into the garbage. He did thousands of dollars' worth of damage to her car and garage before she discovered him the next day.

Raccoons eat just about anything, and their clever hands allow them to open doors and latches. They may kill chickens and eat eggs. They will kill the fish in ornamental ponds. They don't have to wash their food but will if water is nearby.

Raccoons can climb, but they rarely burrow. To keep them out of the garden, where they can be very destructive, use a welded wire fence with small openings and a single electric wire at the top.

Raccoons are game animals and protected in most states. If you have a raccoon problem, talk to the DNR in your area to see what your options are. You may be given a permit to trap or kill them.

Opossums

Opossums rarely get in homes, but they do like to live in barns, especially if animals are fed there. Many people tolerate them because they do a pretty good job of killing mice and rats. However, opossums carry several diseases that can infect livestock and can eat or contaminate a lot of feed.

Opossums prefer meat but will consume some garbage and grain products. They eat chicken eggs, but most don't kill chickens. Opossums move away from humans slowly. They can fight ferociously when they have to, so don't go near them.

> **Country Color**
>
> Opossums have more teeth—50—than any other North American animal and are the only marsupial (an animal with a pouch for the young; think kangaroo) in North America.

Opossums are active all year round. Their babies are born after a short gestation time and climb into the mother's pouch, where they stay for several weeks. Opossums can have two or three litters a year of five to nine babies, but few babies make it to adulthood. When they emerge from the pouch, the babies stay with Mom for a few weeks and then disperse.

Contact your local DNR if you want to kill or trap opossums. In some areas, they are considered game animals.

Rabbits

Rabbits can do a lot of damage to the landscape but rarely harm humans. Young trees and shrubs are most at risk in the winter and gardens in the summer. Rabbits are very prolific, and a population that is not controlled may quickly zoom out of control.

Rabbits need places to hide near their feeding spots, so eliminating brush piles, heavy weeds, and overgrown areas near the garden will help. They don't climb, so to keep bunnies out of your garden, install a fence around it that's buried about a foot in the ground. Enclose all young trees with wire fence around the bottom 2 or 3 feet. The fence must be higher than your normal snow line by a foot or so. Things like blood meal, hair, soap, etc. may protect some plantings if the bunnies aren't very hungry. Be sure to rotate and renew the bunny repellant frequently.

Rabbits are active in the early morning and evening. They may breed two to five times a year and produce four to six young at a time. New rabbits are sexually mature in about 3 months. Baby rabbits begin feeding when they're 3 weeks old and are weaned in another week or two.

Dogs and even cats can do a good job discouraging and controlling rabbits. They are a favorite food for feral cats and many other predators, and between predators and cars, few baby bunnies survive.

Bats

Bats are a wonderful part of nature and deserve to be protected when they are in their natural habitat. But their natural habitat is not your home, and bats should not be tolerated in homes. You don't get rid of bats because you're afraid of them but because it is unhealthy to live with them. Bats carry other diseases besides rabies. Their excrement is extremely corrosive and can erode wiring, cause structural damage, and cause quite a stink. Although the reproduction rate of bats is slow—one baby a year—huge colonies of bats can build up in a home over time.

When you see one bat in your home in the summer, it may have just wandered inside by mistake. If you open a window or door, it might just fly out. Or you can put on heavy gloves to capture it and throw it outside. One bat doesn't necessarily mean you have a problem.

If, however, you see many bats throughout the warmer months in your home, you hear scratching and squabbling in the walls during warm months at night, or you see clouds of bats departing through a hole in your home at dusk, you have a problem.

For many people, the best way to deal with bats is to hire a professional exterminator. If you aren't afraid, don't mind climbing, and are a little handy, you can do what's necessary.

> **Sinkhole**
>
> Never handle bats with your bare hands, even if they're dead. Pets found with bats should be quarantined if they haven't been vaccinated for rabies.

Eliminate bats by locking them out. Go outside on a warm evening at dusk and watch where the bats come out of your home. There may be several places; bats can get in and out any place that's more than $1/4$-inch wide. Look around chimneys, under eaves, near attic vents and windows, etc. Close the openings except one or two. Bat babies do not fly until the end of August, so if you trap them inside to die, the smell and insects will cause many problems. In early fall, wait until after dusk when the bats have left and close the remaining holes.

You can purchase special bat excluders that allow bats to fly out but not get back in. With these, you can work in daylight if you mark the holes you found at night.

Dealing With Burrowers

Moles and groundhogs are burrowing animals that can give homeowners a lot of headaches. Moles do mostly cosmetic damage, but groundhogs can seriously undermine foundations, break an animal's legs, or destroy a garden.

Moles

Moles make tunnels or mounds in your yard while looking for insects and worms to eat. They do not eat bulbs, plant roots, or seeds. You can get rid of grubs but still have moles because their diet consists of a lot of earthworms, which healthy lawns need. Moles make home tunnels they use frequently and a lot of feeding tunnels they may only use once. Moles are territorial animals, so often you'll have only one or two in your lawn doing all that damage.

The best way to deal with moles is to use a harpoon-type trap. Smash down their tunnels until you find ones that are pushed back up every day, and place your traps in those tunnels. The traps don't use bait, so set them according to label directions.

Chewing gum, ultrasonic devices, windmills, rat poison, filling tunnels with water, and using car exhaust don't work to eliminate moles. A few poisons are on the market just for moles; these sometimes work if placed in home tunnels.

Groundhogs

Groundhogs dig large tunnels and also eat huge amounts of garden produce. They can both burrow and climb. To protect your garden, install a fence that's buried in the ground a foot or so and that has an electric wire at the top.

Groundhogs sometimes eat rat poison you put in their tunnels, especially early in spring when food is scarce. They need quite a bit to kill them. They can be trapped with apples or carrots but are quite wary of traps. You can also shoot them with a rifle or shotgun. Watch for them to be active in evening or early morning.

Gas fumigant cartridges can be effective if you locate all tunnel entrances. Seal all the tunnel openings but one, light and insert the cartridge, and seal the hole. Watch for smoke that may escape from an unfound entrance.

Or you can fill in burrows as soon as you find them. If you fill the tunnels frequently enough, some groundhogs will give up and move on.

Controlling Rats and Mice

Sooner or later, all country homes, new or old, will have mice or rats. The most important thing to remember when dealing with rodents is to remove food sources, limit places to hide, and regularly inspect and control procedures. To control rats and mice you must be very conscious of prevention and early elimination.

A mouse can get through a $1/4$-inch opening, so seal and caulk all holes in foundations, around pipes, and under doors. Store all feed in rat- or mouse-proof containers. Clean up spilled feed promptly, and feed animals so their food dishes are empty at night. Use trash cans with secure lids, and pick up any garbage or food scraps. Clean up trash piles close to buildings and junk areas inside. In barns, try to keep everything off the floor and away from the wall by 6 inches or so.

Signs of rat infestation are tunnels in the ground, holes gnawed in walls, greasy spots around the holes and regular paths, and damage to feed and other items. Mice damage is similar but smaller. Mice often make little nest balls of chewed items in drawers or containers. Rats are very secretive and suspicious, and you won't see them in the daytime unless the population is high. Mice are less careful and may be seen scooting across the floor in broad daylight.

In a country setting, regular use of poison rat and mouse bait provide the maximum control. Bait stations should prevent pets and livestock from getting to the poison and out of sight of children. Most feed stores carry a good selection of bait stations and poisons. Rotate the type of poison used from time to time to keep rodents from building immunity to the product or learning to avoid it.

Traps work better with mice than rats. Glue traps are not recommended because you then have to kill the animal after it's caught. Whatever you use, empty traps often.

Unwanted Birds

Songbirds and birds of prey are protected by law and cannot be destroyed, no matter how much of a pest they become. English sparrows, starlings, pigeons, and sometimes crows are the only birds homeowners are free to kill.

Birds are best discouraged from eating fruit by protecting the fruit with netting. Check the netting each day to be sure no birds are trapped in it. Things like inflatable owls and shiny pie plates may work for a few days, but birds are smart enough to disregard them after a while. Rotating such devices may give you protection for long enough to harvest a crop.

If birds of prey are robbing your chicken coop, you need to roof your coop. If the birds are swooping down on birds at a feeder, remember that they need to eat, too.

If woodpeckers are drumming on your home, they may be doing it for one of two reasons. They might be looking for insects in wood siding or may be making lots of noise to attract a mate and mark territory. If insects are a problem, seal the wood with paint or wood sealer. If the woodpeckers are just making noise, try dangling a loose piece of black netting down from the roof over the area they're working on. After they've been discouraged from the habit for a few weeks, you can remove it.

Geese can become a nuisance in some areas. Dogs can be trained to scare away these birds. Even a low fence or strands of rope or wire between water and lawn areas can keep geese out.

Slithering Snakes

Snakes are beneficial creatures, and many are endangered species. Don't kill them just because they startle you in the garden. Learn to identify poisonous snakes in your area, but don't kill them unless you have to. True poisonous snakes are rare around homes. If your crawl space has a den of rattlesnakes in it, you might have a legitimate snake problem. If you live in the far south and a 20-foot python is roaming the neighborhood, you have a legitimate problem. In these cases, get expert help to deal with the snakes.

If a snake gets in your home, put a small shallow dish of water inside a dark bag or pillowcase near where you saw the snake. The snake will probably crawl in for water and hide, and you can then pick it up and put it outside. Try to remove other sources of water to be sure the snake goes for the bait.

Help with Large Predators

In some remote areas, homeowners might have to deal with such things as alligators, bears, cougars, and coyotes. Most of these animals are protected, but in many areas, you might be allowed to shoot them in self-defense or to defend livestock. Report large animals around your home to your local DNR if they become a problem. The DNR will help you with control tactics.

Never encourage these animals by feeding them, either by accident with garbage and pet food, or deliberately. Large predators are needed in nature and should be left alone if they don't cause a problem.

The Least You Need to Know

- Try to co-exist with wildlife, but don't live with it inside your home.
- Live traps aren't always kind.
- To prevent problems in the first place, don't feed wildlife.
- Check your local game laws or with your local Department of Natural Resources before dealing with animal pests.

Chapter 25

Attracting Wildlife

In This Chapter

- ◆ Improving your property for wildlife
- ◆ Feeding wildlife
- ◆ Attracting animals and birds to your property

Some people get so excited about seeing wildlife on their property after they move to the country that they want to do whatever they can to get them up close for observation. Other people move to the country and are disappointed that they don't see much wildlife, such as when a new home is built on bare cropland. They want to start doing things to make the property attractive to wildlife. If you want nice landscaping, fruit trees, or a vegetable garden, be very careful about what animals you attract close to your house and garden. If you're careful to maintain a natural setting and selective about what you want to attract, you may be able to attract wildlife without giving up on your hostas.

And then there are those who want to hunt. There's nothing wrong with managing your property so you can get that trophy buck within walking distance. But it's hard to mix hunting with up-close observation. Never hunt within 200 feet of a dwelling.

Whatever your goals, in this chapter, I cover the do's and don'ts of attracting wildlife to your country property.

Making Your Property Wildlife Friendly

Even the smallest piece of property can become a haven for many species of birds and animals, although it might require a bit of work on your part before the critters will come. What kind of work, you ask? That depends. Look at what you have, what plans you have for landscaping and food crops, and what type of animals you want to welcome into what areas. But rest assured, improving your property for wildlife will probably improve it for you, also.

The most species of animals and birds will be attracted to diverse plantings and the "edge" type of habitat (more on this in a bit). Food plants are important, but animals and birds also need water, places to hide, and places to raise their young. The more needs you can meet on your property, the more animals you'll see.

If you're starting with old, bare cropland, get some trees started first. Cluster them to the north and west of your property to block the wind and then scatter trees throughout. Use a diverse selection of trees that suit your climate and soil conditions. Use shrubs and fruiting plants around the edges of your tree belt. If you have a lot of land, you might want to plant some actual crops to feed wildlife. (More about that later.)

If you have room, let some of your land begin a natural transition from bare land to forest. Trees and shrubs will begin growing after a year or two. Try to remove invasive, non-native species like autumn olive, but leave the rest alone. This area will attract a lot of different animals, and they will change with the transition.

What to Plant

It's not necessary to stick to all native plants to attract wildlife, but native plants do need to be a part of your plan. Native plants are trees, shrubs, wildflowers, and other plants that naturally grow in your area. Local animals and birds are adapted to using them for food and shelter.

Every area has different native plants, and the soil and other uses of your property also define what types of plants will grow well. But diversity is key in providing good animal habitat. A windbreak row of blue spruce looks nice but will be less attractive to wildlife than a mixture of spruce, pines, and deciduous trees and shrubs. Some people like the dense forest look, but animals and birds like a variety of cover and open areas, called "edge" habitat.

Food plants are important to attract animals to your property and attract more species than artificial feeders do. Food plants may be browse (small trees and shrubs), grasses, legumes, fruits, berries, and seeds. And of course, if you're interested in seeing large predators, like hawks, owls, and foxes, you need to attract small animals for them to eat. Some woody plants and vines that are always appreciated are crabapples, mulberries, cherries, nut trees, dogwood, mountain ash, serviceberry, native grasses, red and white cedar, oaks, manzanita, blueberries, holly, Virginia creeper, sumac, firethorn, bayberry, cranberry, cotoneaster, elderberry, currants, yews, and sassafras.

Non-native and ornamental plants also can provide food and cover for wildlife. Most fruits attract a wide variety of animals and birds. Leave the seed heads of flowers like coreopsis, Echinacea, zinnias, sunflowers, cosmos, penstemon, cleome, and larkspur for the birds.

> **Country Color**
>
> To find out what plants would attract wildlife in your area, contact your local county Extension office or your local conservation district office or Department of Natural Resources office. These organizations can guide you in selecting good plants for wildlife in your area.

Managing Forested Land

One common misconception many people have when they purchase wooded land is that they should never remove a tree or change anything on the land. However, managed land, or land where trees and brush are selectively removed or added, is healthier and carries more wildlife than land left to its own devices.

A deep, dark forest is a climax stage in nature's plan and has fewer inhabitants than a younger forest or forest with clearings. Removing some of the older trees allows younger trees of different species to grow and also allows light to reach the forest floor and help other plants grow. And if your stand of trees is all one species, such as pine or oak or maple, you risk losing all those trees if a disease or exotic pest comes along. Start by harvesting any sickly or damaged trees and then perhaps some of the largest trees to let in light. Replace some of them with other species of trees or shrubs.

If you have the skills, tools, and time, you can thin the woods yourself. Sometimes someone will take out what's needed in exchange for the wood. In some cases, you may even be paid for the trees. Just be sure you and the guy with the saw agree on what trees will be removed.

> **Rural Rule**
>
> Leave the occasional dead tree standing, as this provides homes and food for many animals. A few dead logs on the forest floor and piles of brush also provide homes and food.

It's important to leave some meadows, or clearings; your lawn area around your home in the middle of trees, for example. Shorter, thick brushy shrubs, preferably with berries, should transition the forest from clearing. This could be ornamental shrubs at the edge of your lawn.

In the arid Southwest, your landscaping will need to be different, of course. Plant brushy shrubs to provide cover, and any fruiting plants that will grow will be especially welcome. Water is an important draw for wildlife here, too.

Managing or Providing Wetlands

Wetlands are rich in animal, bird, and plant species, and should always be protected. Many endangered species of amphibians, reptiles, and birds need wetlands. You may not want to locate your home too close to wet areas of the property, but don't fill them in or drain them. (This may be prohibited in your area anyway.) If you don't have a pond or wetland area, you might want to construct one.

In ponds and wetlands for wildlife, let natural vegetation grow. Cattails, willows, and rooted water plants provide shelter and food for many species. Do remove any invasive species such as Purple Loosestrife, water hyacinths, and Asian Milfoil because they choke out more desirable plants.

Manage the mosquitoes that come along with wetlands with products like BT, a natural bacterial disease that infects only mosquito larvae (it's safe for the fish). Fish, even minnows, will also eat mosquito larvae.

If you don't have room on your property for a large natural pond, even a small ornamental pond will benefit wildlife. Ornamental water features with running water and shallow areas are especially attractive to birds.

Wildlife Food Plots

If you have the space and inclination, you can even plant crop areas to attract animals such as deer and turkey. If you like to hunt, this is a better way to go than providing bait piles or salt blocks, as animals feed more naturally and are less likely to pass on disease.

Although different types of food plots attract different species of animals, many crops attract a variety of species. Try grasses and grains, or things like root vegetables and pumpkins. In some areas, food plots might attract animals you don't want, such as bears or wild pigs, so you might not want to locate food plots too close to your home or to agricultural crops.

Check With the Experts

What will do well as a food plot varies from region to region, so contact your county Extension office, your local conservation district office, or the Department of Natural Resources in your area for information on what to plant.

In some cases you may even find funds available to plant food plots. Some private organizations such as Pheasants Forever also offer help and sometimes even provide funding.

Planting and Managing

Some equipment and time are involved with managing food plots. You need to get the crop planted, which involves a plow or tiller and seeder. Some crops, such as alfalfa, need to be mowed from time to time to keep it growing.

Consider getting a soil test before you plant, and you may need to amend the soil or fertilize to grow your intended crop. Most food plots are not treated for pests, but if something threatens to wipe out the plot, this may be necessary to save it.

Food plot crops are generally not harvested—the animals do that—but spring cleanup, removing leftover stubble and debris, may be necessary.

> **Country Color**
>
> Just like farm crops, food plot crops need to be rotated to keep the soil healthy and avoid disease buildup. This means changing the crop grown in an area each year.

Attracting Deer and Elk

Wildlife food plots and managing woodlands are the best way to attract deer and elk. In dry areas, providing a water source also helps. Deer and elk like dense brush, even swampy areas, to bed down in. Put these areas near food sources, and you might get lots of these critters on your property. Surround the food plots with unmowed shrubby areas at least 15 to 20 feet deep.

Salt blocks like those sold for cattle attract deer and elk. Carrots, apples, turnips, pumpkins, sugar beets, hay, grains, and various pelleted mixtures are sold for deer.

Preferably, keep deer and elk away from homes and let them eat naturally, not nose to nose over a pile of food you put out. If you simply must see these animals from your home, at least put the food away from the house. Scatter the feed instead of dumping it in a pile.

Before you start the practice of artificially feeding deer and elk, find out what the game laws about feeding are in your area. Some areas experiencing disease problems prohibit feeding deer, and some limit the amount of feed that can be put out in one day.

Attracting Songbirds

Millions of people feed birds, and in the country, bird feeders attract a host of wonderful species. Birds you attract rarely do damage to your home or landscape and pose little threat to humans. Besides bird feeders, you need to provide natural food plants, shelter, nest material, and water to bring birds to your yard.

Water is very attractive to birds, especially running water or light sprays. Birds like to bathe in shallow areas that are close to cover but still fairly open. Birds even like mud puddles in the spring when they're building their nests.

Rural Rule

Empty and scrub bird baths every few days to prevent disease and mosquitoes.

Most birds are territorial, and although water sources and feeders may become neutral ground, fighting and bickering are natural. Most bird song is actually a male announcing his territory.

Natural Cover and Food

Birds' needs for cover and nesting areas differ from species to species and differ from season to season also. Most songbirds are birds of the "edge," preferring to nest in dense areas somewhere near open areas and sources of food. Some birds need cavities in trees to nest, and others need deep grass and brush because they nest on the ground. Still others like to nest in open, flat, but undisturbed areas on the ground. The more different areas you can provide on your property, from tall trees, to dead trees, to thick shrubs and tall grass, the more different species of birds you will attract.

Birds do like to nest close to a food source because raising babies is hard work. Providing many sources of food helps territorial birds find places to raise babies. This is best accomplished with natural sources of food.

Not all birds will eat at feeders, and even those who do rarely get most of their diet there. If you want to see lots of birds, plant things that feed them and manage your property so insects and other prey are available.

Hummingbirds and even some other birds are attracted to flowers with nectar, and red and orange colors attract them the most. Plants that attract hummingbirds include trumpet vine, salvias, honeysuckle, bougainvillea, beebalm, columbine, canna, nicotiana, weigela, azalea, fuchsia, and petunias. Sprinkling these flowers liberally through your landscape will assure you of their presence if they're in your area.

Other birds eat seeds, and sunflower is a favorite. Sunflowers are easy to grow in a sunny location. If you can sneak some into the landscape, the birds will love you. Thistles are not the most attractive plants, but leave a few in out-of-the-way places for the birds.

> **Sinkhole**
>
> Avoid pesticides of any type on your landscape to protect birds. Birds are very susceptible to death from chemicals applied to the lawn or to kill insects on crops.

Bird Feeders

Providing a variety of bird feeders that you can see from the house will add much enjoyment to your day and help songbirds survive. Birds need food in the winter, but they really appreciate it when they are raising young in the spring and summer. In northern areas, the variety of birds you can attract to a feeder increases in the summer.

Birds like feeders placed in the open but close enough to cover that they can get to it quickly. Feeders should be high off the ground; 4 or 5 feet is good. Wherever you put your feeder, be prepared for the mess of hulled and spilled seed that piles up. Keep this raked up, or move the feeder from time to time or your grass will die.

The three types of seed best for feeders are thistle or niger seed, oil sunflower seed, and millet. All the other stuff added to bird feed such as milo, buckwheat, cracked corn, etc. is generally wasted and only feeds the squirrels (or the rats at night). Some birds eat cracked or whole peanuts and occasionally safflower seeds. Some new feeds add dried fruit or fruit flavor, but these ingredients aren't worth the added expense. Suet is a hit in the summer as well as the winter. Always use a wire suet feeder that keeps the suet from being carried off. Believe it or not, a simple dish of jelly attracts orioles and some other birds in the summer. Try grape; it seems to be well liked. Orange halves and raisins also attract birds. Most types of nuts are appreciated, but use unsalted nuts.

For hummingbird feeders, you don't need to buy special mixes. Just boil water, add table sugar, and let it cool. Use 1 cup sugar with 2 cups water. You don't even need red dye in it. Red attracts the hummers to the feeder, but after they've found it, they'll keep coming back, regardless of color. If you have many hummers in the area, hang several small feeders 10 to 15 feet apart rather than one large one. Hummingbirds fight all the time, even males and females, and the feeders become aerial battle-grounds.

Orioles eat out of feeders similar to hummingbird feeders with perches. However, I've found that they much prefer jelly over sugar water. Set a dish of jelly under a covered, tray-type feeder with lots of room for perching. To help them find it at first, cut an orange in half and attach it cut side up on top of the feeder.

If you want to attract birds like doves, quail, and pheasants, a flat tray on the ground with oil sun-flower seed and millet, and maybe a little cracked corn, does the trick. Either pick up this tray at night or be sure the feed will be eaten by nightfall.

Squirrels, raccoons, and even larger animals are sometimes attracted to bird feeders. Squirrels are particularly hard to discourage, but putting your feeders inside fenced yards with dogs really helps. Be sure there's nothing over the feeder they can jump down from. Oil or grease poles, and buy or make metal squirrel baffles.

Bring feeders in or put them inside metal garbage cans with lids at night to discourage raccoons, opossums, and rodents. If bear or other dangerous animals start visiting, it's time to stop feeding for a while.

Once a week in warm weather, scrub your bird feeder with a stiff brush and warm water with a little dish soap. Rinse with a mixture of 1 cup bleach to 10 cups water, and let it dry in the sun before re-filling. This helps keep diseases that kill birds in check.

Sinkhole

Birdseed is often infected with the eggs of various grain moths, which hatch in stored grain and eat the seed. If you notice fine webbing, fine crumbs, and small worms, the seed is infested. It isn't as nutritious as clean grain, although safe to feed, and the moths could infest your house and become pantry pests. If you store your seed in the freezer, or at least freeze it for a week, you will have few problems.

Birdhouses

Some birds will never use a birdhouse, but many birds that won't come to a feeder can be attracted with houses—bluebirds, swallows, purple martins, and wrens among them. Wood ducks can be attracted to a pond or wetland area with the proper nest box. Even some owls will use nest boxes.

Building birdhouses is a good activity for older children and gets them interested in birds. Birds don't care about color, so kids can express their artistic side when decorating the birdhouses. In hot areas though, white or light colors help reflect heat from the house.

Birdhouses need to be built with the species they are meant to attract in mind. They need the proper "door" size and inside dimensions. You can find many sources and plans for building your own birdhouse. The Audubon Society, nature centers, your state Department of Natural Resources, and your local Extension office are good sources for plans.

You can hollow out gourds and hang them for birdhouses, and many other recycled products can also be used. Wrens might actually use the tiny decorative birdhouses you buy for garden décor if you don't plug the hole. Barn swallows appreciate small "shelves" attached to the rafters in barns and sheds for nest building.

Rural Rule

Birds are attracted to a mesh bag filled with nesting material such as dryer lint, short pieces of cotton yarn, pet or human hair, or straw. Never include any nylon string or yarn.

Remember when you place your birdhouses that birds are territorial and won't use a box too close to another pair of the same species. Purple martins and some swallows are exceptions; they like to breed in colonies. Place boxes designed to attract different species a few feet apart.

Attracting Game Birds

Some large birds such as pheasant, grouse, quail, and turkeys can be attracted to feeders, but the best way to get them on your property is to plant some crops they like to eat and provide some cover for them to nest. Ducks and geese also feed on crops, especially during migration periods, and come to ponds and wetlands to nest. For game birds, grain crops like corn and wheat are preferred. If you can stagger crop-ripening dates with something ripening from mid-summer on, you'll get more game birds.

Sometimes quail and ducks nest close to human activity, but most large birds prefer to nest in undisturbed areas. They won't nest where your dogs are running every day or where your kids play. With the exception of wood ducks, these birds nest on the ground and their young are up and moving in hours after hatching.

If you can provide some islands in your pond, ducks and geese are happy to nest there. They also like to nest on unmowed banks and in shrubby areas. Wood ducks need a nest box suspended over water or close to water on a pole. Turkeys, grouse, quail, and pheasant nest in tall grass and weeds. Leave fields unmowed until late July to help them. Turkeys and some quail roost in trees at night and prefer to be near wooded areas.

About "Orphan" Animals

About 90 percent of baby animals that people feel have lost their mothers and need to be saved are not really orphans. People should leave baby animals where they find them in most cases and just try to keep predators and children away.

Mother deer and rabbits leave their babies alone at first except for brief periods of time to feed them. This is because the babies have no scent to attract predators, and Mom does. Leave them where you find them. Mom is nearby. Other animal moms are frightened away by humans or are off hunting or eating. And some may return and attack you with zealous maternal instinct if they hear their baby squalling.

If your child brings you a baby animal, have him or her show you where it was found and return it near there. The scent of your hands won't keep Mom away. Teach children to observe and never touch babies without first consulting an adult.

It's illegal to keep and raise the babies of most game animals, regardless of what happened to Mom. They need to be turned over to a licensed animal rehabilitator. Call a nature center or your local Department of Natural Resources to find out who in your area is qualified and licensed.

The Least You Need to Know

- ◆ Cover and nesting areas are as important as food to attract animals and birds.
- ◆ Feeding in a natural way with food plants is better than putting out food piles.
- ◆ Attracting wildlife you want may also involve attracting unwanted pests.
- ◆ Most wild animal "orphans" have a mom nearby and shouldn't be touched. It's illegal to raise many types of wildlife, and babies should be brought to licensed wildlife rehabilitators.

Glossary

acre An area of land 43,560 square feet, 4,840 square yards, or 160 square rods.

aquifer A confined, distinct area of groundwater.

artifact Something made by humans, generally in an earlier time and with archaeological interest. Arrowheads, old pots, and remains of homes are artifacts.

auger A giant corkscrewlike tool powered either by a gasoline engine or a PTO (power take-off) shaft off a tractor that bores holes in soil for wood or metal posts.

buck A male rabbit, goat, or deer.

casing A metal or plastic pipe that holds and directs ground water from an aquifer to a home.

chicken wire Also called poultry netting, chicken wire is lightweight wire fencing with six-sided openings either 1 or 2 inches wide. It's generally inexpensive, but not very strong and rusts quickly.

cockerels Baby male chickens or roosters.

colt A young male horse or pony.

cord A legal measurement that denotes a stack of wood 4 feet high, 4 feet wide, and 8 feet long.

culinary herbs   Herbs used for cooking.

doe   A doe is a female rabbit, goat, or deer.

Extension program   Extension programs are a cooperative effort between the U.S. Department of Agriculture (USDA), your state Department of Agriculture, a college, and your county government. More than 3,000 Extension offices exist, in almost every county of the United States. The Extension office offers a wide variety of information and advice on agriculture, gardening, natural resources, nutrition, food safety, parenting, money management, community planning, small business start-up, and much more. The Extension program also offers the 4-H youth program.

face cord   A face cord, stove cord, or rick, is not a legal measurement and can be different in different areas. It's generally a stack of wood 4 feet high and 8 feet long but varies in depth. It, along with a *stove cord* or *rick*, are not legal measurements and can be different in different areas.

farrier   A person who works on horse and pony feet, trimming and shoeing them.

filly   A young female horse or pony.

flue   A pipe or shaft that carries smoke and exhaust gases away from a furnace or fireplace. It can be metal, ceramic, clay, brick, or plastic, depending on the appliance.

gelding   A neutered male horse or pony.

grafted trees   A piece of a tree with good fruit inserted into a tree grown for strong, hardy roots and certain growth characteristics. The two parts grow together and become one tree.

hens   Female chickens that have started laying eggs.

kindling   When a rabbit gives birth. Also small pieces of flammable material used to start a fire.

leach field   A series of perforated pipes that allow liquefied waste to percolate down into a layer of sand and gravel and eventually into the soil.

mare   An adult female horse or pony.

microchip   A tiny plastic chip with your identification on it your veterinarian can insert with a needle under your pet's skin. Most animal shelters and many vets have scanners used to pass over the pet to detect the chip and access your information.

no wake   A rule on lakes and ponds in certain areas where boats must move slowly and not cause waves. It may be for quiet and safety or to protect wildlife or shorelines.

perk test   A perk test involves digging a hole and filling it with water to see how well it drains. It's done to evaluate the suitability of soil for a septic field. It should be done by a professional.

poaching   Shooting or otherwise killing animals outside a legal hunting season or without a license.

pollinate   Pollination occurs when a pollen grain from the male part of one flower is carried to the female part of another flower. If the female part of the flower is receptive, the pollen grain makes a tube down to the eggs inside the flower ovary, and the male sex cell contained in the pollen grain unites with an egg. That's called fertilization. A certain number of eggs must be fertilized and become seeds for a fruit to form.

posthole digger   Also called a clamshell shovel, this tool has two curved shovel blades that face each other. You move the handles apart to get the blades apart, jab them into the soil, and move the handles together to pick up soil to remove it from the hole. It is used to make tight holes for wooden fence posts.

posthole driver   A heavy piece of pipe with a weighted, closed end and two handles. You put the open end over a metal post and lift it up and let it fall, driving the post into the ground. They are inexpensive and nice to have around.

PTO (power take-off) shaft   A shaft rotated by a tractor engine used to power pulled or stationary implements. They are one of the main differences between farm and garden tractors. They are very useful but also very dangerous and should never be used without a shield.

pullet   A baby female chicken or hen.

ram   An adult male sheep.

rod   A measurement equal to 5.5 yards or 16.6 feet.

rooster   Also called a cock, a rooster is a male chicken that has become sexually active, generally when he begins to crow.

section   A mile square, or 640 acres.

septic system   The system by which country homes handle the disposal of waste from the toilet, sinks, laundry, etc.

stallion   An adult male horse or pony that's not neutered.

steers   Castrated male cattle, generally raised for meat.

sump pump   A pump that sits on the basement floor or in a hole under the home and pumps water out of the house if water rises to a certain point.

tack   Items put on a horse, such as halters, lead ropes, saddles, bridles, etc., or things to groom the horse with such as brushes and hoof picks.

thatch   An accumulation of dead grass leaves and other vegetation. It's not harmful unless it builds up to more than a couple inches but should be removed before reseeding the land so seeds have contact with the soil.

township   An area that consists of 36 sections.

wellhead   A pipe sticking out of the ground that connects directly to the well. In modern homes this is outside; in older homes it may be under the house.

wench   A pulling device. With ropes or chains, you attach one end to a bumper, pass the rope or chain around a strong stationary item—such as a post or tree—and back to a cylinder turned by the power source—such as your engine or a hand crank. Then pull out the vehicle.

wetlands   Areas where water is close to or at the surface of land at least seasonally. They can be swamps, bogs, marshes, or fens. Wetlands are extremely valuable because they filter storm runoff, protect land from erosion, and are the nursery or home of thousands of animal and plant species.

Additional Resources

In this appendix, I give you some further resources you can use to find more detail on some of the topics I mentioned earlier in the book.

General Country Living

Your county Extension office

Extension programs are a cooperative effort between the U.S. Department of Agriculture (USDA), your state Department of Agriculture, a college, and your county government. More than 3,000 Extension offices exist, in almost every county of the United States.

The Extension office is the place to go for a wide variety of information and advice on agriculture, gardening, natural resources, nutrition, food safety, parenting, money management, community planning, small business start-up, and much more. The Extension program also offers the 4-H youth program.

Each state's Extension service provides many online resources, printed material available at local offices, and Extension agents or educators in the offices you can speak with about problems and questions.

To find your county Extension office, go to www.csrees.usda.gov and click the links to your state and county. Or look in the phone book under the government section.

United States Department of Agriculture (USDA)
www.usda.gov
The USDA is a surprisingly good source of information on many subjects, including plant and animal problems and information, emergency preparedness, septic and well information, food and nutrition, and wildlife and natural resources, among many others. The USDA offers many online informational brochures, and you can also get many of their publications in print for a small fee.

Animal and Plant Health Inspection Service
www.aphis.usda.gov
This is a department of the USDA that deals with plant and animal problems.

You can also call 1-800-999-6779 and ask how to request a catalog of publications. Most libraries have some publications on hand, and can access a catalog and even request information for you.

Emergency Management and Preparedness

Federal Emergency Management Agency (FEMA)
500 C Street SW
Washington, D.C. 20472
1-800-621-FEMA (1-800-621-3362)
TDD/TTY users: 1-800-462-7585
www.fema.gov

American Red Cross
National Headquarters
202 E. Street NW
Washington, D.C. 20006
www.redcross.org

Vegetable and Fruit Gardening

The Vegetable Gardeners Bible by Ed Smith is a good guide to healthy soil and veggies.

Fruits and Berries for the Home Garden by Lewis Hill is a good beginner's resource for these crops.

The Gardener's A–Z Guide to Growing Organic Food by Tanya Denckla is a great book for organic methods.

For gardening questions, you can also contact your Extension office.

Raising Chickens

American Poultry Association
PO Box 306
Burgettstown, PA 15021
724-729-3459
www.amerpoultryassn.com
This organization has a magazine and online information.

Storey's Guide to Raising Chickens by Gail Damerow is an easy read for beginners and is packed with information.

Chickens in the Backyard: A Beginner's Guide by Rick Luttmann is also great for beginners.

Bee Keeping

American Honey Producers Association
Mark Brady
3307 Sanger Creek Way
Waxahachie, TX 75165
214-356-6791
beeman52@sbcglobal.net or pegbrady55@sbcglobal.net
www.americanhoneyproducers.org
Go online for information and links to sellers of bee supplies. Call or write for more information on producing honey.

Keeping Bees and Making Honey by Alison Benjamin and Brian McCallum is a great book for beginners.

The Backyard Beekeeper: An Absolute Beginner's Guide to Keeping Bees in Your Yard and Garden by Kim Flottum and Weeks Ringle—I highly recommend this book for beginners and intermediate beekeepers.

Raising Rabbits

American Rabbit Breeders Association, Inc.
PO Box 5667
Bloomington, IL 61702
309-664-7500
Fax: 309-664-0941
info@arba.net
www.arba.net
ARBA has a good magazine, online information, and an informational guidebook to raising rabbits plus a guide to showing rabbits.

Raising Rabbits Successfully by Bob Bennett is an older book but considered one of the top rabbit books by many rabbit owners.

Keeping Horses

There's a lot of information on horses available online, in bookstores, at the library, and through associations and clubs. My favorite horse books include the following:

Horse Keeping on Small Acreages by Cherry Hill

The Complete Idiot's Guide to Horseback Riding by Jessica Jahiel

My First Horse and Pony Care Book by Judith Draper, Elwyn Hartley, and Matthew Roberts (This is written for young adults, but it's good for all beginning horse owners.)

Index

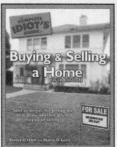

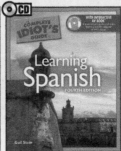